I0793187

IMAGES
of America

EDEN

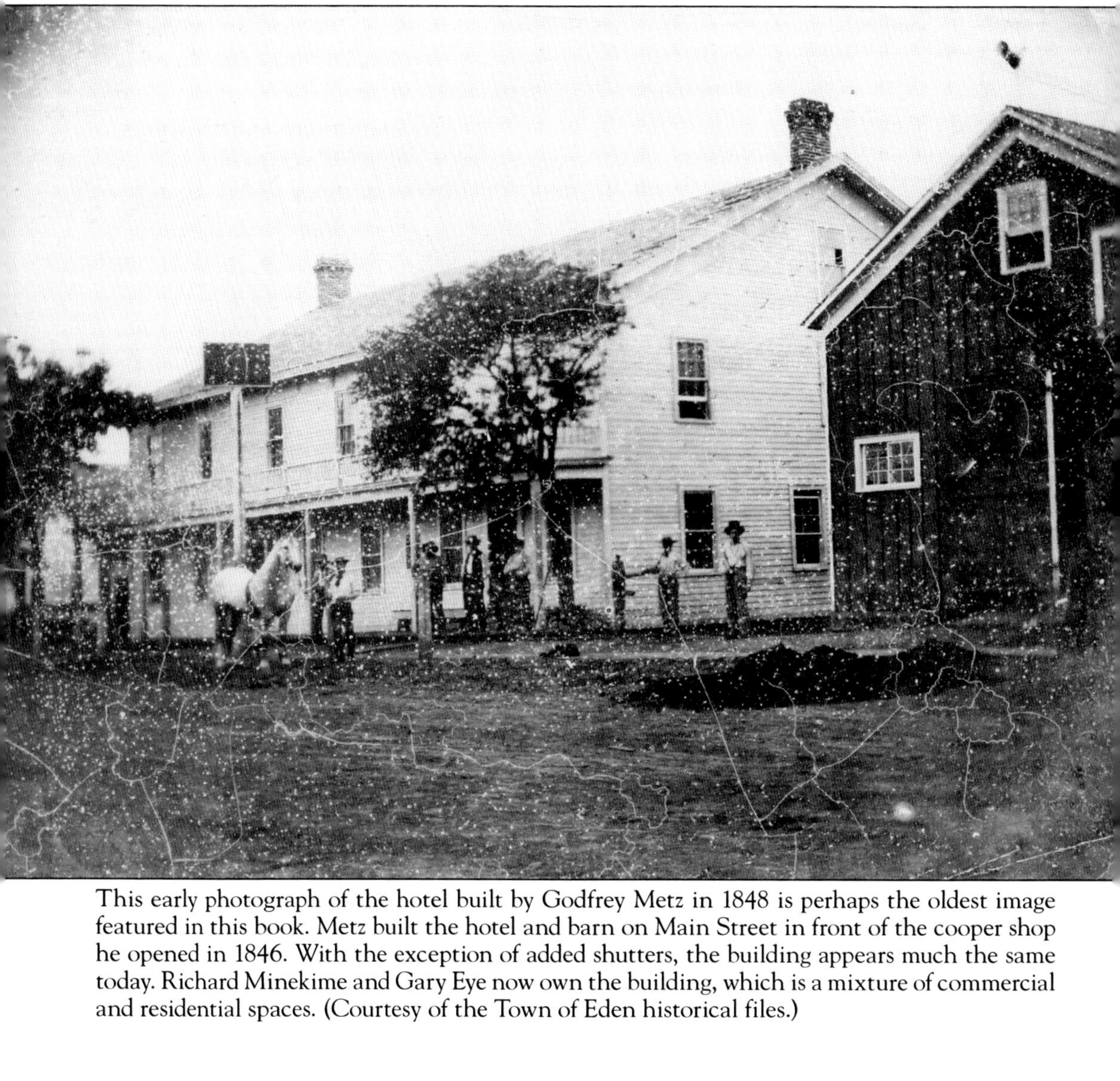

This early photograph of the hotel built by Godfrey Metz in 1848 is perhaps the oldest image featured in this book. Metz built the hotel and barn on Main Street in front of the cooper shop he opened in 1846. With the exception of added shutters, the building appears much the same today. Richard Minekime and Gary Eye now own the building, which is a mixture of commercial and residential spaces. (Courtesy of the Town of Eden historical files.)

On the Cover: The Town of Eden celebrated its sesquicentennial in 1962. Residents dressed in period costumes and posed in front of the Roeller Hotel, which was built 114 years earlier by Godfrey Metz. Howard Roeller is the man riding the high-wheel bicycle, also known as a penny farthing. (Courtesy of the Town of Eden historical files.)

IMAGES
of America

EDEN

Susan Minekime

ARCADIA
PUBLISHING

ISBN 978-0-7385-7457-8

Published by Arcadia Publishing
Charleston, South Carolina

Printed in the United States of America

Library of Congress Control Number: 2010936919

For all general information, please contact Arcadia Publishing:
Telephone 843-853-2070
Fax 843-853-0044
E-mail sales@arcadiapublishing.com
For customer service and orders:
Toll-Free 1-888-313-2665

Visit us on the Internet at www.arcadiapublishing.com

To my husband, Dick Minekime, who introduced me to Eden, and to my parents, Jean and the late Barney Carlson, who taught me to appreciate times past.

Contents

Acknowledgments

The creation of this volume has been akin to doing complicated jigsaw and crossword puzzles at the same time. Reconciling conflicting information has been a challenge, and I have done my best to accurately depict the stories within the captions. I am exceedingly indebted and grateful to the late Doris Anderson for the tremendous time and effort it must have taken her to complete her various historical works about Eden. Without her *Informal History of Eden*, *Sketches of Eden History*, and her three-volume work *The History of Eden*, this book could not have been written.

My sincere appreciation goes out to the many individuals who so kindly shared information and searched out and loaned photographs for inclusion in this project. Their enthusiasm kept me going! Many thanks to the following: Ferris Randall, Stirling and Jean Brusehaber Muck, Walter Henry, Sheila and James Landon, Elton and Frances Palmerton, Warren Hickman, Julia Laing-Meyers, Bob Maltby, Jean Klug, Harold Bley, Gary Nobbs, Frank and Linda Meyer, Bob Kehe, Loreena Smith, Cheryl Colvin, Jack Gavin, Marvin and Jayne Cohoon, George Zittel, Bill Feasley, Jennifer Soule, Jane Gould-Badger, Don Hunt, Bill Laing, Bettyann Neifer, Eugene Winter, Kate Riedel, Hal Leader, Rich Kegler, John Conlin, Karen Spaulding, Pat Agle, Ron Salzman, Lois Friedrich, Don and Lolly Rebmann, Karen Smith, Carol Lewis, Rosemary Smutz, Peggy Skotnicki of the Buffalo and Erie County Public Library, the librarians at the Buffalo and Erie County Historical Society, and Tony Annunziato of SASi (Suburban Adult Services, Inc.). Thank you also to Marlene Bowman and my daughter, Gretchen Minekime, for proofreading the text and to my husband, Dick, and so many others who offered their support. Unless otherwise noted, all images are from the historical files of the Town of Eden.

INTRODUCTION

The town of Eden has its roots in the westward movement that took place in the decades following the Revolutionary War. Our young country was rapidly expanding in 1796 when a group of Dutch bankers purchased a vast tract of land encompassing 3.3 million acres in the most western part of New York State. The Holland Land Company employed Joseph Ellicott to survey their holdings, a job that he and a crew of 130 men accomplished over a period of three years. By 1801, the land had been surveyed into townships and ranges, and the Holland Land Company had established its main land office in Batavia. For the next 30 years, the company developed its holdings mostly through the direct sale of land to pioneers making their way west from New England and eastern New York State.

The area that was to become Eden was a densely forested wilderness in a huge township called Willink. It was into this wilderness that Eden's first settler, Deacon Samuel Tubbs, ventured in 1808. Tubbs, his wife, two sons, and a nephew, James Welch, came up the Eighteen Mile Creek from Lake Erie and settled in what is now Eden Valley. Upon his encouragement, Welch's two brothers, John and Elisha, made their way west in 1809 to join the new settlement at "Tubbs Hollow." Many others were not far behind. The 1810 census reported about 4,000 people living in Willink. Since the town covered such a great area, it was decided to subdivide it into four towns, Eden, Hamburg, Concord, and Willink. The towns of Boston and Evans were spun off from Eden several years later.

John Morgan Welch, Elisha Welch, and their brother-in-law, John Hill, deserve much of the credit for getting the town going. Between 1810 and 1818, John Morgan Welch bought up several hundred acres of land from the Holland Land Company. In the process of the backbreaking work to clear the land, he found himself with so much excess wood that he simply burned what he did not need. His original home, a log cabin, was located somewhere on the land bordered by Main and George Streets. Down in the valley at Tubb's Hollow, Elisha Welch built the first sawmill in 1811 and the first gristmill in 1812, thus establishing what developed into Eden's first thriving mill community. Also in 1811, John Hill settled with his family in what is now the hamlet of Eden. It was known then as Hill's Corners and later as Eden Center. Hill is credited with naming the township Eden when the various settlement areas were incorporated on March 20, 1812.

At the first town meeting, held in 1813, John Twining was elected the supervisor and John March the town clerk. It was voted to raise $200 for the building of roads and bridges—a good idea, as most of the land was still unbroken forest. Once the War of 1812 ended, the town began to grow quickly. Those choosing to settle in Eden were faced with a variety of obstacles that needed to be overcome in order to survive. Virgin forests needed to be cleared, shelters for humans and livestock built, and crops planted. The danger of wolves, bears, and panthers was ever present. Fortunately, relationships were generally good between the new settlers and the native people who frequently passed through town. Money was scarce, and the barter system of exchanging goods was widely practiced, even for the payment of land. Twenty-first-century folk can hardly imagine how primitive life was and what a struggle each day was. Forging a new life in the wilderness was not for the faint of heart!

Two natural resources, the land and the Eighteen Mile Creek, made the area attractive for settlement. Eden's three milling communities at Eden Valley, Toad Hollow, and Clarksburg took full advantage of the creek's water power to run sawmills and grind grain. Word of the fertile soil in Eden had reached many who eventually made their way to the area. They were not disappointed. Initially everyone in town was in some way working in agriculture, forming the basis for the legacy that continues today. As the forests gave way to agricultural fields and goods began to be more available, life was still hard but not so much of a struggle. During the 1830s, frame houses began to replace the log cabins that sheltered the early townsfolk. Jobs became more diversified, and the original settlement areas thrived with stores, post offices, mills, cheese factories, and other businesses.

Opportunities for education and the practice of religion were priorities from the first days of the town. Eden's first teacher, Rowena Flack, conducted classes at home as early as 1812, and the first school was organized in 1814. Over the next several decades, one-room district schools began popping up throughout the town. Providing a good education for Eden's children began early and continues today. Pioneers also brought with them a desire to practice their religious faith. It was not easy, and the devout often traveled significant distances for worship. Congregations gathered as early as 1813, with the Baptists being the first denomination to formally organize in 1816. At least seven different churches had been established by the 1850s, including a large community of Quakers.

Before the advent of the railroad in Eden, the town, like so many others across the country, was basically self-sufficient, especially by modern standards. The opportunities fostered by railways enabled the business and industrial community to expand in numerous ways. Travel for the sake of pleasure was something entirely new. The latter part of the 19th century saw people on the move and involved in more activities that connected them to the world at large. Civic involvement, fraternal organizations, study groups, and travel excursions expanded social and intellectual horizons. As recreational time increased, music, drama, service clubs, and churches fed the mind and the spirit.

Other factors left indelible changes on the town. The invention of the telephone and the installation of electricity and indoor plumbing brought comfort and convenience to peoples' lives. The automobile and mechanization of farm equipment significantly changed the way people lived and worked. As the Civil War left its mark, so did World Wars I and II. The Roaring Twenties, the Great Depression, and the postwar boom of the 1950s also created major societal changes that were reflected in the lives of Eden residents.

From its inception to the present day, Eden has been a beautiful place to live. As the town approaches its 200th birthday in 2012, reflecting on its past seems appropriate. Some may look through these pages and feel nostalgia for the old days, when the rhythm of life followed the seasons and life was simpler and more relaxed. Others might find themselves wondering how our forefathers could get by without the modern inventions and conveniences taken for granted in the 21st century. Whatever one's reaction, it is hoped that this work will create an awareness and increased appreciation of the heritage of all who have ever called Eden home.

One

Down in the Valley

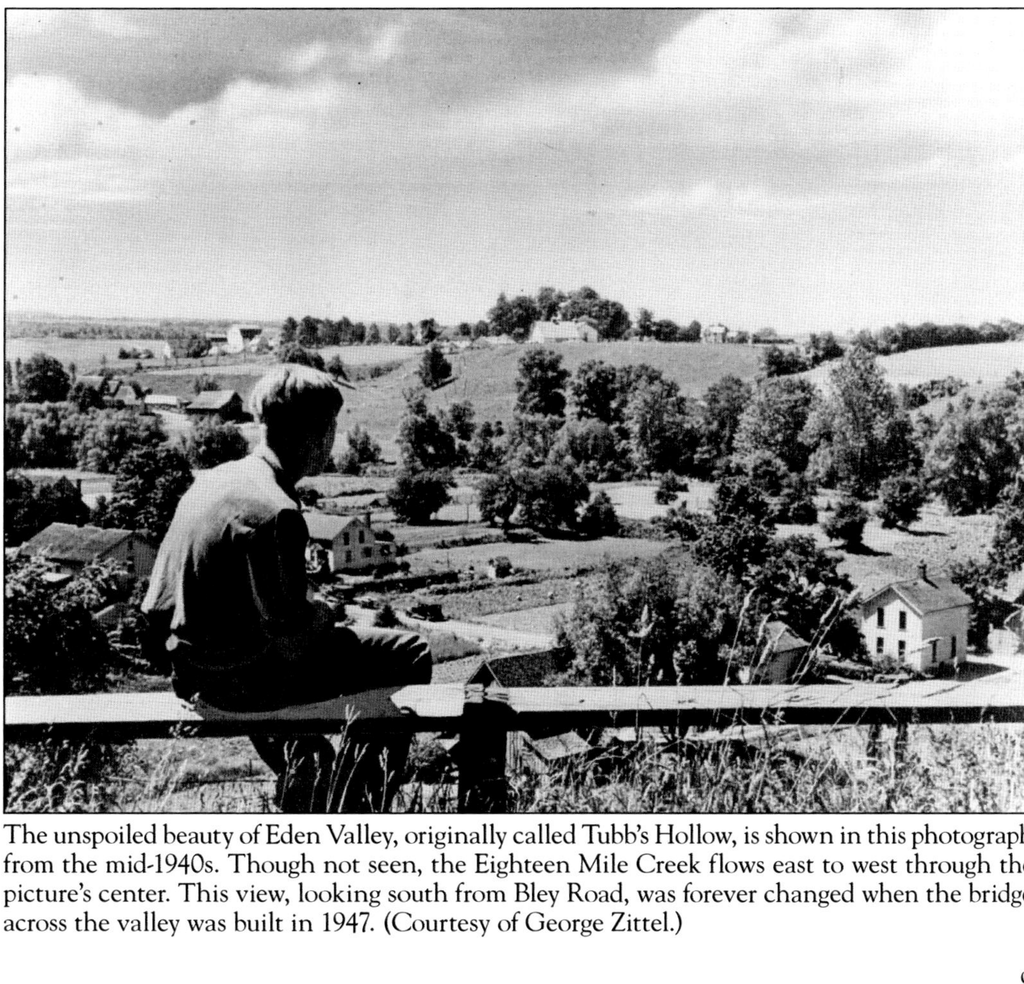

The unspoiled beauty of Eden Valley, originally called Tubb's Hollow, is shown in this photograph from the mid-1940s. Though not seen, the Eighteen Mile Creek flows east to west through the picture's center. This view, looking south from Bley Road, was forever changed when the bridge across the valley was built in 1947. (Courtesy of George Zittel.)

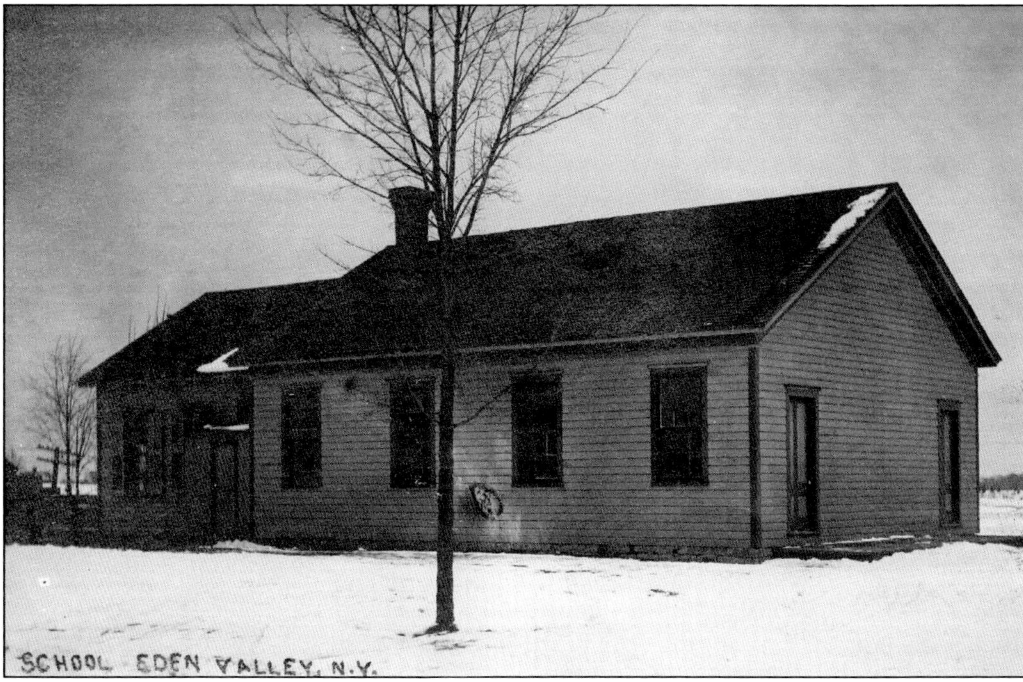

The Eden Valley schoolhouse, built in 1831, was located on North Boston Road on the valley's north side around the corner from the old state road. Records from that year show that school was in session for eight months. The teacher's annual salary was listed as $44.25. Doris Anderson, author of the three-volume *History of Eden*, taught here during the 1920s. The building was replaced with a brick schoolhouse in 1936.

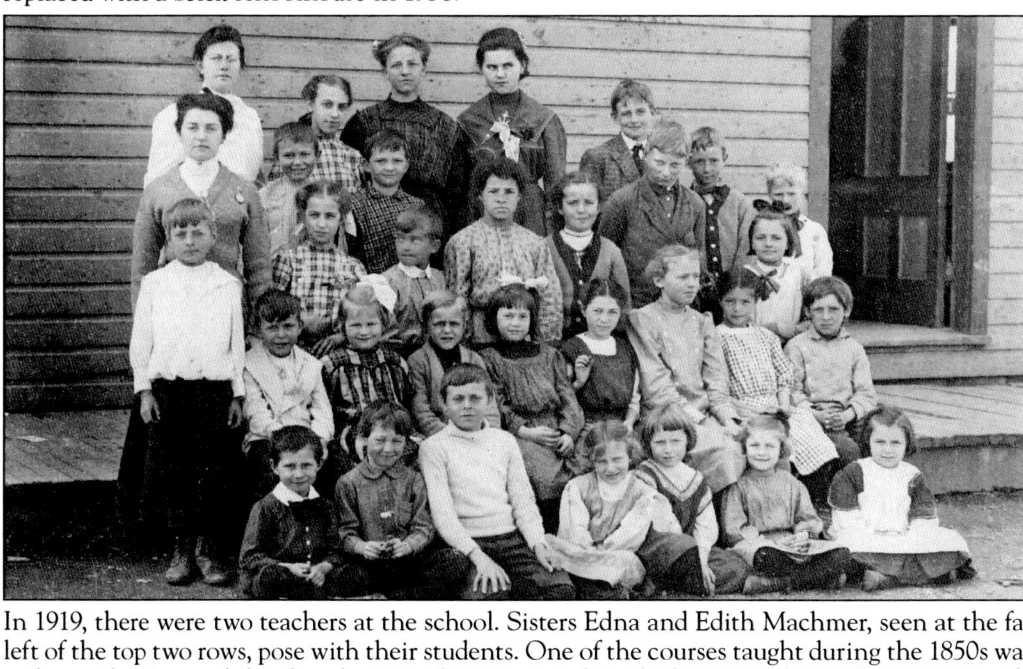

In 1919, there were two teachers at the school. Sisters Edna and Edith Machmer, seen at the far left of the top two rows, pose with their students. One of the courses taught during the 1850s was orthography. It was defined as the "art of writing words with the proper letters," or more simply stated, spelling. Other subjects included philosophy and astronomy.

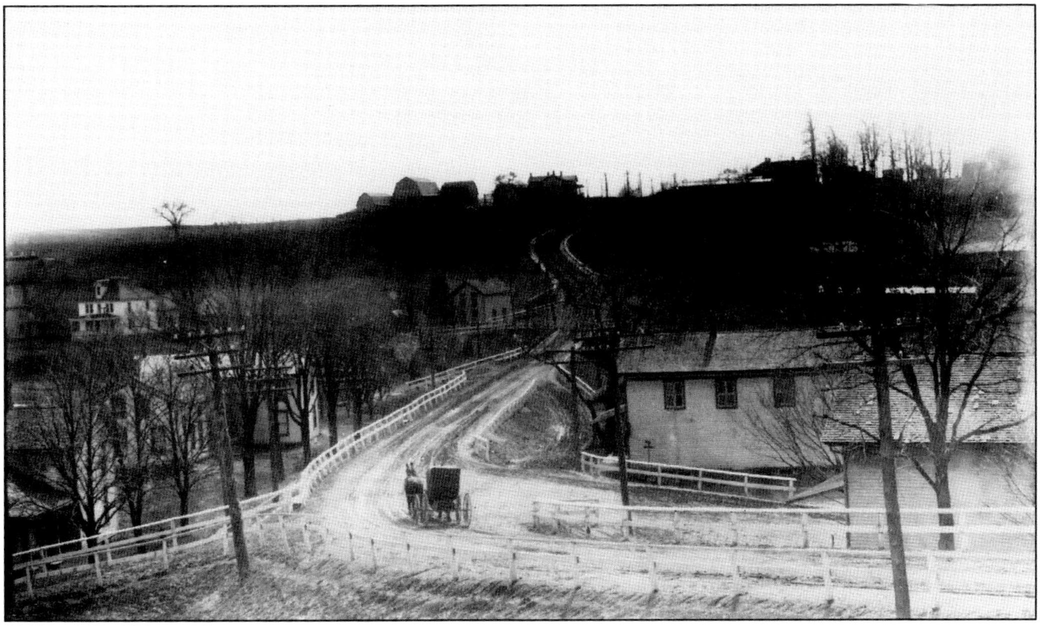

In earlier days, Eden Valley was a thriving mill community, complete with stores, a cheese factory, a post office, and a saloon. This photograph from about 1900 shows a traveler making his way down the steep and treacherous road on the north side of the Eighteen Mile Creek. Across the bridge, the west end of Jennings Road joins the road leading out of the valley towards the center of town.

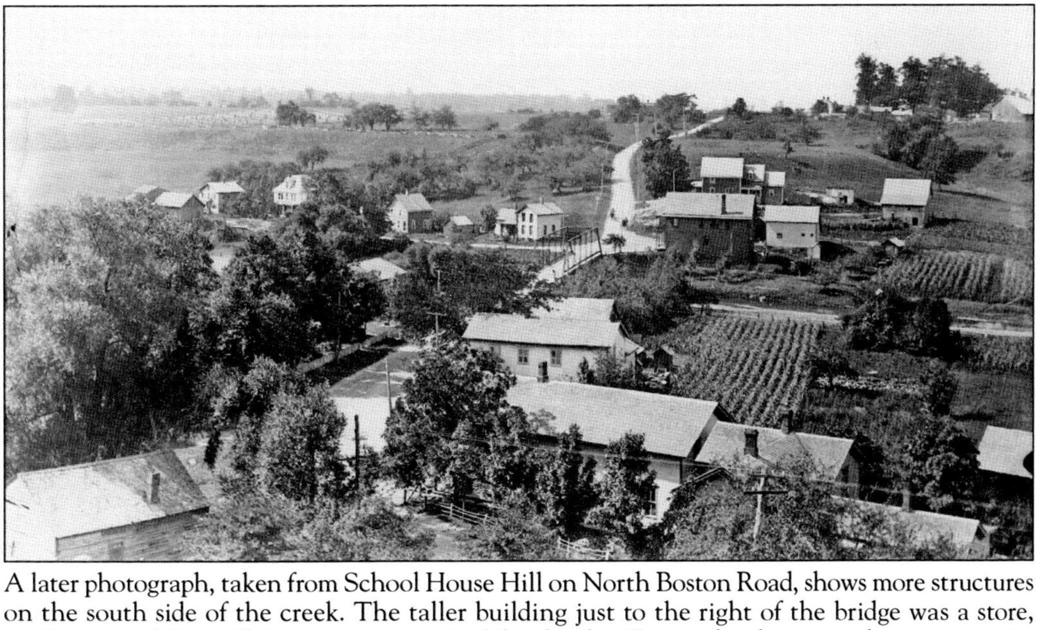

A later photograph, taken from School House Hill on North Boston Road, shows more structures on the south side of the creek. The taller building just to the right of the bridge was a store, residence, and farm all in one—very typical for the day. Except for the store, the structures in the picture remain today as residences.

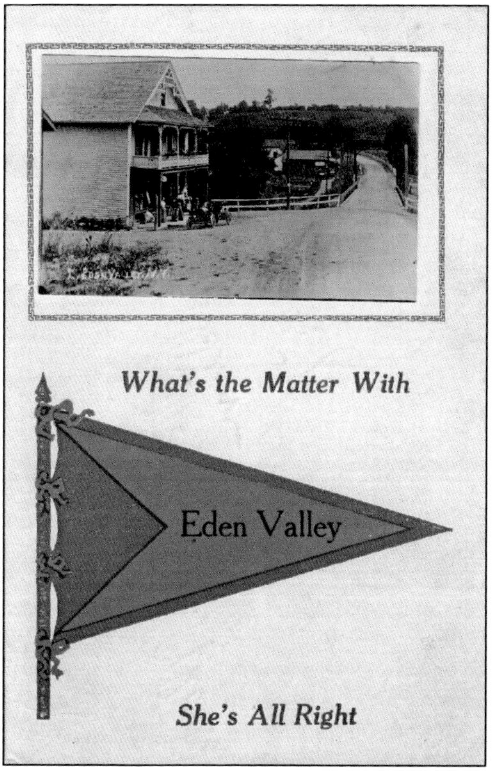

This postcard from 1900 sings the praises of Eden Valley. Among the retail establishments in the valley was this store built by Frank Webster and later run by William Klimaszecki. It was located on the south side of the creek. The building was destroyed by fire, and a residence now stands on the property.

Apparently, these ladies thought everything was all right with Eden Valley. Enjoying the cool waters of the Eighteen Mile Creek are Gertrude Richardson Tooley (left) and Edith Ketchum. The Richardson family owned and ran the gristmill in the valley during this time. This image and several others of the valley and mill were made from glass negatives around 1895.

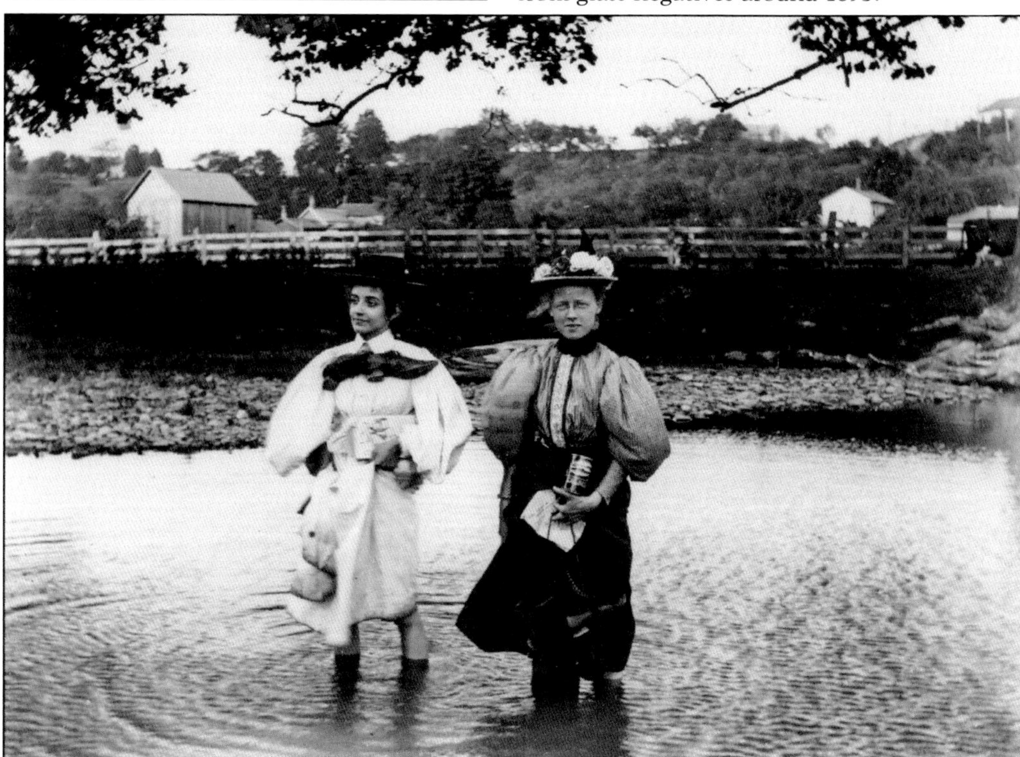

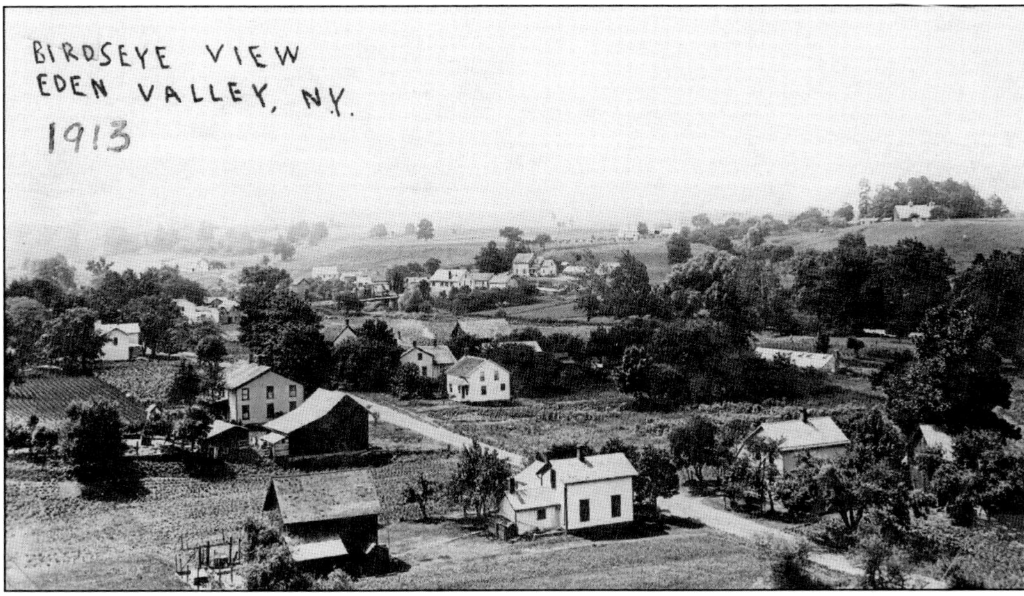

This 1913 picture shows Mill Road in the valley looking toward the southeast. At that time, most everyone's property was a small farm complete with cows, goats, pigs, and chickens. Outhouses and wells for water were the order of the day. The grove of trees below the barn at the upper right is thought to be the site where Samuel Tubbs established Eden's first homestead in 1808.

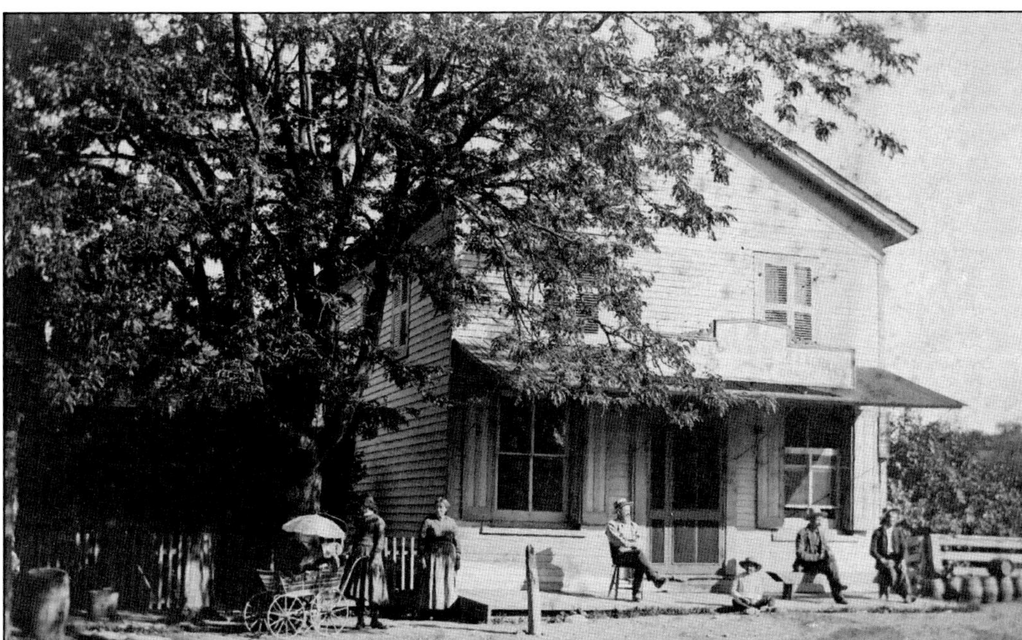

A group of unidentified valley residents is seen posing about 1870 on what appeared to be an idyllic day. The building at the foot of the hill on the north side of the creek was for many years one of the retail establishments in the valley. The store's name was the Eden Valley Stock Exchange. Maps from the period indicate that the owner was A.D. Martin. (Courtesy of Lois Friedrich.)

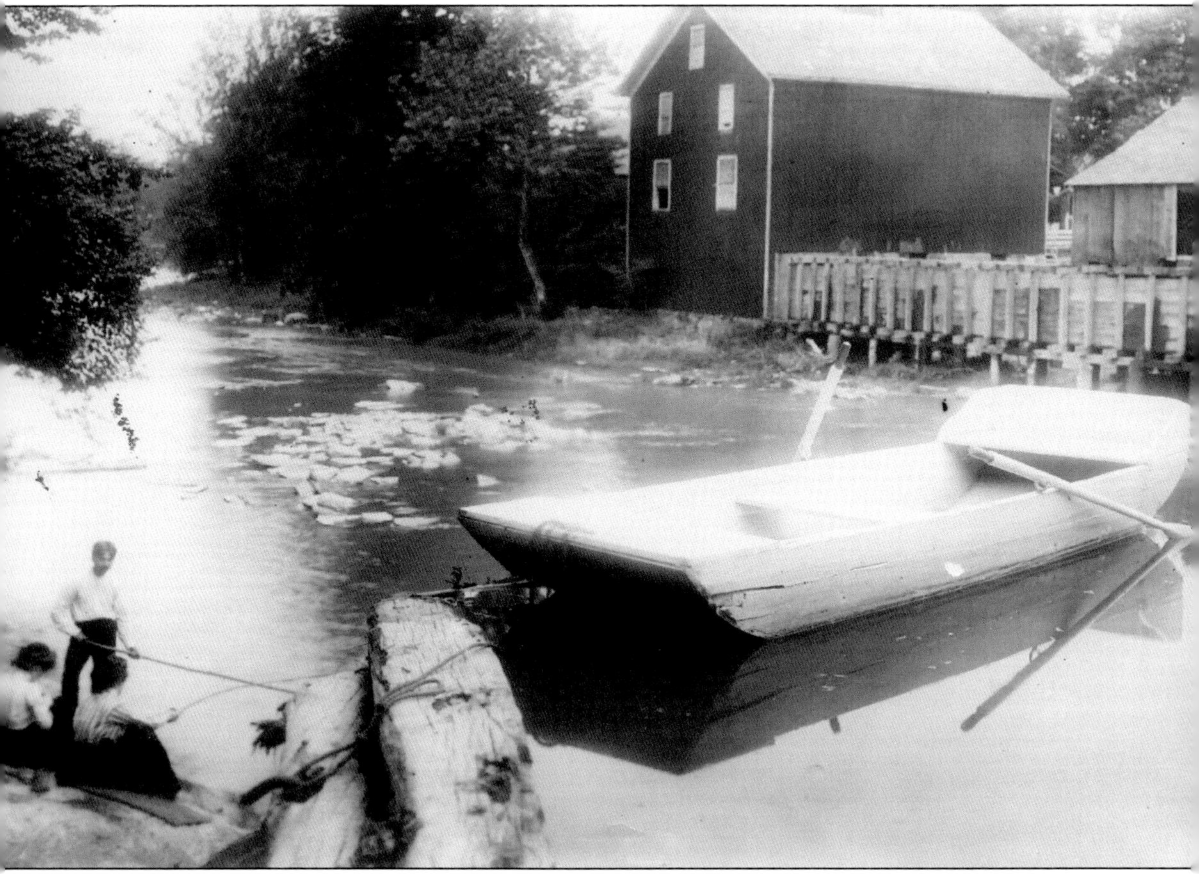

The centerpiece of Eden Valley has long been its gristmill. Most recently known as Croop's Mill, the structure pictured is situated on the site of Eden's first mills built by Elisha Welch in 1811 and 1812. The mill was sold to Asahel Richardson in 1859. He and his sons ran the mill for 56 years, becoming well known for the quality of their buckwheat flour. Richardson sold the mill to Leo Schumer, who later sold it to Clement Croop in 1918. This 1890s view of the mill shows the dam in the creek and the sluiceway that directed water into the mill to run the mechanisms that turned the grist wheel. The dam was made from heavy planks and timber. High water and spring ice floes necessitated constant maintenance and repair. In 1930, the dam "went out," and Croop, finding it beyond repair, was forced to seek an alternative power source. Croop's solution was to use a modified Buick engine powered by natural gas. He ran the mill for nearly 40 years.

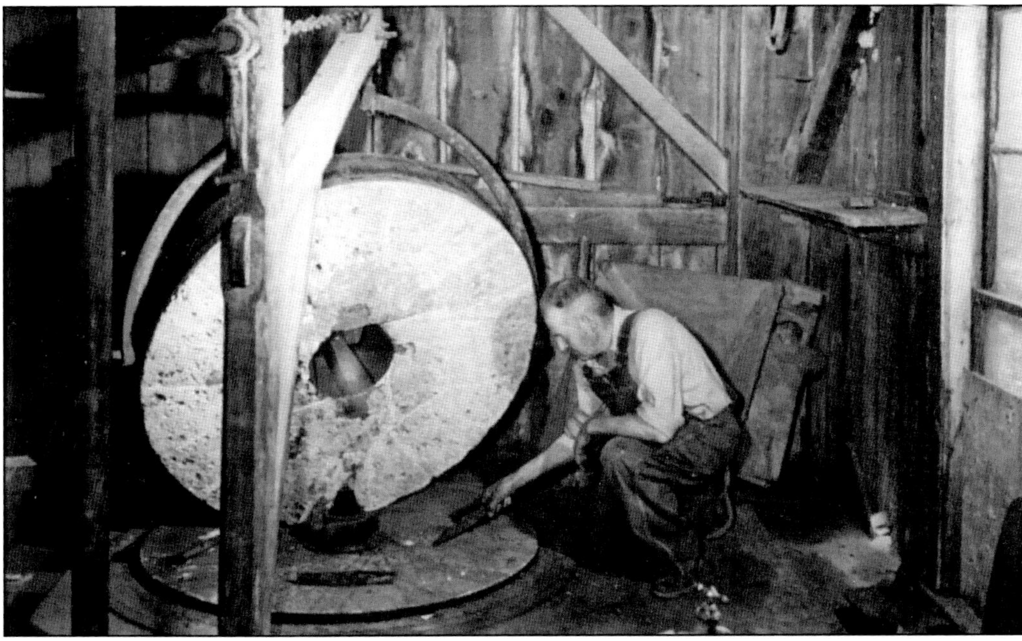

The mill's two large stones, imported from France, worked together to grind grain—one rubbing in a circular motion over a stationary one below it. During Eden's sesquicentennial celebration in 1962, Clyde Welch Sr. demonstrated how the stones were sharpened or "dressed." At the time of the picture, the old grist wheel had ground more than its share of grain, and the mill had ceased operation several years earlier.

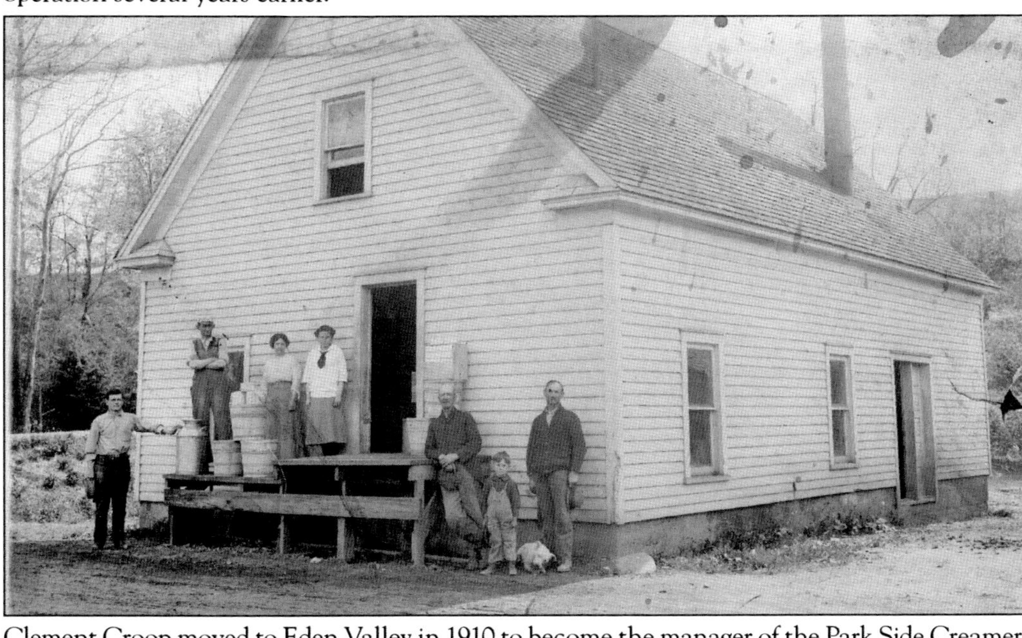

Clement Croop moved to Eden Valley in 1910 to become the manager of the Park Side Creamery Company, which he later purchased along with the mill. Butter and cheese were the main products produced from the milk received from area farmers. Later, after a large walk-in freezer was installed, the creamery made and sold Valley Velvet Ice Cream to area retail stores and at the Erie County Fair in Hamburg.

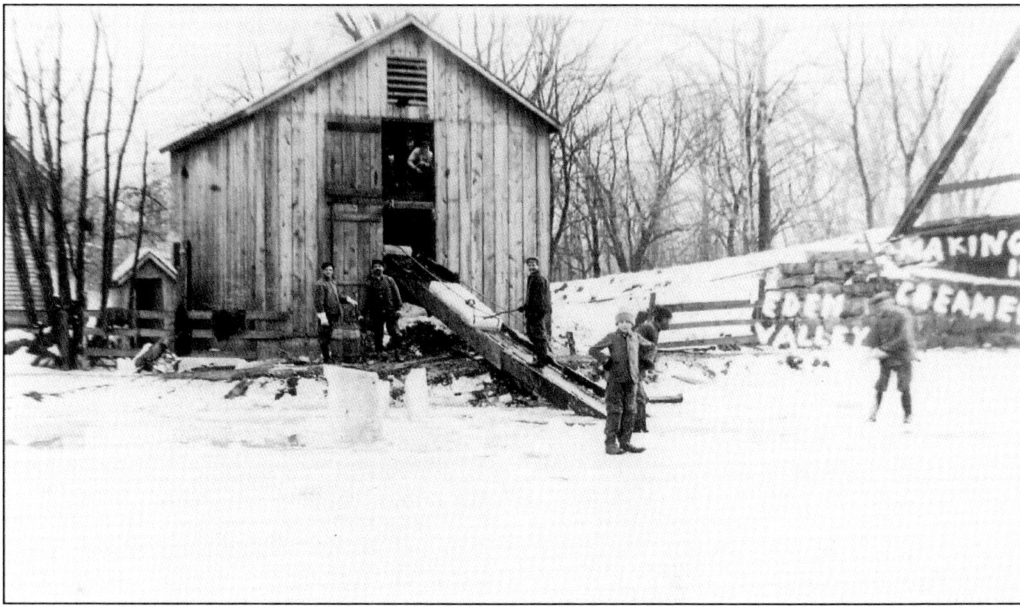

Next to the creamery was the icehouse. Making ice involved cutting large blocks of frozen creek water and storing them between layers of straw or sawdust in the icehouse for use during warmer weather. The icehouse supported not only the creamery but also a cider mill. Every fall, local apples were pressed into sweet juice that was sold in glass gallon jugs. (Courtesy of Jean Klug.)

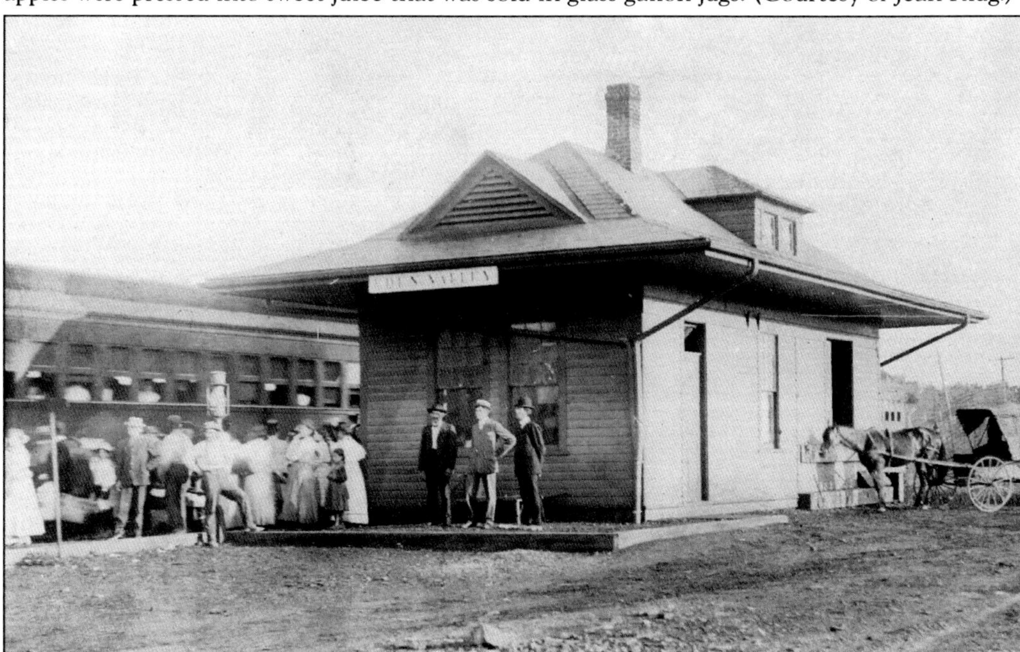

The Erie Railroad depot at Eden Valley was located just off Bley Road. This 1899 photograph shows travelers waiting for one of the trains that carried people into Buffalo. Until the 1930s, commuter trains were very popular, but the increasing popularity of the automobile caused ridership to steadily decrease. Present-day residents nostalgically recall being able to take the train into Buffalo until 1950. (Courtesy of Jean Klug.)

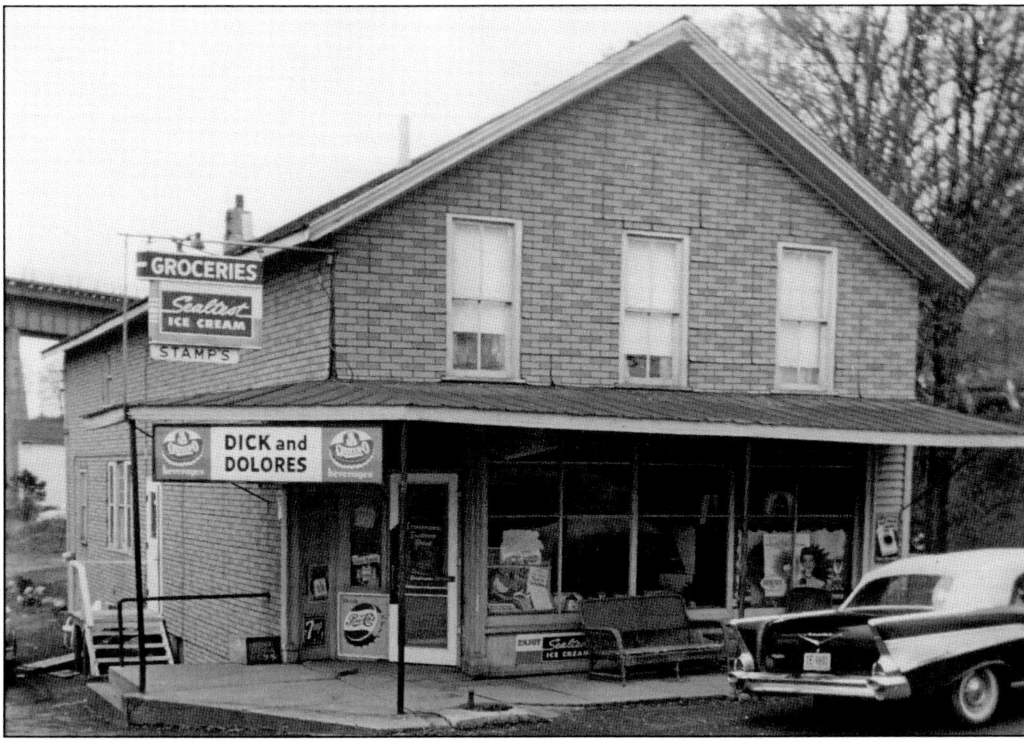

As the 20th century progressed, business and commerce in the valley began to wane. At the time this picture was taken in 1958, William and Rose Marie Donovan owned this store. The building had obviously seen better days, especially when compared to the earlier photograph seen on page 13. The store ceased operation, as such, some time in the 1960s. (Copyright Buffalo and Erie County Historical Society, used by permission.)

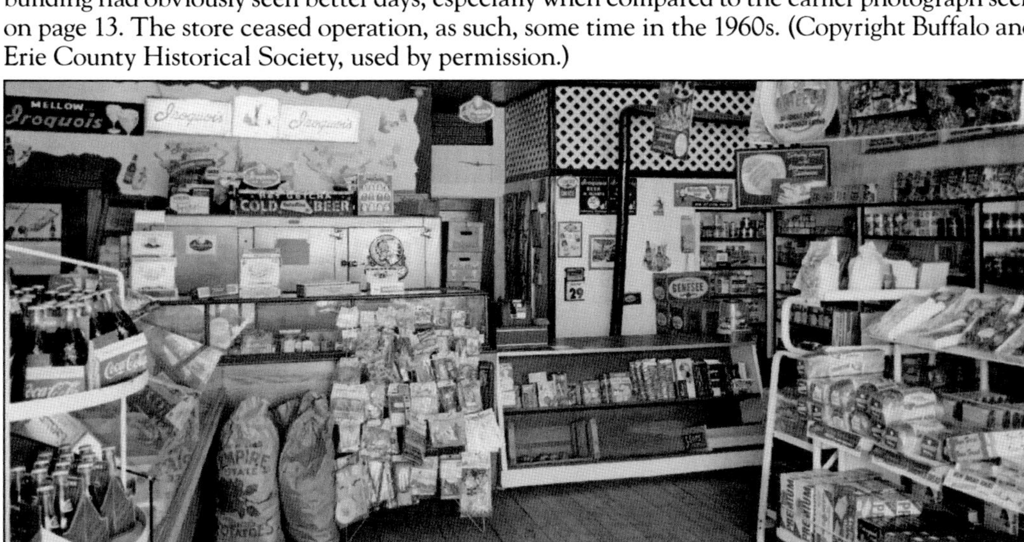

The interior of the Donovans' store shows a typical corner grocery of the 1940s and 1950s. The wooden floor probably squeaked and was uneven. Sealtest ice cream and Stroehmann's Sunbeam bread were still made. Mellow Iroquois beer, one of the most popular brands in the Buffalo area, was available, and Coca-Cola was only in bottles. There was a gumball machine on the counter. (Copyright Buffalo and Erie County Historical Society, used by permission.)

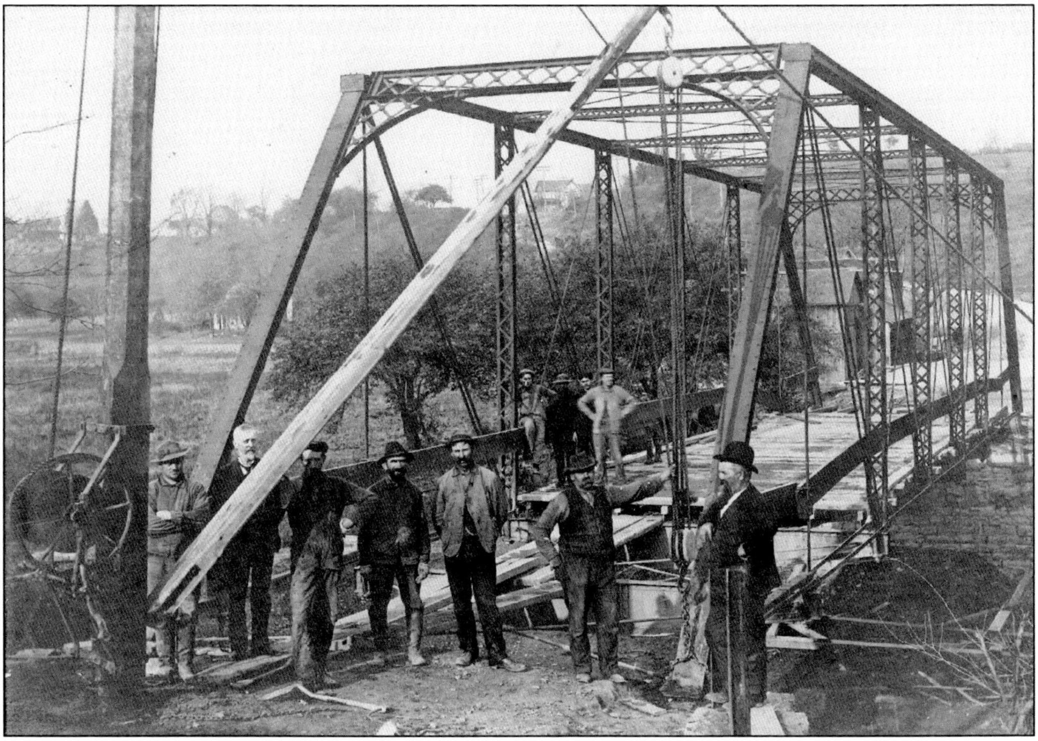

Recycling was alive and well in the early 20th century. In 1914, this iron bridge replaced the original span on Eden Valley Road. That replacement was not new but was from Water Valley in Hamburg, where a new bridge was erected. The old valley bridge was then taken to Kromer's Mill to replace the wooden covered bridge that crossed the creek there on Old Church Road. Confused?

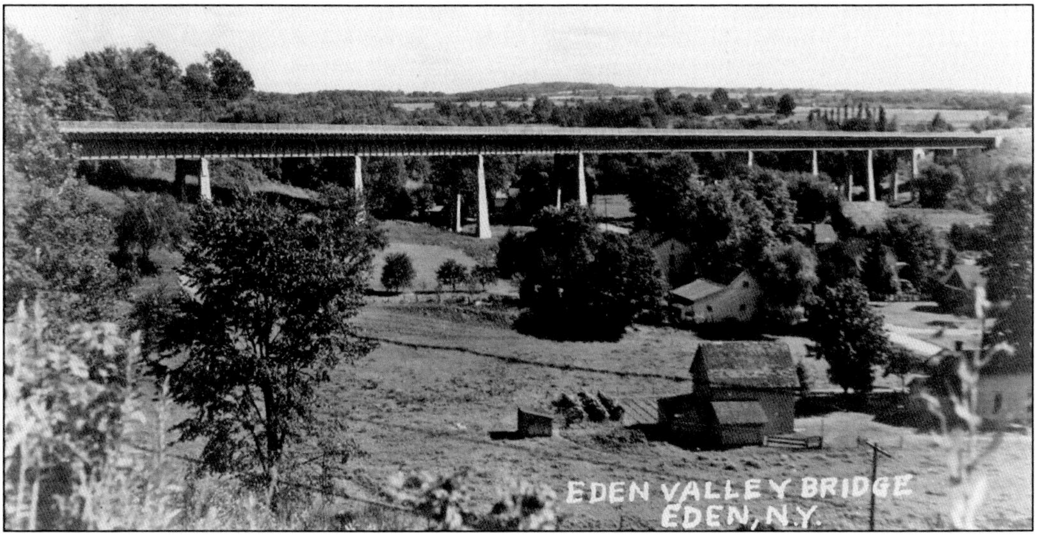

The bridge spanning Eden Valley made vehicular travel across the creek much easier for motorists. Town Supervisor Ida Landon proudly cut the ribbon to open the new bridge in October 1947. Amid much fanfare, hundreds of people walked from the center of town to gather on the bridge for the ceremonies. The bridge, costing $600,000, was the first major postwar construction project in Erie County. It was replaced in 1991.

Two

Eden Center Streetscapes

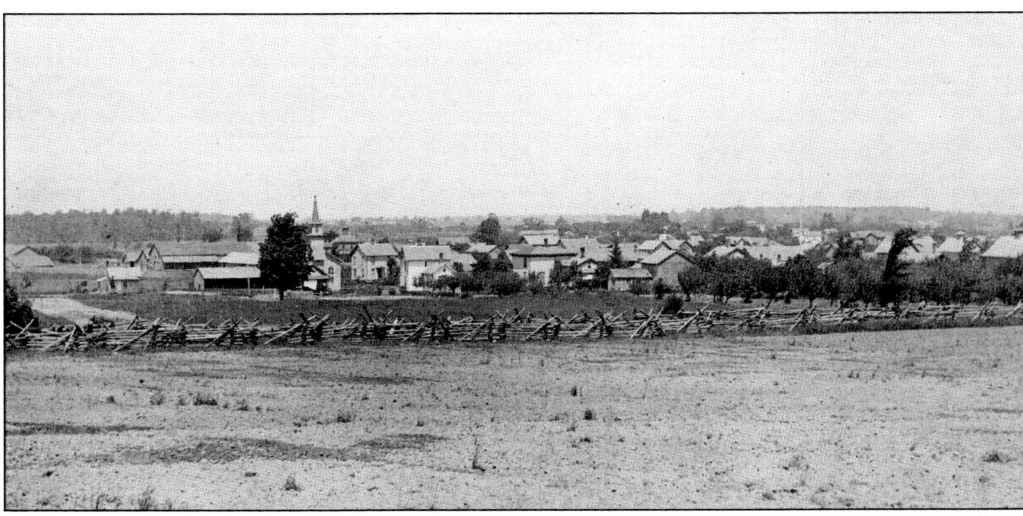

In the early 1890s, Eden was a well-established small town. In Eden Center, commercial and retail establishments existed side-by-side with garden plots, horses, chickens, and milk cows. The railroad was an important link to the city of Buffalo and points south. This view from near Second Street looks west towards Main Street. St. John's Church, now Faith Bible Church, is left of the center of the photograph.

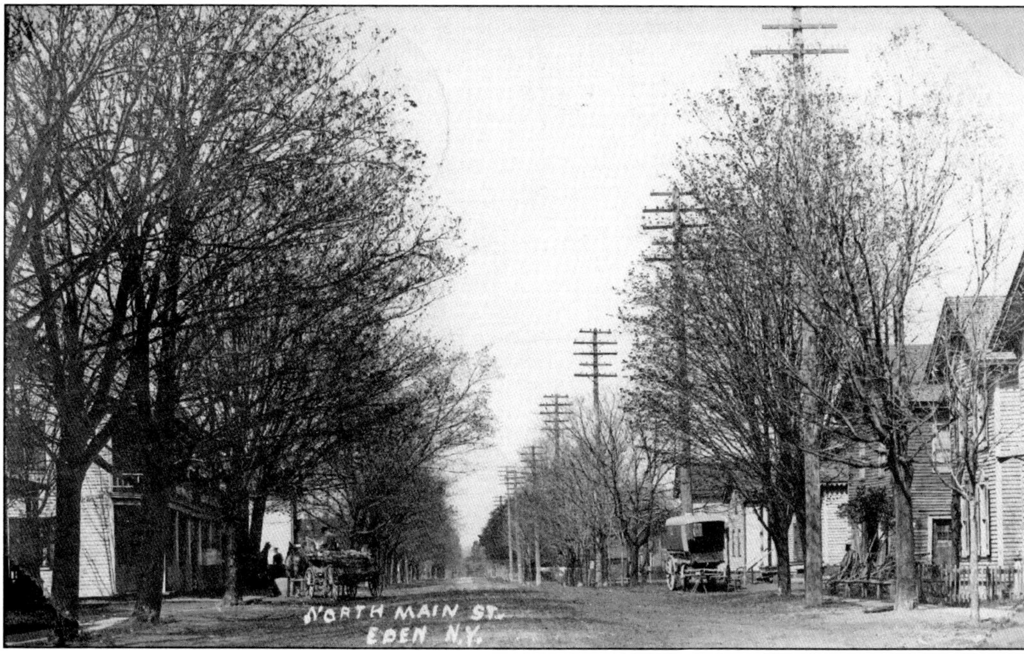

Looking north from the four corners of Main and Church Streets, the poles in this photograph indicate that it was taken sometime after 1902, when the telephone came to Eden. Electricity was not installed until shortly before World War I. The Roeller Hotel is on the left side of the wonderful tree-lined street. The two structures on the far right are now Eat'sa Pizza and Eden Chiropractic.

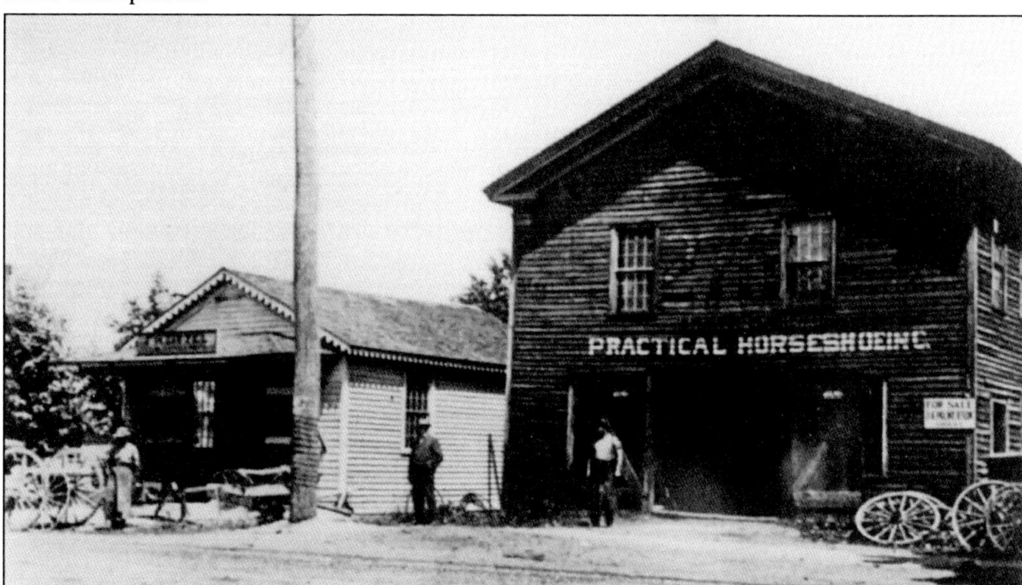

Two vital trades in the 19th and early 20th centuries were harness making and blacksmithing. Zittel Bros. Harness Shop and M.A. Hines blacksmith shop were in operation during the period from 1860 to 1922. The site of the harness shop, on the left, is approximately where O'Brien's Pub is today. The blacksmith shop was moved to South Main Street and was part of the Eclipse Metal Manufacturing plant.

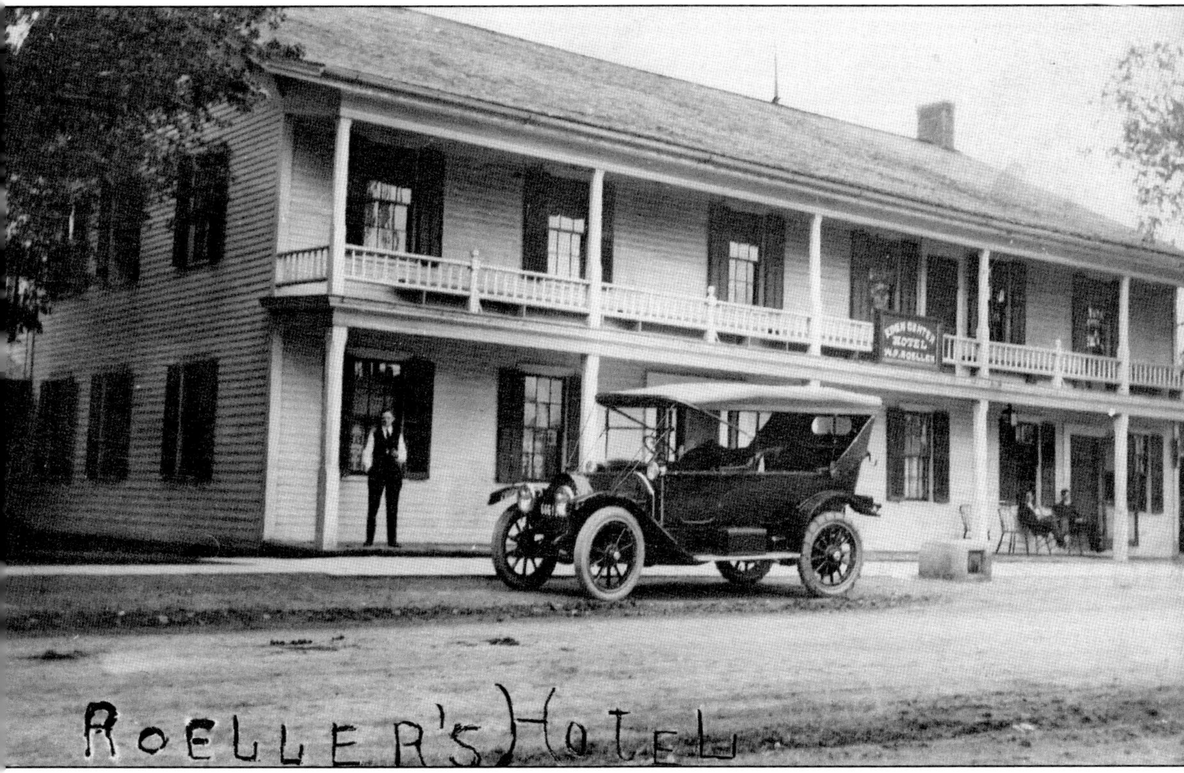

One of Eden's best-known landmarks is the Roeller Hotel, built by Godfrey Metz. In 1846, Metz built a cooper shop in town near the four corners. Using horsepower, he manufactured flour and apple barrels until 1858, when he installed the first steam engine in town. The hotel, built in 1848 in front of the cooperage, was a regular stop for the coaches traveling the road from Buffalo. On East Church Street, Metz built a spot called the Birch Woods. Located on the hill just above the present Eden Library, it was a place of entertainment for the town, complete with swings and a dance platform. It was the site of many picnics and Fourth of July celebrations. George Roeller purchased the hotel in 1876, and it remained in his family until 1967. The man standing in this c. 1910 photograph is likely George's son, William Roeller.

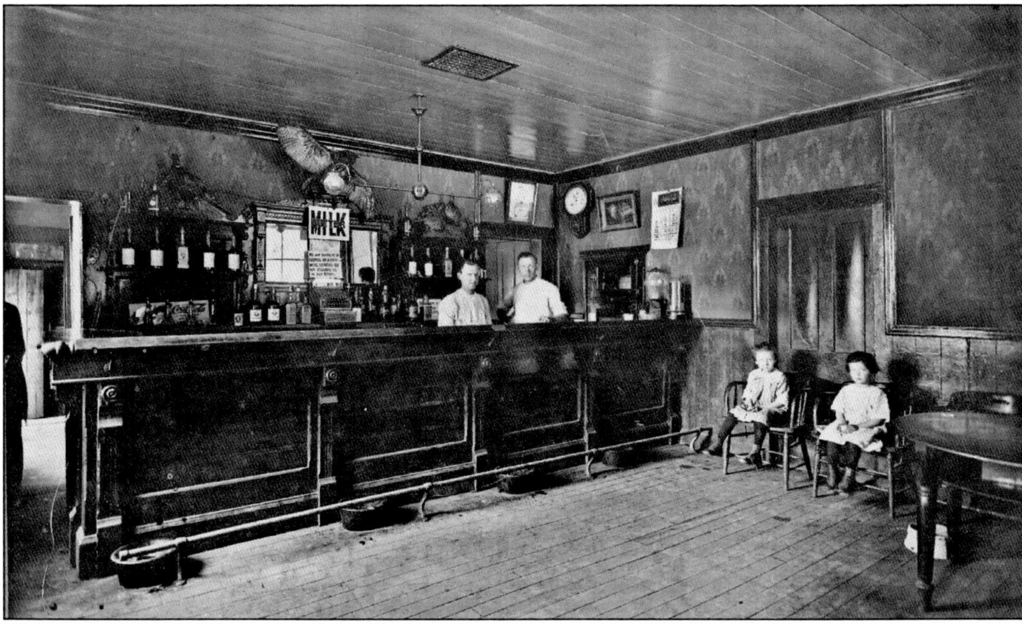

In her *Sketches of Eden History*, Doris Anderson relates a story from a long-deceased resident about how north Main Street was considered "tough." Many of the coopers and railroad men lived in a boardinghouse with a saloon in its basement. Perhaps that had something to do with the singing often heard after hours in that part of town. Inebriated individuals were frequently spotted on the street, especially on payday. The Roeller Hotel bar is pictured above.

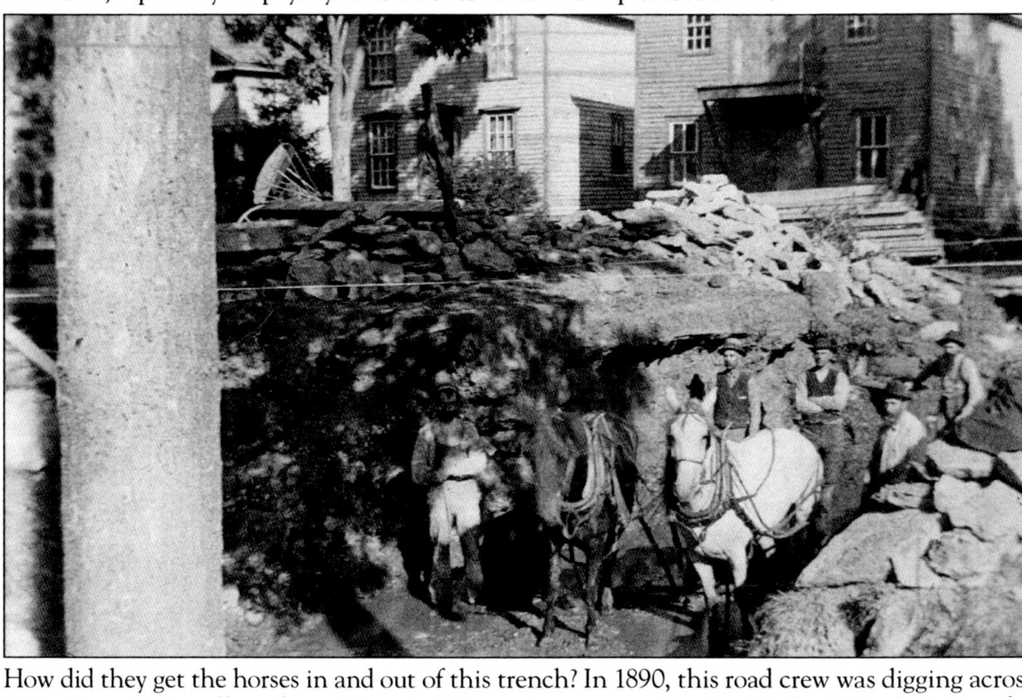

How did they get the horses in and out of this trench? In 1890, this road crew was digging across Main Street to install a culvert. Many in Eden today are unaware that Ryther's Creek runs under the road in this spot just north of Green Street. Workers Louis Keehn, Matt Schreiner, and George Nyhart, and two unidentified men are standing in front of the Baldauf basket factory.

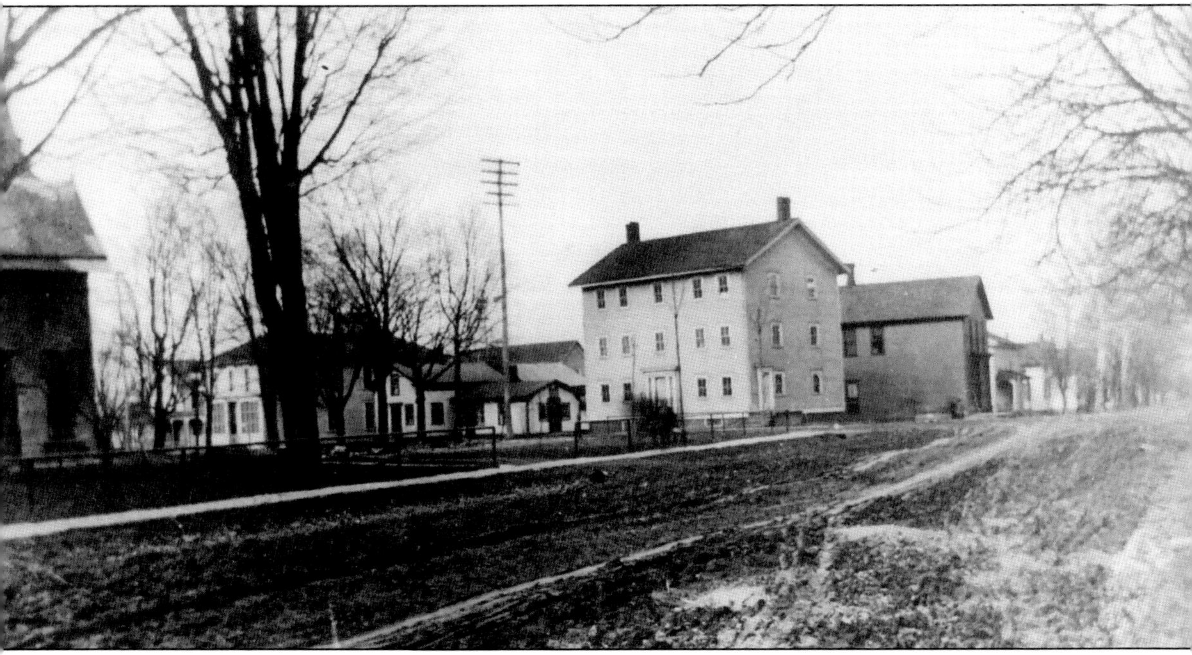

This imposing three-story structure on the southwest corner of Main Street was known at different times as the Redfield Building and Ellicott Square. The original building on this site was a log tavern built by Dr. William Hill, father of John Hill, founder of Eden Center. Dr. Hill was a former Revolutionary War surgeon and also a Methodist minister. Upon his arrival in town in 1814, he decided he was too old for either of those occupations, so he opened the tavern! Subsequent owners Asa Warren and James Green added space and made changes. In 1858, Homer Redfield remodeled the building extensively, adding the third story. During its lifetime, the building housed Redfield's law office, apartments, Miss Emaline's Select School for Girls, two dentists' offices, the town clerk's office, a bakery, a shoe shop, and a meat market in the basement. It was the hub of activity for young Eden. Martin Stinson renamed it Ellicott Square when he purchased the building in 1919. Three years later, it was torn down and replaced by the brick structure that stands today. This photograph was taken in 1910.

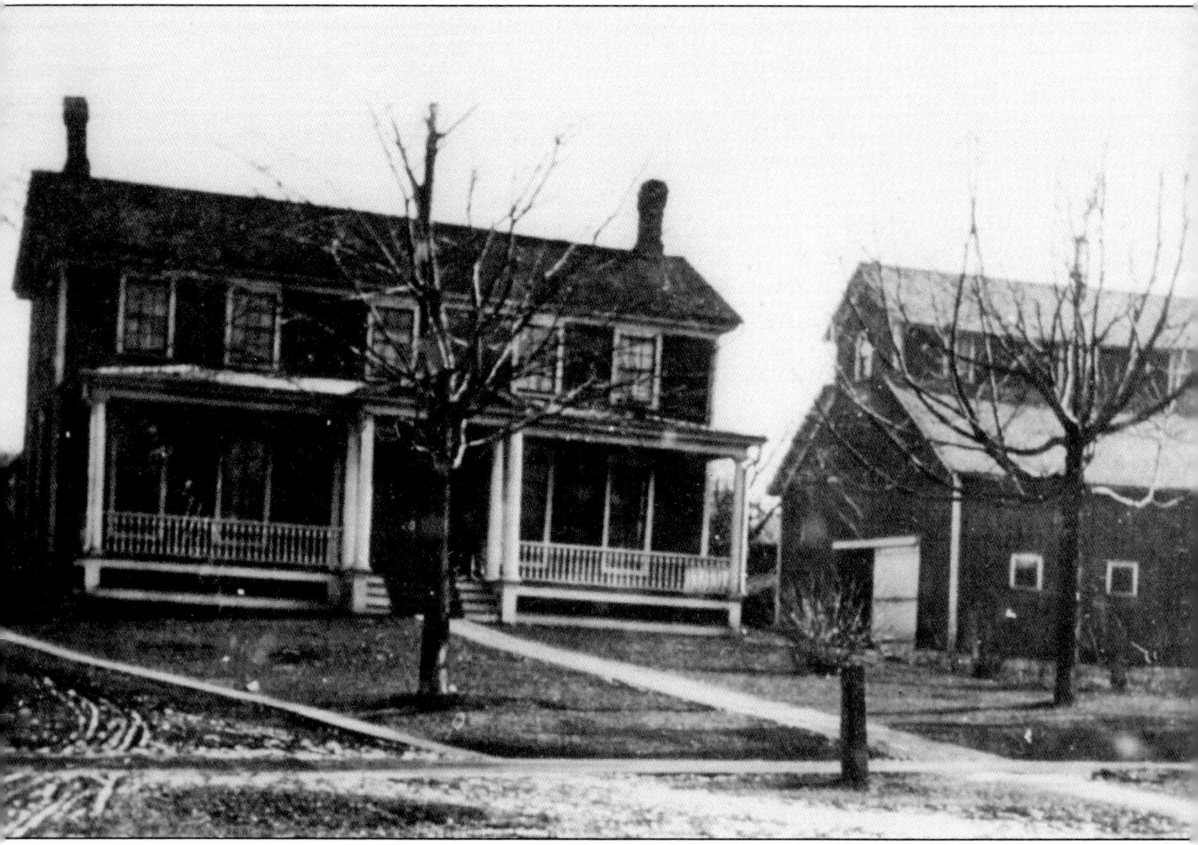

Three years after it officially became a town, War of 1812 veteran Col. Asa Warren arrived in Eden. He built what was probably a one-room home on Main Street in 1815. A grander structure eventually replaced it. He also built a gristmill on the Eighteen Mile Creek that he sold to Alexander Kromer in 1848. Warren became one of the fledgling town's most prominent figures. He was town supervisor, a tavern owner, and president of the Eden Temperance Society, though not all at the same time. He was an ardent supporter of public education and a social activist. During the Civil War, Warren's home was a stop on the Underground Railroad. In 1867, Luther Landon acquired the property for $4,000 from Warren's heirs. In the 1880s, Landon's son, Horace, maintained a stable of fine horses, which he ran at a racetrack located on the corner of Main and Hemlock Streets. This photograph shows the Landon house and barn as they appeared in 1900. The Eden Historical Society purchased the house in the 1970s and restored it to Warren's 1840s time period. Today the Asa Warren House is a museum.

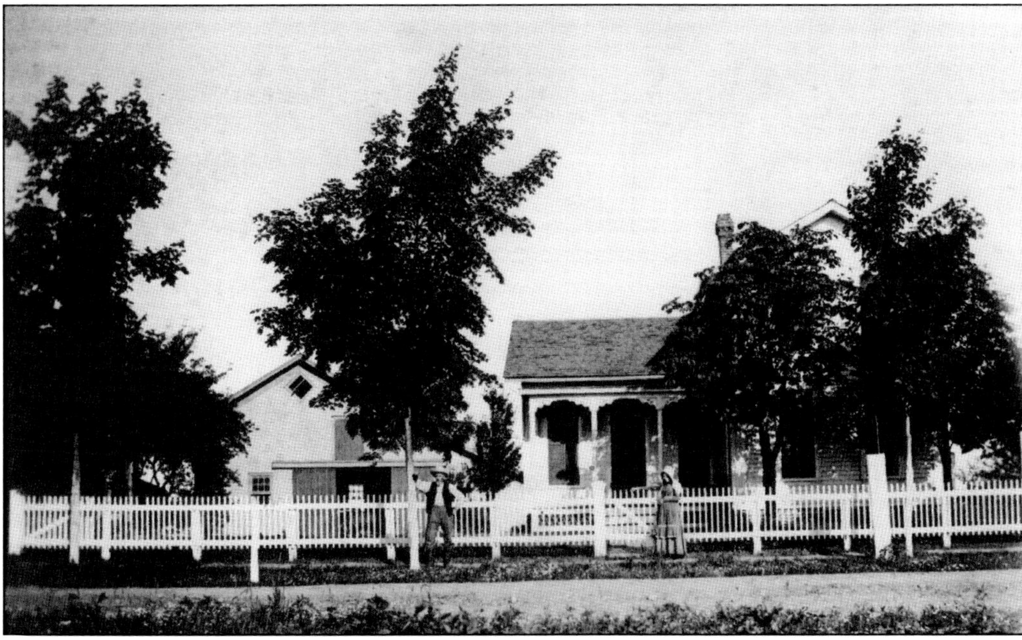

The charming 19th-century fence enhances the appeal of this photograph. Though it is gone now, the house and barn still stand. Standing in front of their home at 8492 North Main Street are Frederick and Magdalena Bauer. The land this house sits on was once part of the vast tract of land that the Welch family owned. It is thought that the barn once was a cooper shop, a logical idea since North Main Street was once known as Cooper Street.

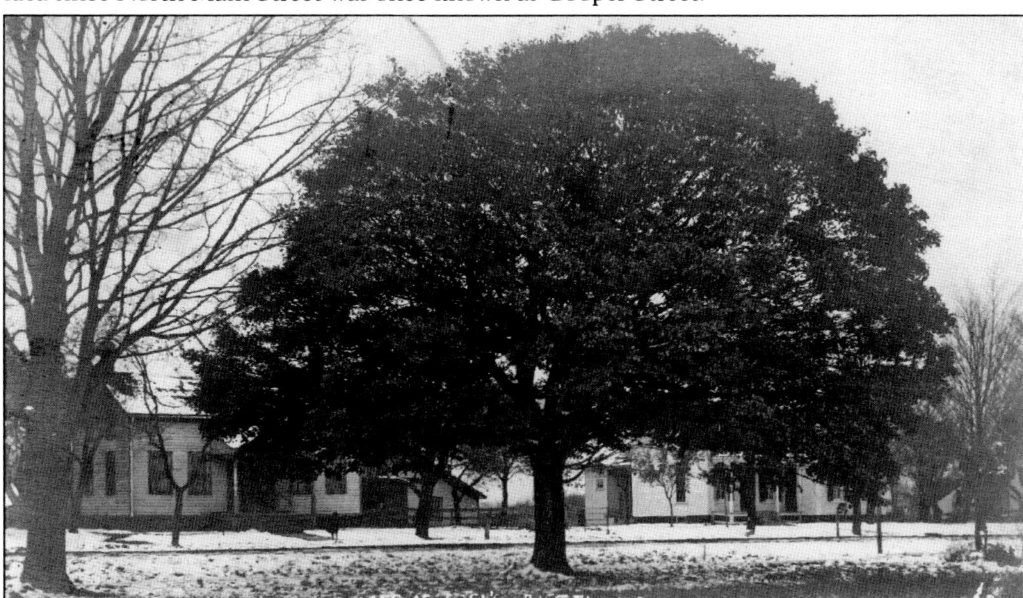

A postcard from 1911 labels this nicely shaped maple as "One of Eden's Pretty Trees." It stood on North Main Street where Roswell Parkway now begins. Nelson and Willis Hill, son and grandson of Eden Center founder John Hill, are credited with planting the trees that once shaded Main and Church Streets. As a boy during the 1920s, Elton Palmerton remembers that this particular one was a great climbing tree.

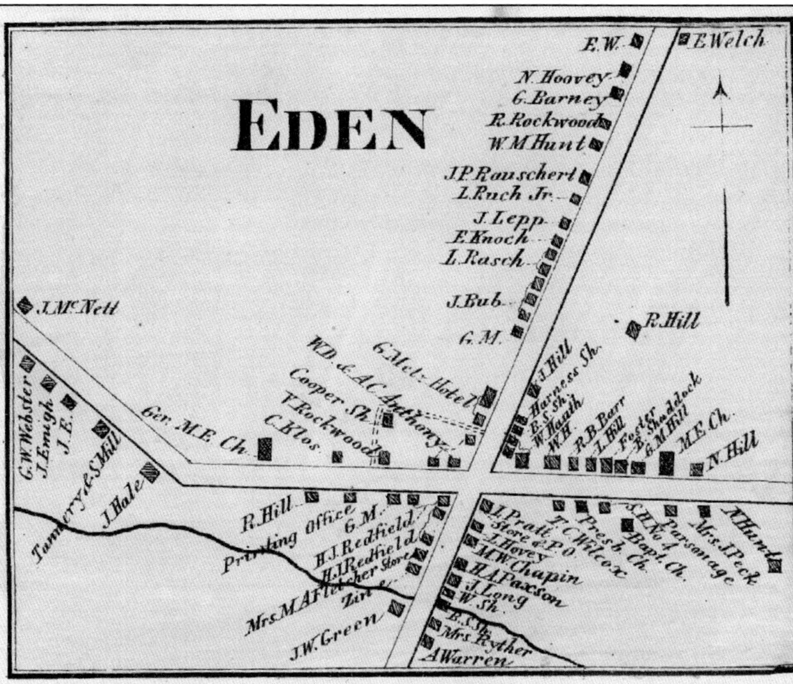

EDEN BUSINESS DIRECTORY.

Lyman Pratt...Dealer in Dry Goods, Groceries, Hardware, Glassware, Crockery, Hats, Caps, Boots, Shoes, Ready-Made Clothing, &c.
Godfrey Metz...Proprietor of Eden Center Hotel, and Manufacturer of Barrels.
H. A. Paxson...Dentist.
John S. Fidler...Printer.
Abram Thorn...Attorney and Counsellor at Law.
H. J. Redfield... " " "
L. Hill...Harness Maker.
Frank Knoch...Prop. Knoch Saloon.
Lewis Rasch...Butcher and Meet Market.
Jacob Long...Carriage and Wagon Maker.
A. D. Martin...Engineer.
Jacob Lepp...Cooper.
Louis Ruch, Jr...."
Christofel Klos..."
John Bub...Shoemaker.
Anton Setter...Proprietor of Saw Mill, 2 1/2 miles N. W. of Eden Center.
J. W. Green...Resident.
P. Baldauf...Carpenter.

This map of Eden Center is from the 1866 *New Topographical Atlas of Erie County*. Family names of Welch, Hill, Green, Webster, Rockwood, and Hunt are all among those of the earliest settlers of the town. Images of many of the structures shown on the map are featured in this chapter. The business directory lists some of the services available in town. The Ryther blacksmith shop can be seen straddling the creek. Lyman Pratt's store and post office are across Main Street from the Redfield Building. Zittel Brothers Harness Shop and the Hines Blacksmith shop are on the east side of Main Street. Godfrey Metz's hotel and barn are on the west side of the street. There was a tannery and sawmill on West Church Street, and on East Church Street, one can pick out the one-room school and the Baptist church. The structure labeled "Presb. Ch." was really the Congregational church and the site of today's fire hall. The Asa Warren home, shown on page 24, is the last structure at the south end of Main Street on the map.

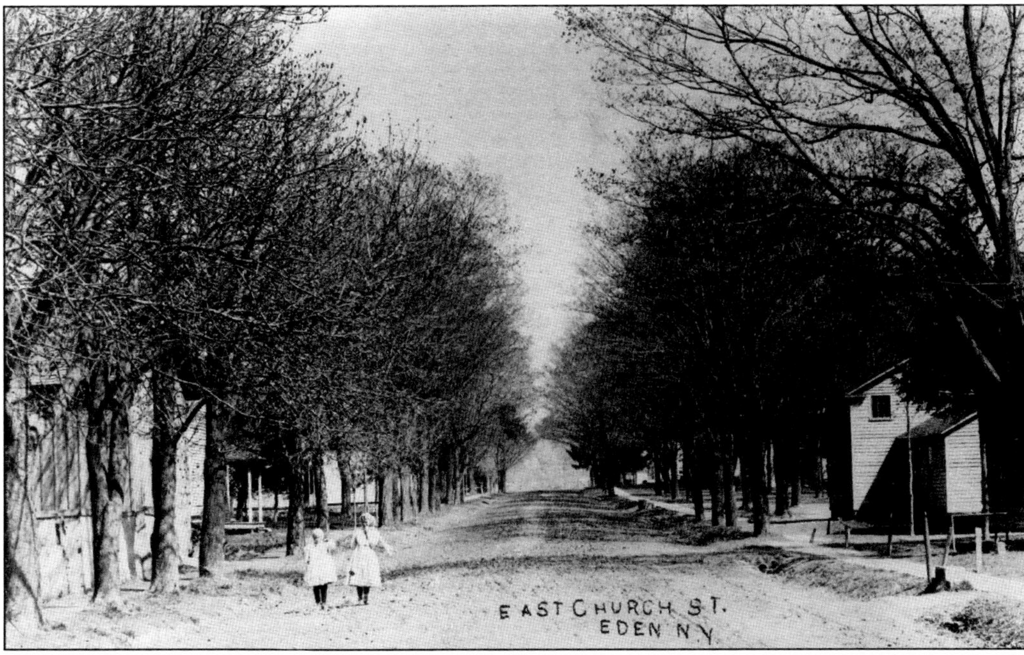

Two young girls prefer the road to the sidewalk in this 1905 picture of East Church Street. The light-colored frame house on the right was located on the site of today's HSBC Bank's parking lot. Dirt roads were the norm for Eden until around 1920, when Main Street was macadamized. Church Street was paved in 1925, but most of the side roads remained dirt for some time.

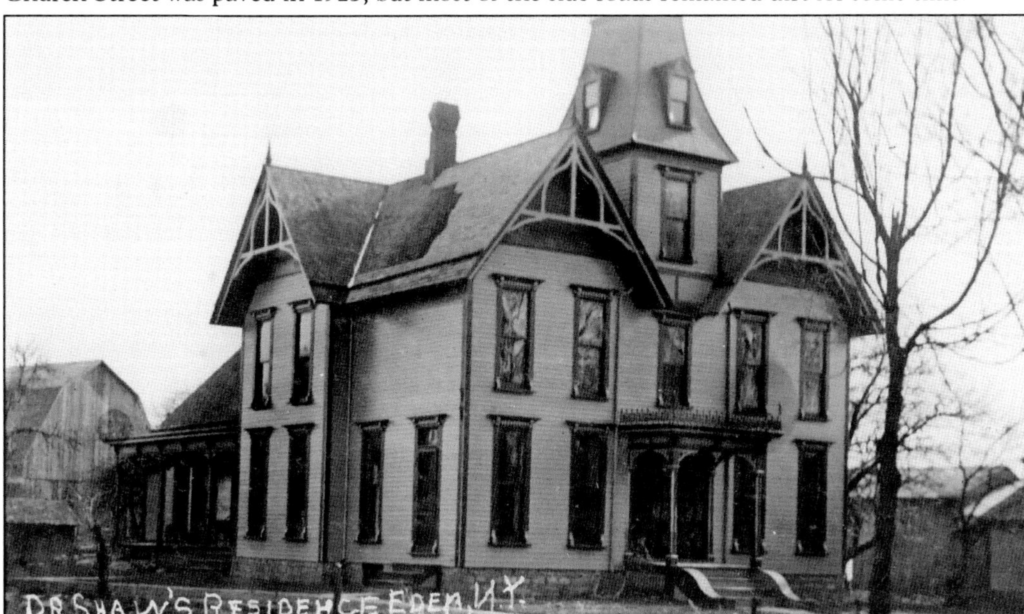

The little girls in the image above spent much of their life in this elegant Victorian home on Main Street. Lucille Shaw Laing and Helen Shaw Parmelee were the granddaughters of Dr. Malin B. and Arminda Shaw, who raised them after the girls' parents both died. Albert Martin built this home for Dr. Shaw in 1880. Upon his graduation from the University of Buffalo Medical School in 1866, Shaw moved to Eden where he practiced for 46 years.

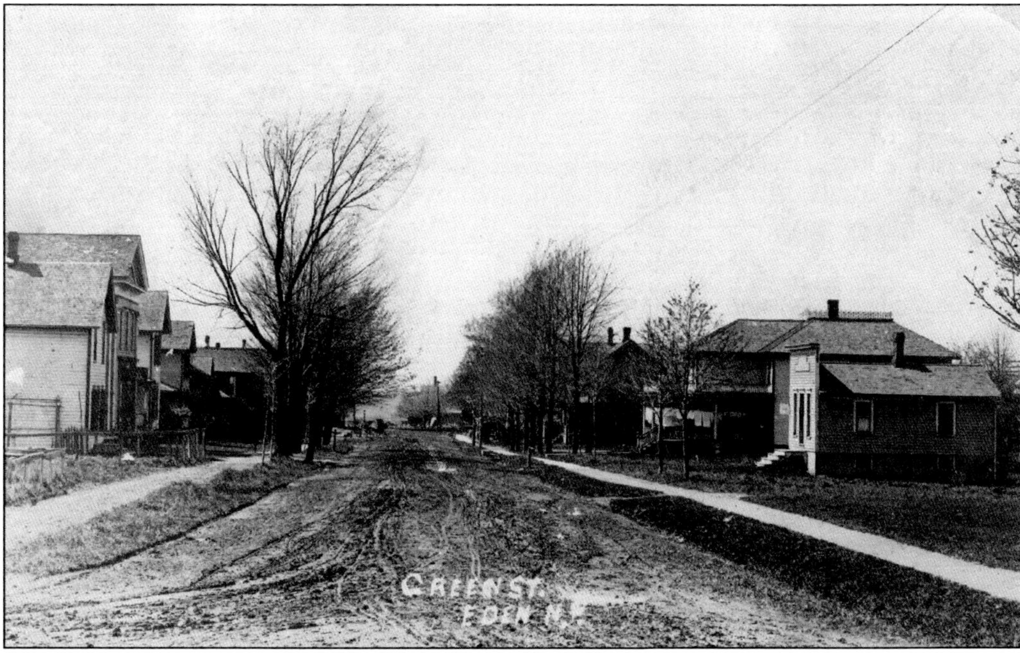

With the advent of the railroad line through town, Green Street became a bustling retail and commercial area. The far end of the street was the location of the railroad, lumberyards, and warehouses for grain and coal. Looking west from Main Street toward the train depot, one can see the Eden Telephone Exchange on the right. Homes and stores lined the street. This photograph was taken about 1910.

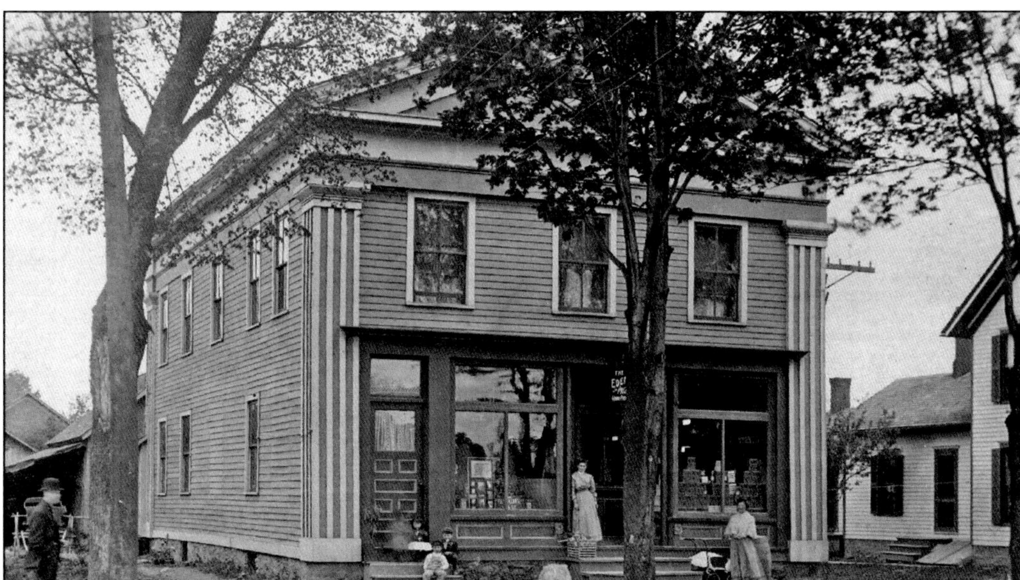

Dickman's Store had an interesting history. The classical structure was built on East Church Street in 1842 for the Eden Academy, a high school that charged tuition. The Baptist congregation bought the building and remodeled it in 1848. It was moved to Green Street in 1895 when the present Baptist church was built. Dickman's Store burned in 1913, taking the homes on either side with it.

Another one of Eden's lovely homes, built by John Vellum in the 1880s, stood on the corner of Main and Green Streets. Duran A. Palmerton acquired the property in the late 1890s, when he came to Eden. He operated his real estate business from the home where he and his family lived for many years. About 1903, Eden's first telephone exchange was located in this home. Palmerton and his son, Jay, acted as night operators.

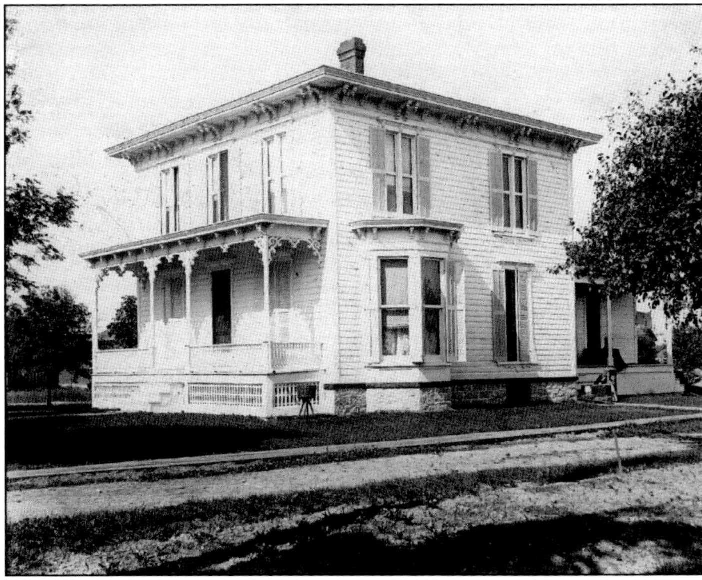

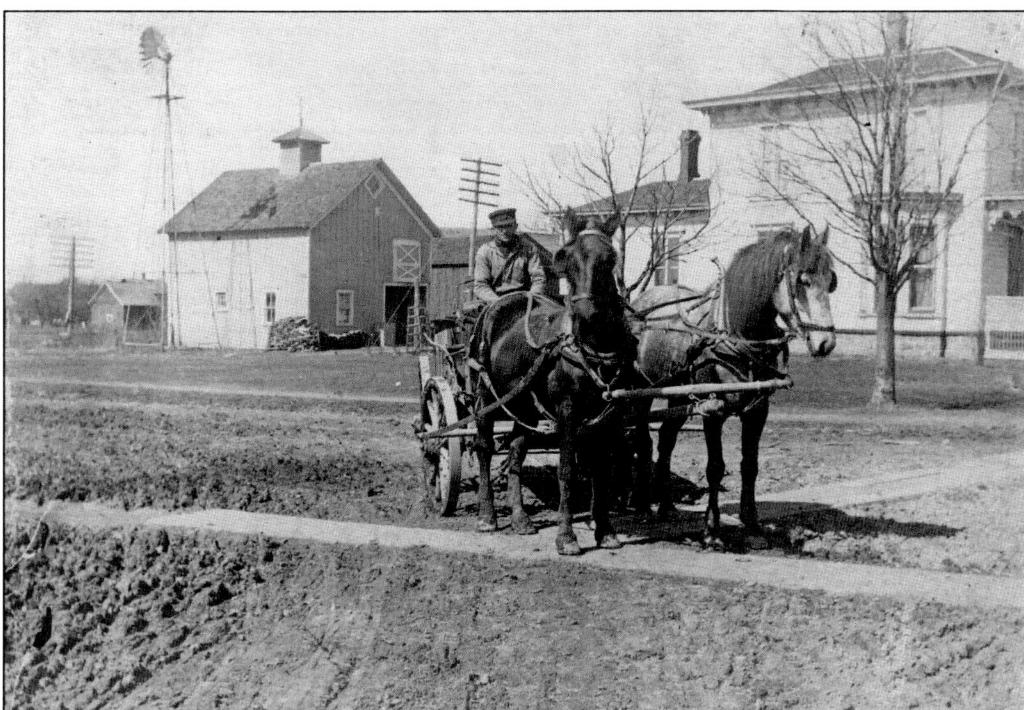

Another view of the Palmertons' home shows their barn, which still stands. The windmill beside the barn was used for pumping water. There were a number of windmills in Eden during the early 20th century. Henry Hickman purchased the first one in 1899 from Redfield and Davis Hardware. Notice the wooden plank sidewalks bordering the dirt roads. The man driving the wagon is unidentified.

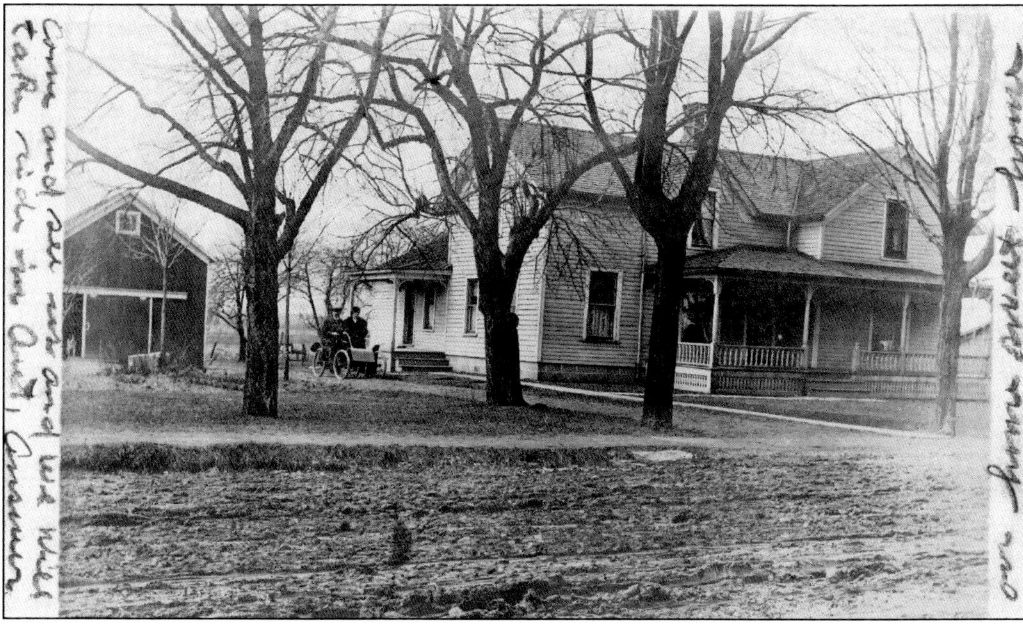

This 1907 photograph is significant because it presages the future. West Church Street residents Fred and Laura Kaufman are shown sitting in their two-cylinder Michigan. It was the first gasoline-powered automobile to be purchased by an Eden resident. Many others soon followed. Doubters were convinced that the car's awful speed would "shatter people's nerves or cause them to go insane." (Courtesy of Bob Maltby.)

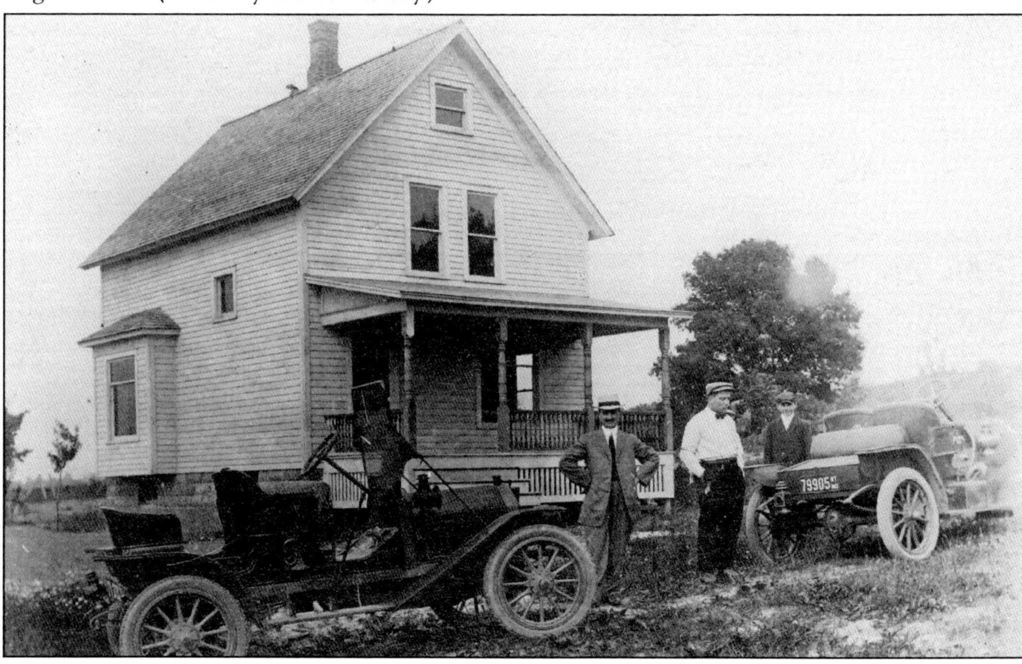

Looking neither insane nor shattered, a dapper-looking D.A. Palmerton stands proudly beside his vehicle. Pictured in front of a Second Street residence are Palmerton, Herman Gumtow, and Isador Greenfield. The license plate on the car to the right reads 1913. That same year, Clarence Henry and Edward Hickman bought the first trucks used to haul farm produce to market.

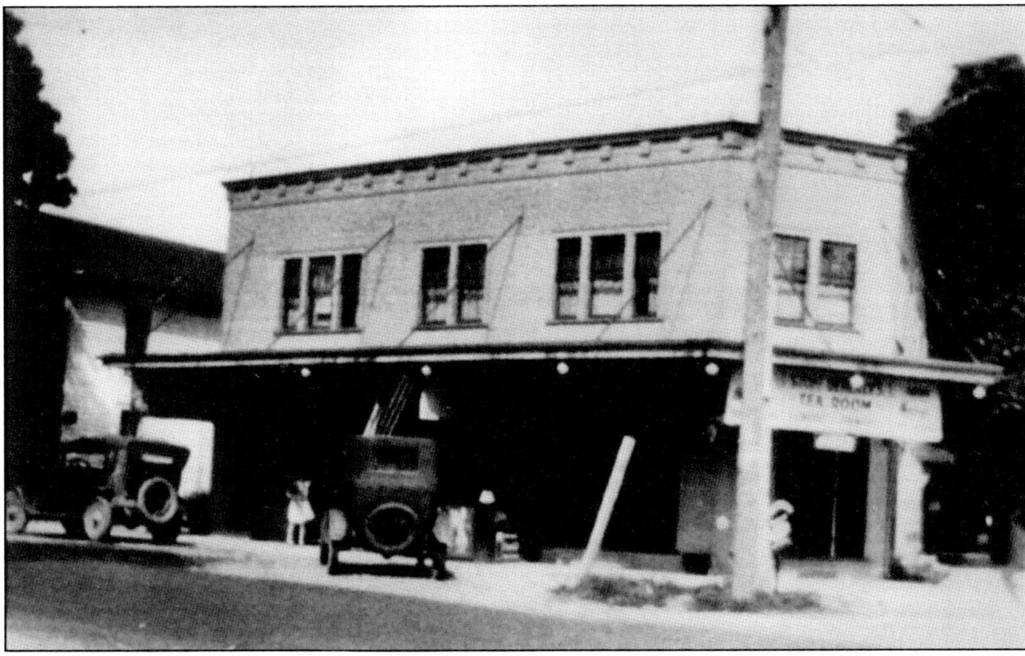

This building is familiar to Eden residents as the Four Corners Café. In the early 1920s, after the removal of other structures, Edward Demerley built this restaurant, Demerley's Tea Room. How long it was actually a "tea" room is not known. At one time, the space was a bar and an ice cream parlor at the same time! Food and drink have been served in this establishment since its first days.

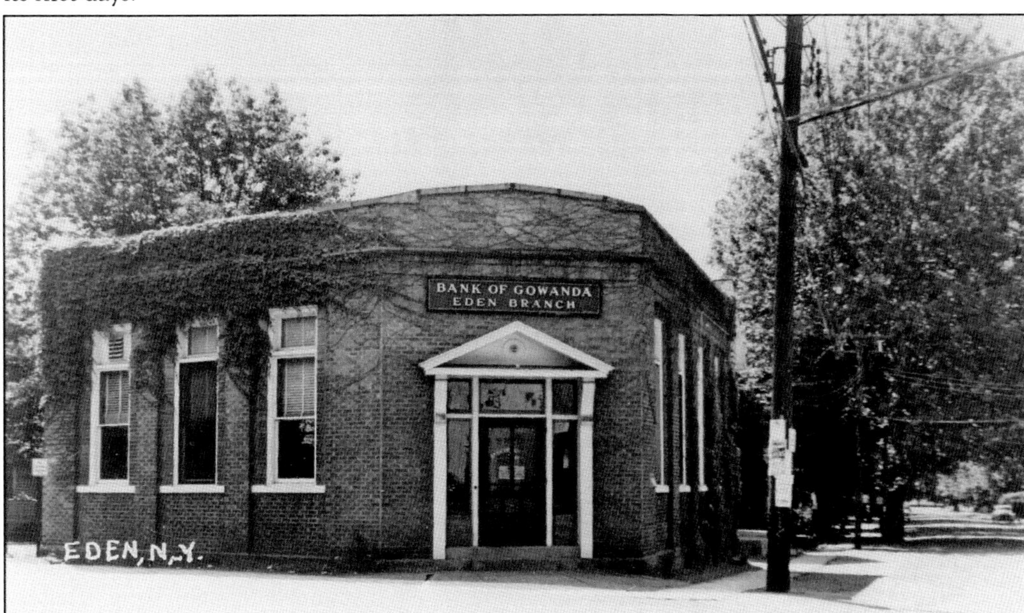

The Bank of Eden was incorporated by several of the town's leading citizens in 1922. They erected this brick structure, which is now home to the Randall Agency. Big excitement came to town in May 1935, when four armed men held up the bank and made off with $10,000. They were apprehended in Cleveland. The bank was sold to the Bank of Gowanda in 1939, as pictured here.

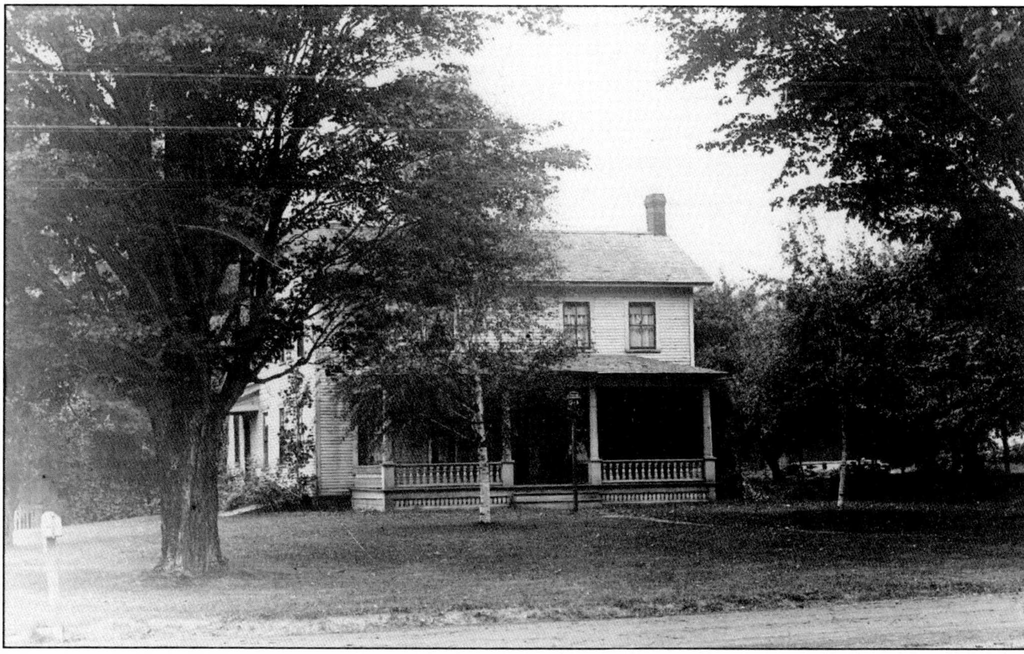

This house, located at 8373 North Main Street, is one of the oldest in Eden. It was built by John Morgan Welch on part of the large tract of land that he purchased from the Holland Land Company between 1810 and 1815. The original part of the house probably dates as far back as the early 1830s. Elizabeth Welch continued to live there after her husband died in 1838.

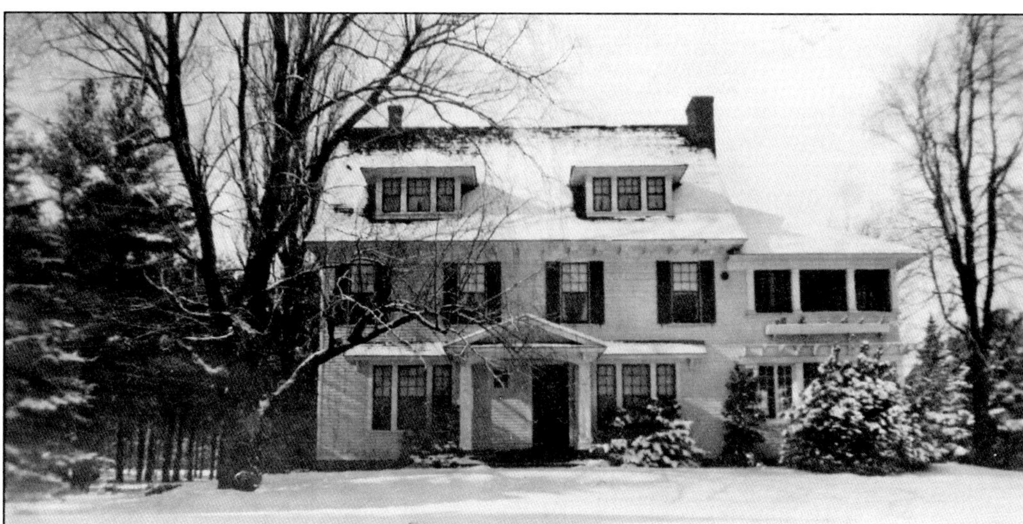

Almost across the street from the dwelling pictured above is the home built in 1903 by Sen. Nelson Welch Cheney. It is believed that John Welch's original log cabin stood on the same site. This is the home as it appeared in 1939 and much as it does today. At various times in the latter part of the 20th century, it was a nursing home and a bed-and-breakfast inn before once again becoming a residence.

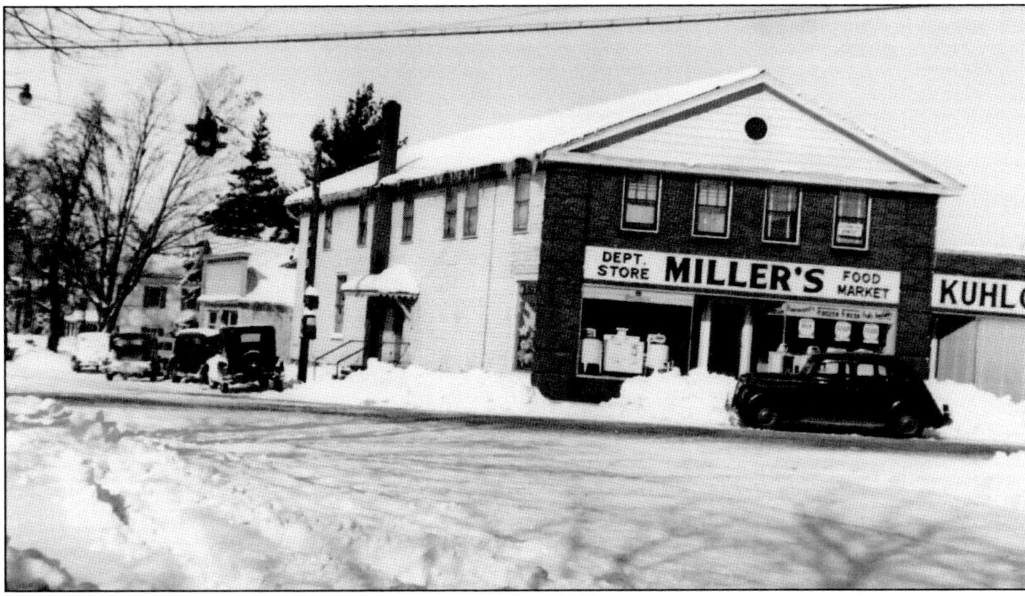

This wintertime photograph from 1937 shows the corner of Main and West Church Street. Miller's Store, now the site of the Chamber of Commerce Park, was a beloved institution for many decades. It was the go-to place for just about everything. The building was completely destroyed by fire on March 12, 1974. A store had existed on the site since 1816.

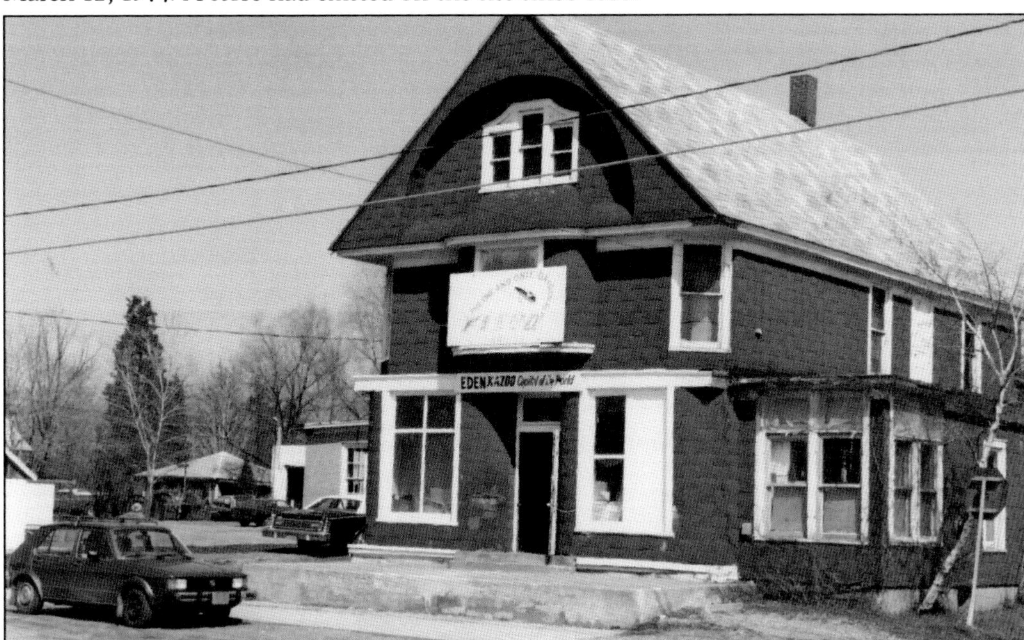

By the mid-20th century, the Kazoo Company was still making instruments on the original machinery, but the building was in poor condition. It was not until 1985 that Robert Bergash of Brimms Industry bought the business and began an extensive renovation of the building. Complete with a new gift shop, the revitalized building shone. In 2002, Bergash donated the building to two local nonprofit agencies, SASi and the Claddaugh Commission. (Courtesy of Rosemary Smutz.)

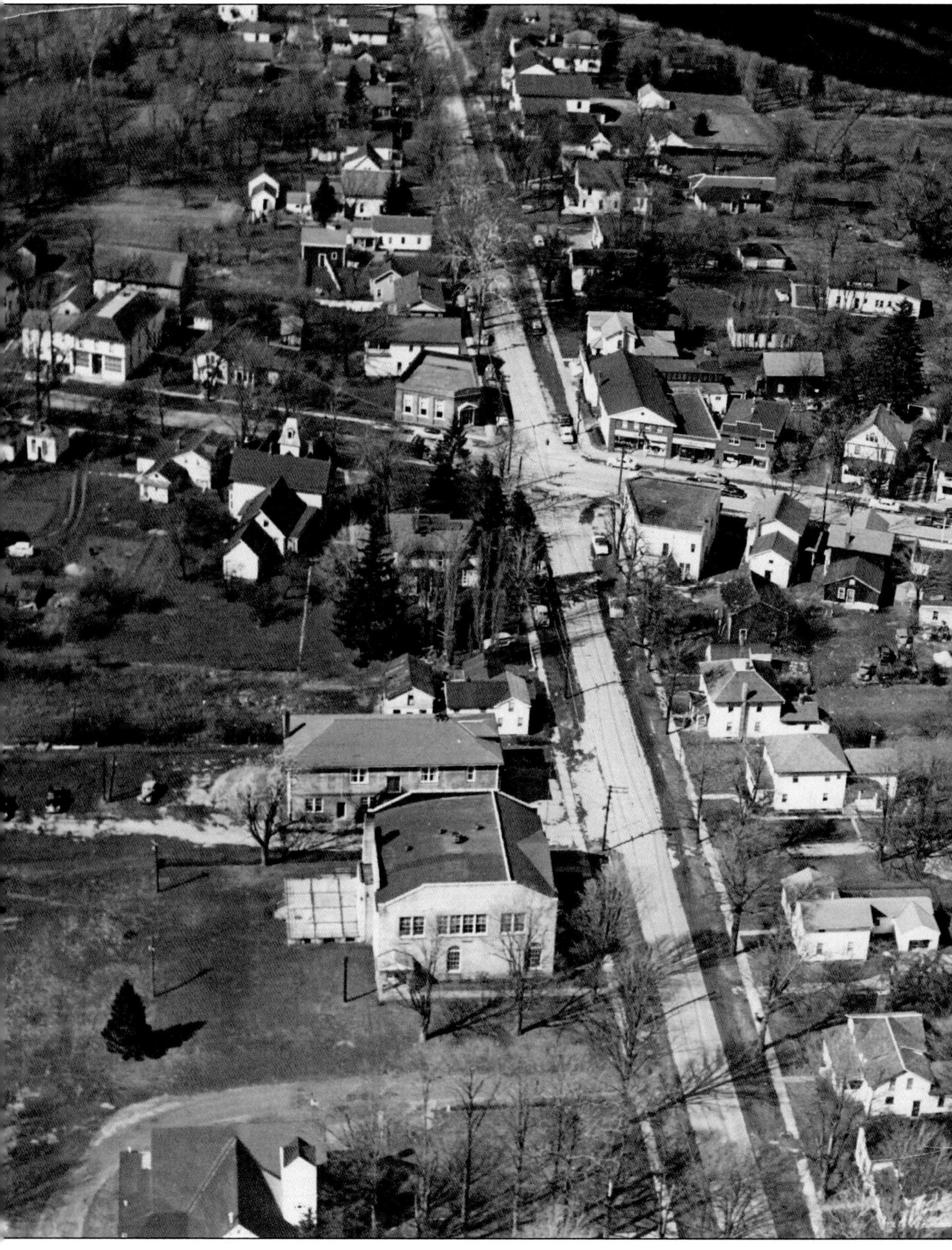

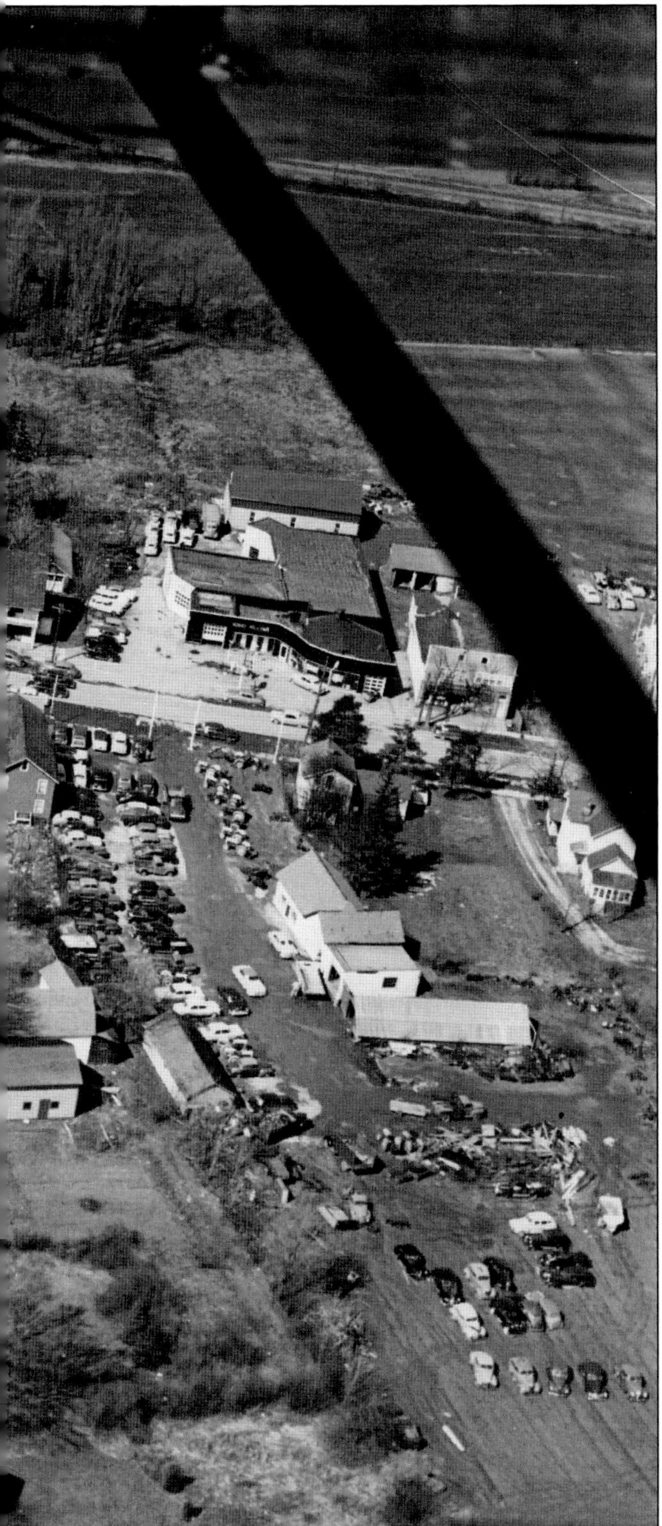

This 1940s aerial view of the center of Eden is worthy of scrutiny with a magnifying glass. Many of the pictured structures remain, while others have disappeared, been remodeled, or been replaced. The town hall in the lower left of the photograph now has two additions. The old building housing the library and fire department was replaced in 1973. HSBC Bank and its parking lot now occupy the corner of Main and East Church Streets. Across the road at Main and West Church Streets is the Bank of Gowanda, now Randall Agency. Across West Church Street, Miller's Store is now the Chamber of Commerce Park. The two buildings between Miller's and the Roeller Hotel are commercial establishments. The Nobbs and Williams Ford Agency is located next to the hotel and also across Main Street. Sharp eyes will pick up other similarities and changes.

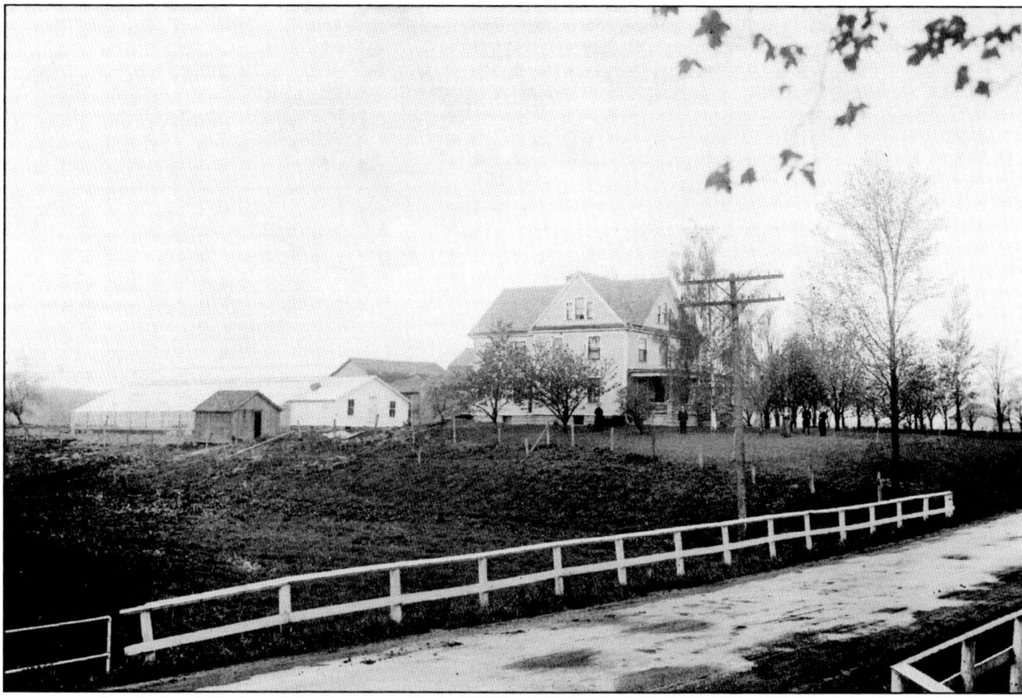

These two photographs illustrate how the appearance of many of the structures in town have either remained the same or drastically changed. The house above should be familiar to everyone who regularly travels through Eden. It is the old Albert Hickman home at 8009 Gowanda State Road. The formal gardens down the hill from the house did not yet exist, and Route 62 looks very different from today's roadway. The house itself, however, is very much the same. The author was astonished to discover that the lower picture is an early image of her own home. Millard Webster built the Old Jennings residence in the 1880s or earlier. Over the ensuing decades, additions and the removal of the porch have significantly altered the structure's appearance. With the exception of one barn, the out buildings have long since disappeared.

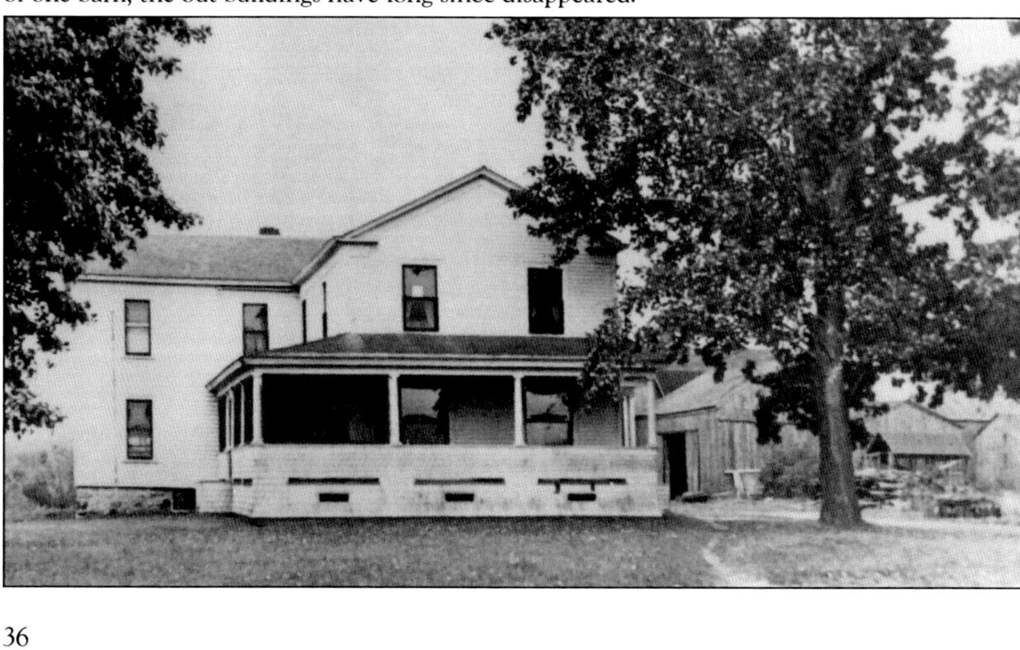

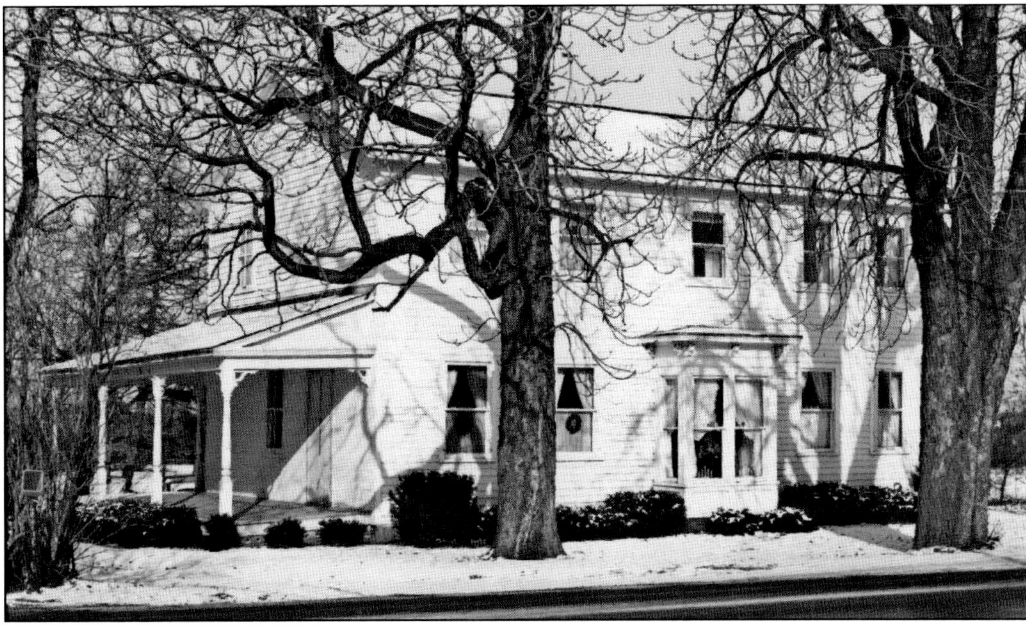

These photographs tell the story of two different fates. A 1981 architectural survey of old buildings speculated that the original portion of the home at 8122 North Main Street, shown above, was one of the oldest in Eden and perhaps Erie County. In the 1830s, under Joseph Thorn's ownership, it was a tavern and stagecoach stop. During the Civil War, the house was part of the Underground Railroad. By the late 1990s, the house was deteriorating, and it had to be demolished in 2009. Today the Bunting/Wilcox home on Jennings Road looks better than in the 1914 photograph shown below. The Buntings were among the earliest settlers in town. This frame house, finished in 1869, is one of the oldest farmhouses on Jennings Road. Few structural changes have been made over the years. The land for Eden High School came from this property.

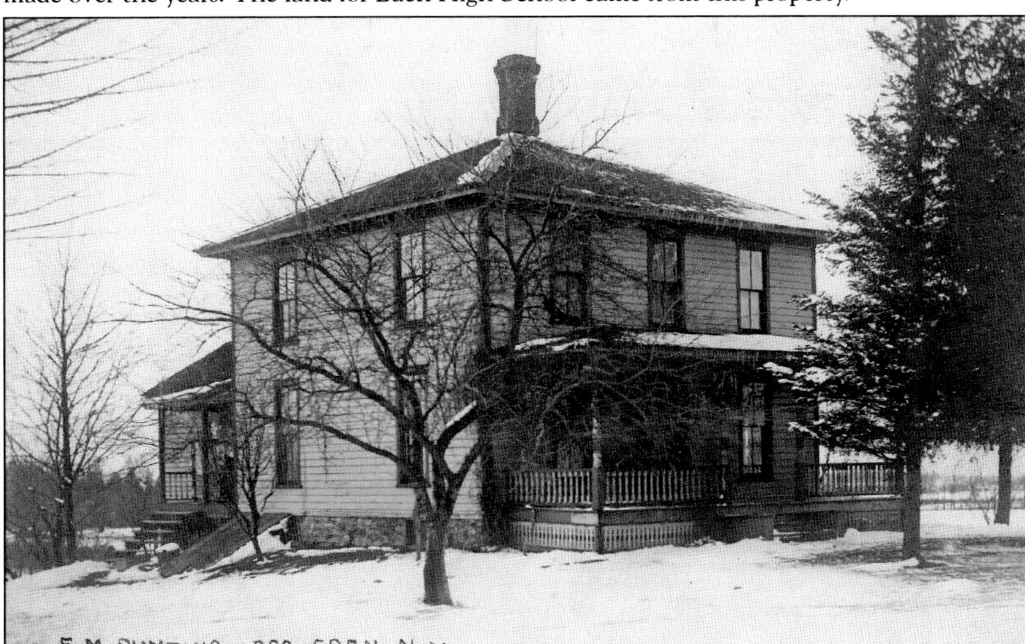

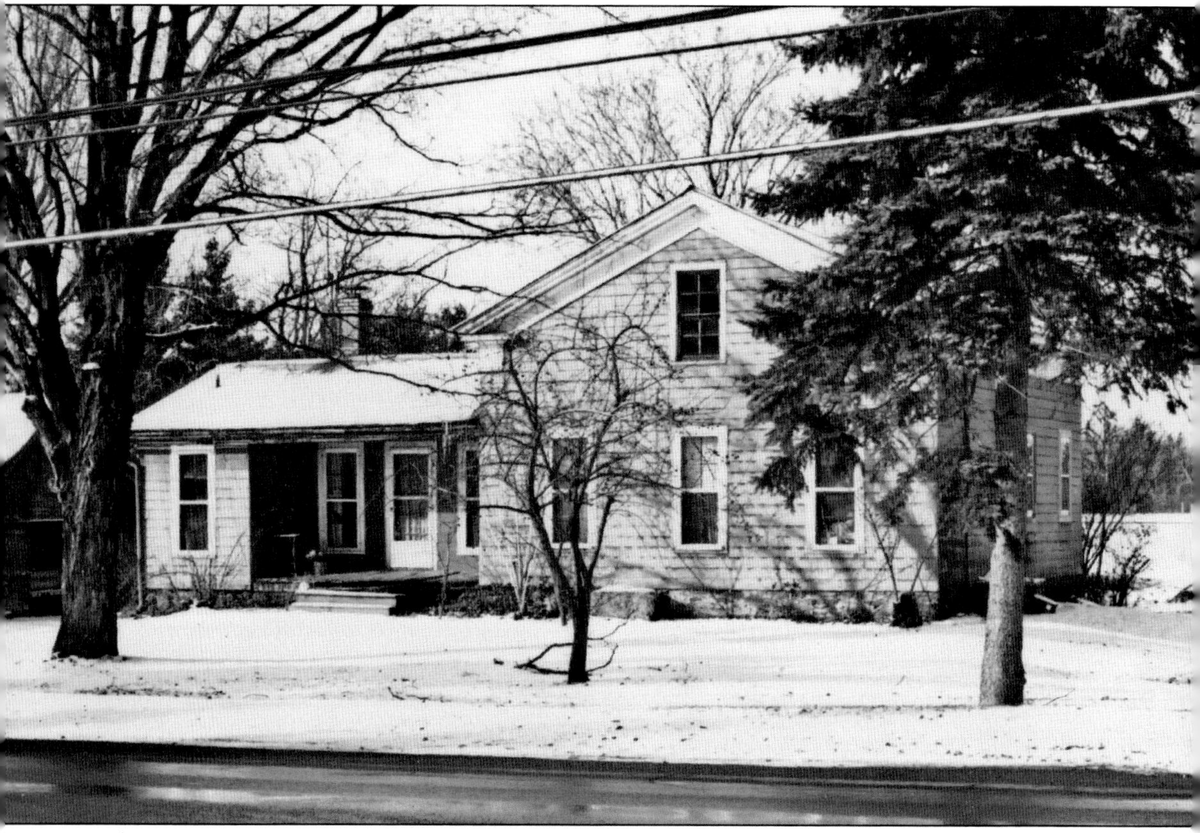

This modest dwelling, located at 8326 North Main Street, is one of the most historically significant properties in Eden. Until 2003, it was the earliest farm in town still belonging to descendants of the original owner. John Morgan Welch settled the Welch Homestead around 1810, after he made the first of several large land purchases on the north side of town. It is thought he might have owned as much as 500 acres. When his brother-in-law John Hill came to Eden, Welch sold him the southern part of his farm. Today that is the center of town. Pioneers generally paid from $2 to $5 per acre. In lieu of cash, goods were often accepted as payment. This frame structure replaced Welch's first dwelling, a crude log cabin, the exact location of which can only be guessed. Though known to be very old, the precise age of the house is undetermined. The back portion is original from the 1830s, and the front is somewhat newer. The property is now home to the newly formed Welch Farm Museum, whose mission is to preserve Eden's agricultural heritage.

Three

East Eden, Toad Hollow, and Clarksburg

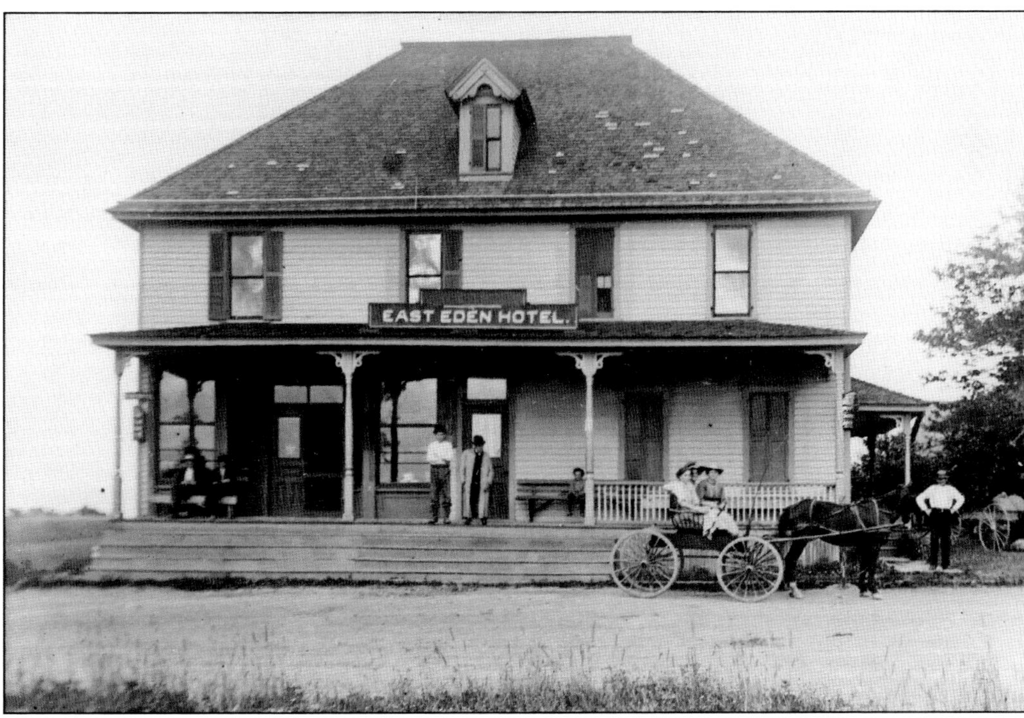

The northeastern quadrant of the town of Eden is known as East Eden. At one time, it was much like Eden Valley, a busy community with its own post office, stores, and tradesmen. William Mumbach, who was also postmaster for a time, built this hotel about 1860. This 1911 photograph shows the hotel a few years after it was acquired by Jacob Wittmeyer, whose family ran it for the next 50 years.

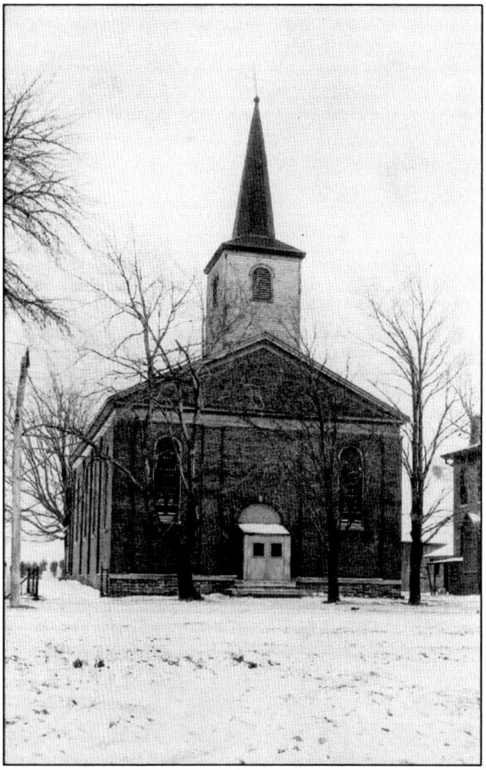

The centerpiece and heart of East Eden is St. Mary's Church. Established in 1835 as a mission of St. Louis Church in Buffalo, it is the second oldest Roman Catholic parish in the Diocese of Buffalo. In 1851, the original frame building, built by parishioners, was replaced by the brick structure that stands today. A walk through the church cemetery is a lesson in East Eden's history.

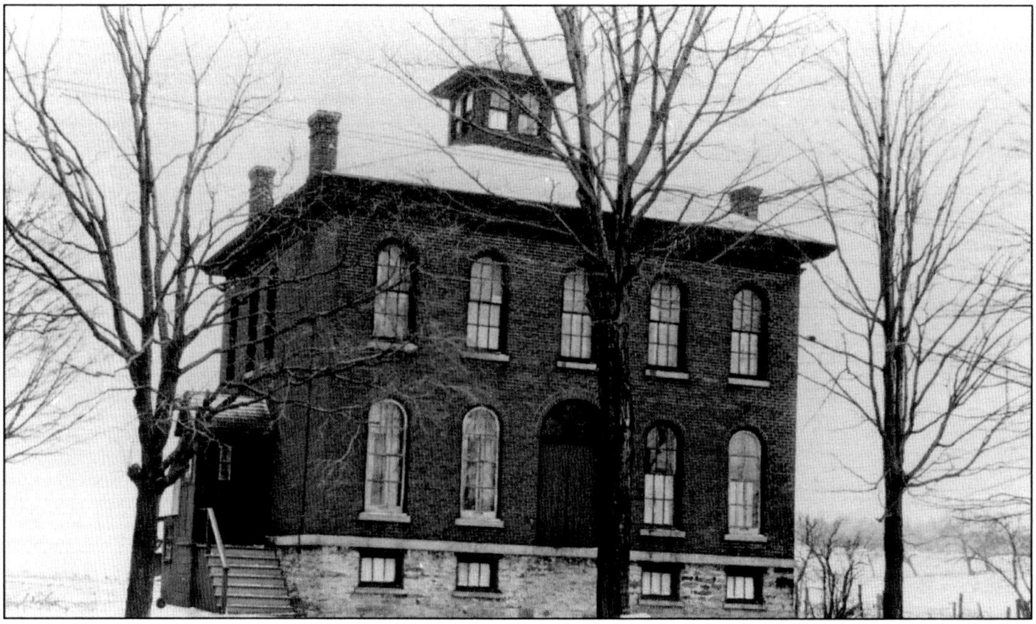

From 1862 until 1970, the Sisters of the Third Order of St. Francis maintained a convent in East Eden and taught at the parochial school. Their first dwelling was a structure built by St. Mary's first rector, the Reverend Nicholas Mertz, as a home for the poor. In 1868, the sisters erected the structure seen above. It was renovated in 1923 and demolished in 1971. It stood where the church parking lot is located. (Courtesy of East Eden Historical Society.)

St. Mary's parochial school was built in 1878. The congregation and the priest, Father Martin Weinards, donated beautiful desks costing $100. Nuns conducted classes in both German and English until the 1930s, when the ethnic nature of the population diversified. Over the years, additions and renovations kept the building updated and equipped. The frame structure on Keller Road was used until 1968, when the school was closed. (Courtesy of East Eden Historical Society.)

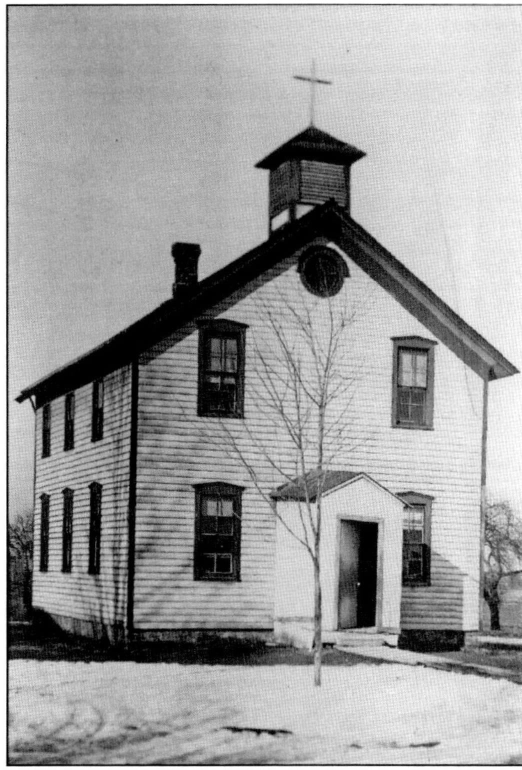

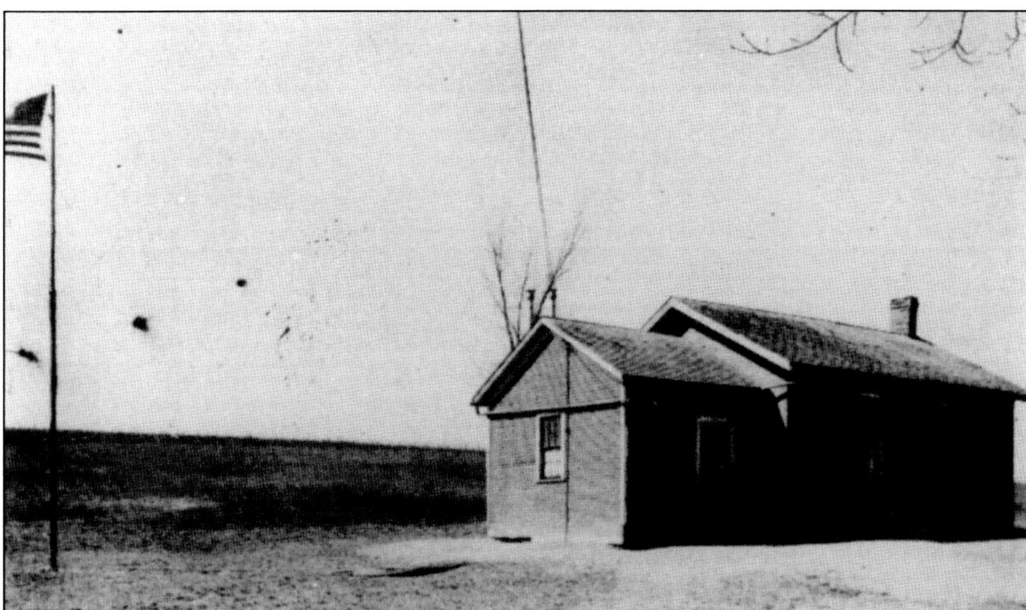

The first district school in East Eden was built around 1836 south of St. Mary's Church on East Eden Road. Records from the 1830s indicate that there were 103 children from ages five to 16 in the district, though it does not say all of them attended school. This picture shows the brick structure built in 1868 to replace the original school. It was located on the corner of North Boston and East Eden Roads.

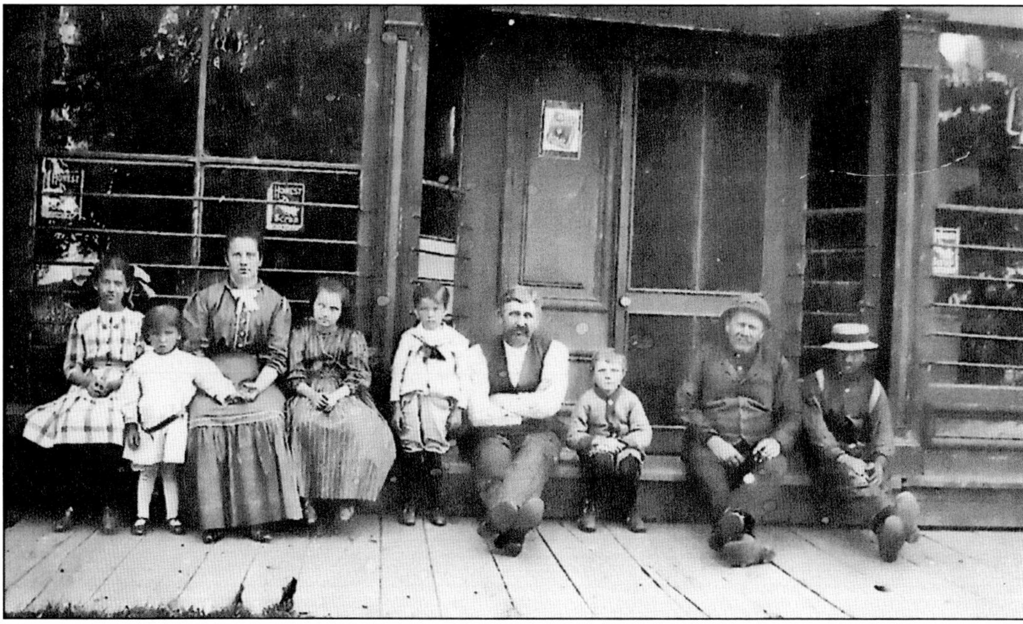

In 1902, George Schwanz and his family (center and left) posed on the steps of their home and business, the Schwanz Hotel on East Eden Road. The hotel served meals and had a saloon, a meat market, and a grocery store on the premises. Originally the ground floor was one large room, but as laws became more restrictive, partitions had to be erected between the saloon and the grocery store. (Courtesy of Eugene Winter.)

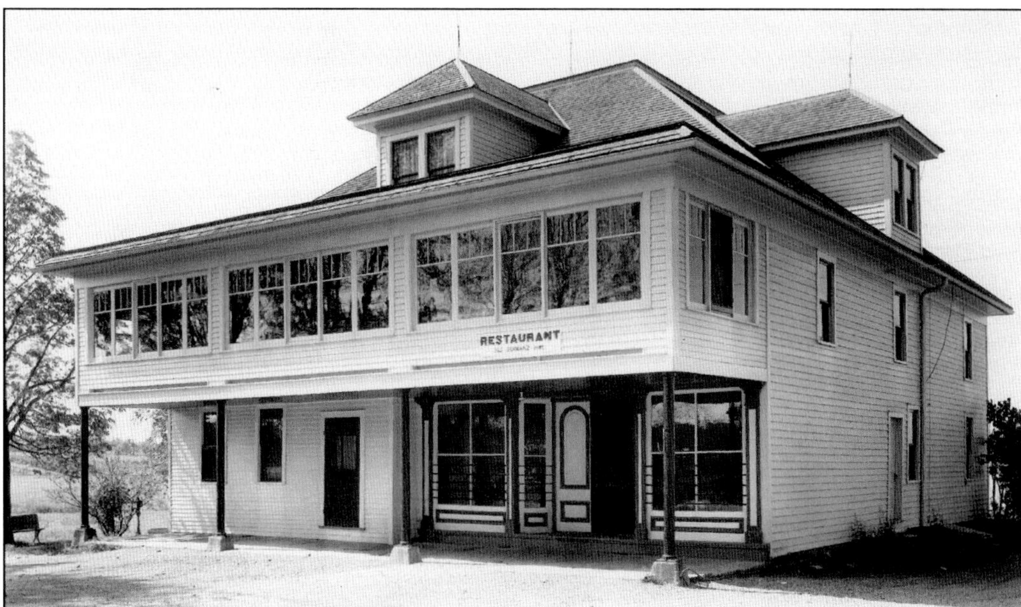

When he grew up, Joseph Schwanz bought the hotel from his father, George. This is how the building looked in the 1930s, when he was the proprietor. The next owner, Joseph Kwilos, ran a grocery store that was a popular meeting place for young people in the 1940s and 1950s. Drinking pop, playing cards, and racing cars on East Eden Road were the favorite pastimes. In more recent times, it was Haag's Store.

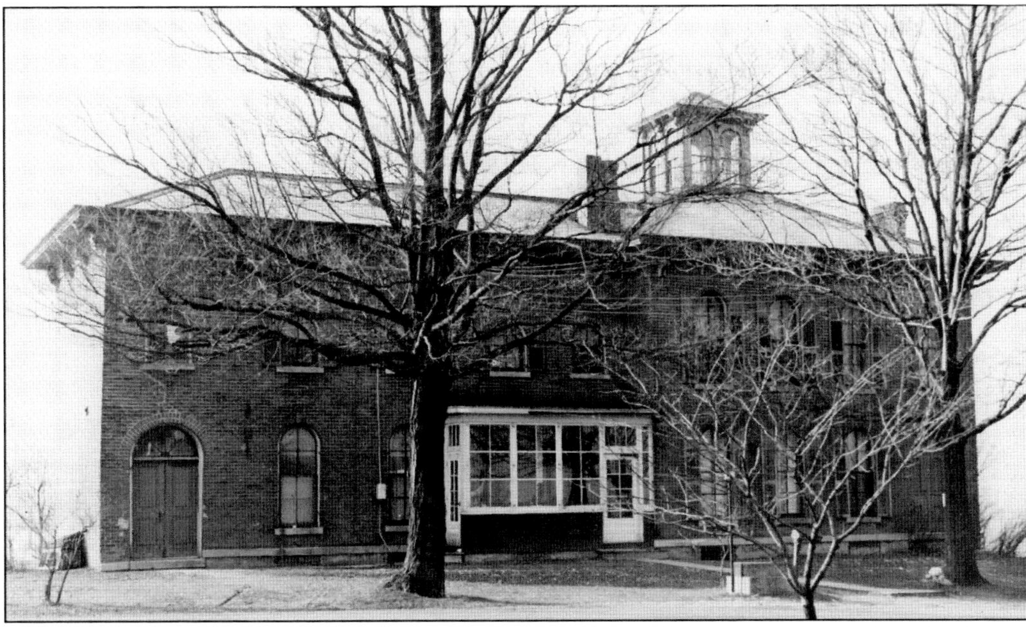

One of East Eden's most distinctive landmarks is the 1850 brick homestead of the Daniel Schweickhardt family on Hardt Road. His brewery, across the street, produced lager from hops and grain grown on his farm. The beer was stored in three hand-dug underground caves. The house, with its distinctive cupola, remains little changed today, but the brewery is gone. This image is from 1951.

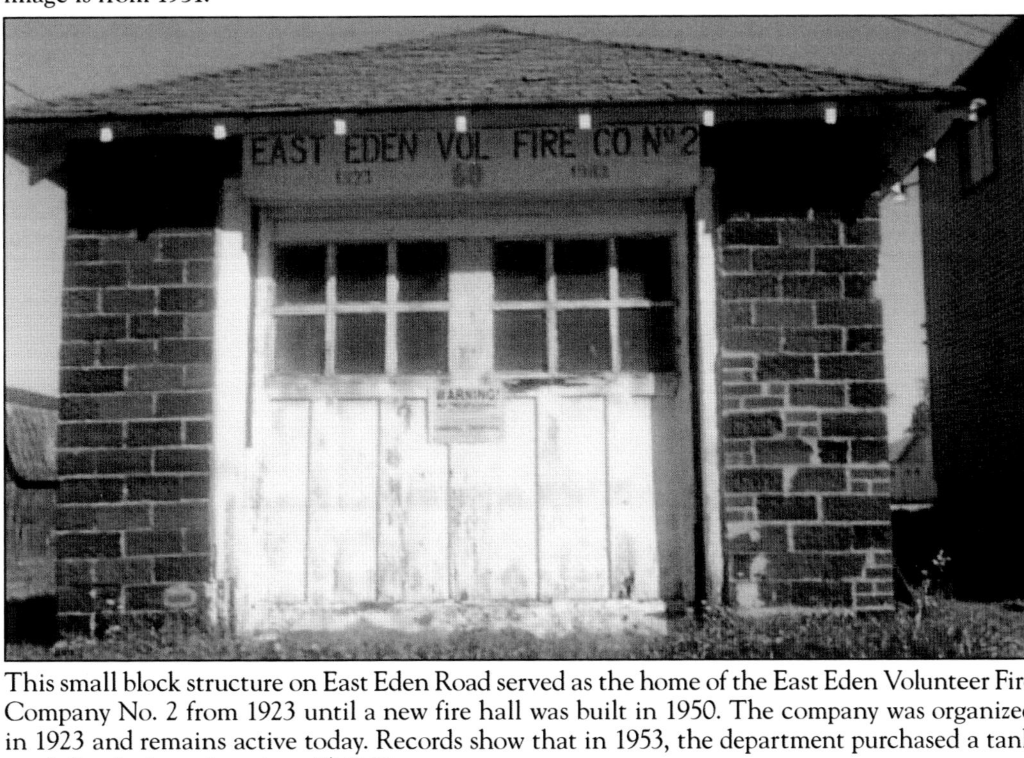

This small block structure on East Eden Road served as the home of the East Eden Volunteer Fire Company No. 2 from 1923 until a new fire hall was built in 1950. The company was organized in 1923 and remains active today. Records show that in 1953, the department purchased a tank truck for the bargain price of $43.10.

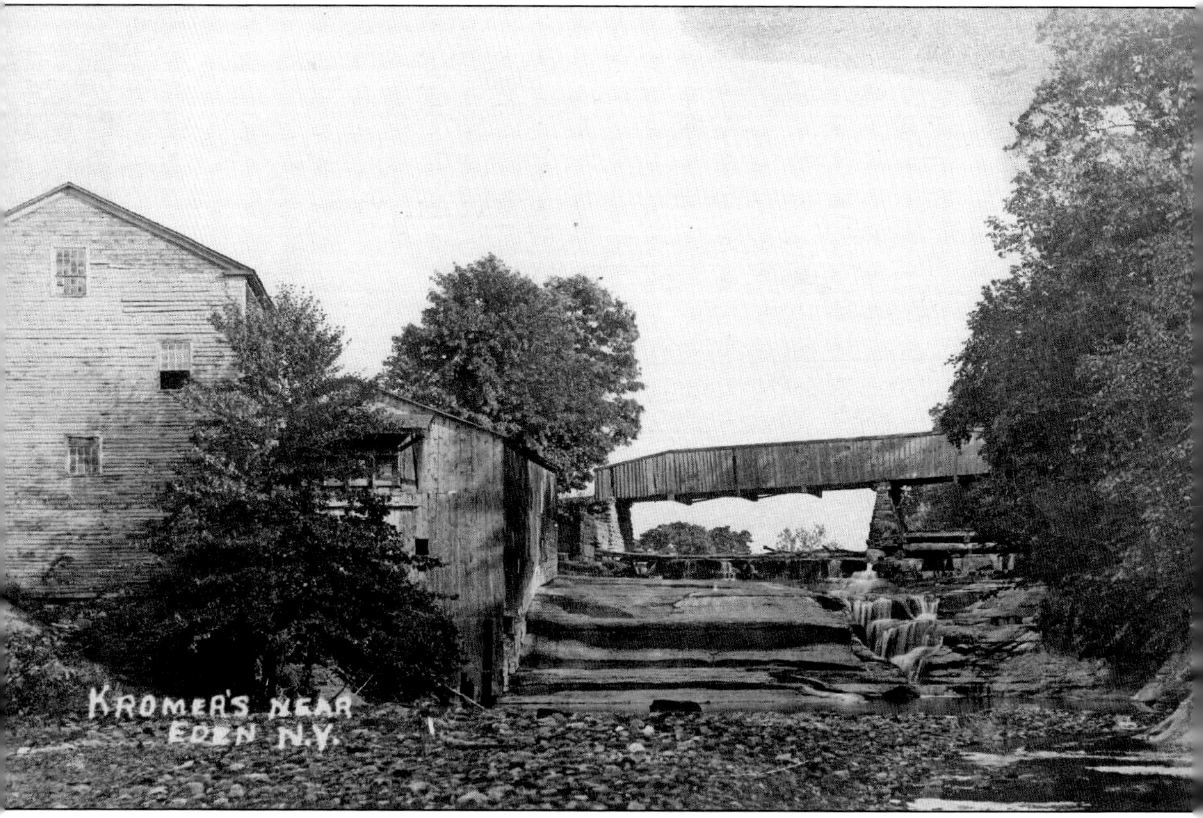

Toad Hollow is a name seldom used these days to specify the area of town along the Eighteen Mile Creek where Sisson Highway meets East Church Street. Kromer's Mill at Toad Hollow has been photographed countless times, yet each picture evokes nostalgia for times gone by. The old gristmill, on the far left, was built by Col. Asa Warren in 1816. Alexander Kromer was so taken with the site that in 1847, he bought the mill, left his tailoring job in Buffalo, and moved to Eden to become a miller. He built the sawmill seen between the gristmill and bridge. Five generations of the family continued the operation in three mills for the next 140 years. Until 1950, Church Street crossed the creek at the mills and wound through Kromer's property. This photograph, taken around 1895, also shows a covered wooden bridge, one of three that once spanned the creek. The mills and the bridge are gone, but the spot by the falls is as picturesque as ever. (Courtesy of Marvin Cohoon.)

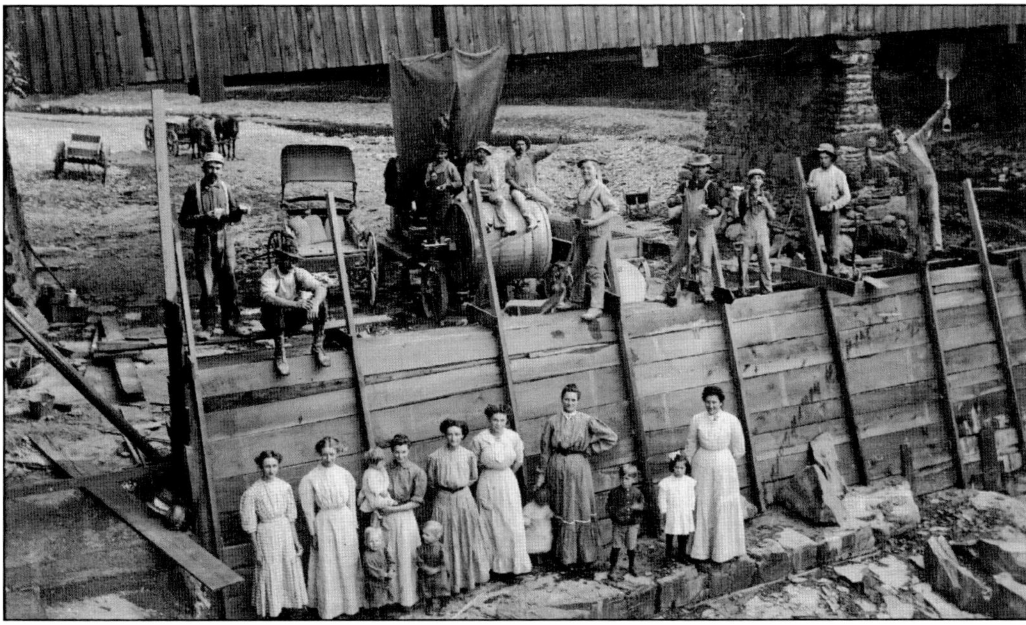

Water levels in the creek could vary significantly, so most mills had a dam to control the flow. Kromer's first one, made of logs, was replaced by a 12-foot-high concrete dam. George Kromer did the engineering and then hired his neighbors to help with the construction of the 70-foot-long structure. Workers and family members are shown here in 1911 during the concrete pouring process. (Courtesy of Marvin Cohoon.)

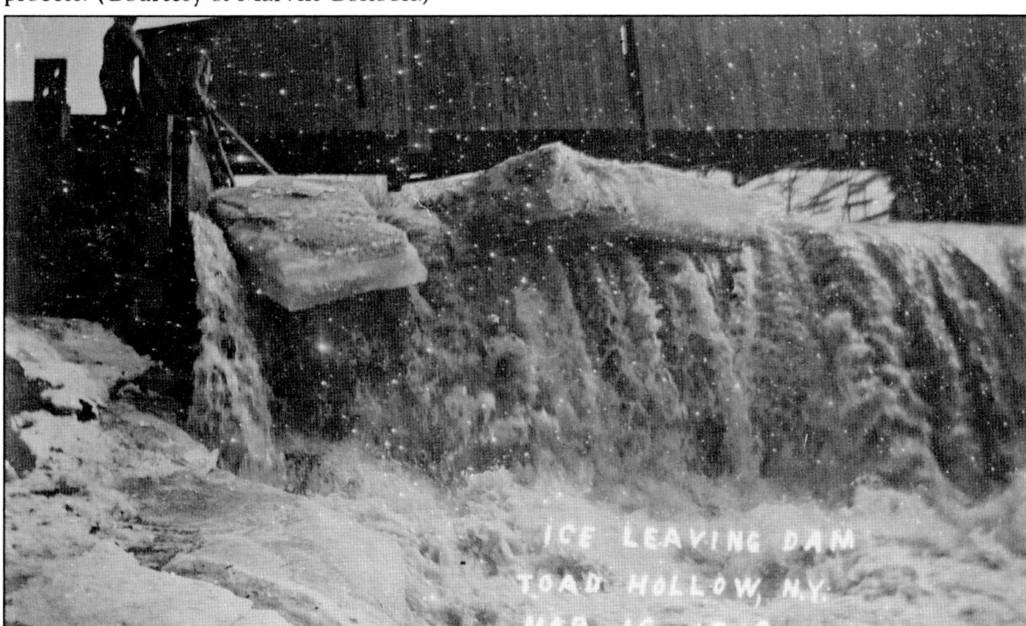

When the creek flooded during the 1912 spring thaw, the new dam was put to the test as water and large chunks of ice flowed over the top. In the late 1920s, a similar situation undermined the sawmill and its turbine box, plunging both into the creek. A new mill that used steam power was built away from the edge of the creek. Electrical power was used from 1950 on.

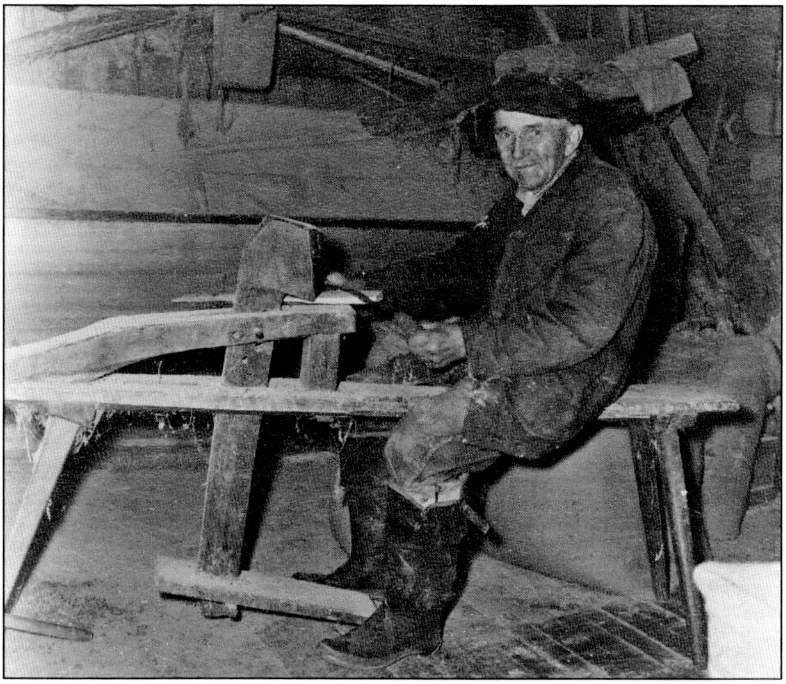

Eighty-two-year-old George Kromer is seen in 1955 using his *schnitzelbunk*, a device designed to make axe handles and shingles. Kromer had worked in the family's mills since he was 13, taking over after the death of his father, Christian. There was nothing pertaining to the mills' operation that he could not handle. In the midst of it all, he raised six children after his wife died in 1914.

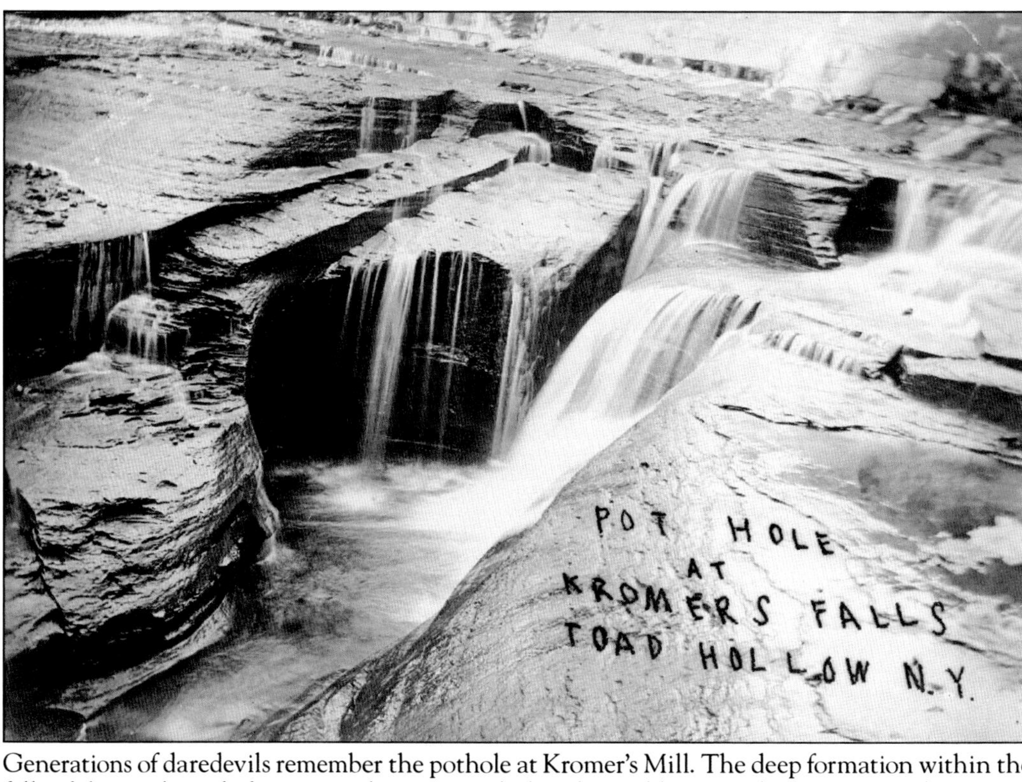

Generations of daredevils remember the pothole at Kromer's Mill. The deep formation within the falls of the creek made for a natural swimming hole. The problem was that it was also dangerous. Men of a certain age remember being told by old Kromer to always wear a white shirt if they dove in. It seems that the shirt would make them easier to spot if they did not come up again.

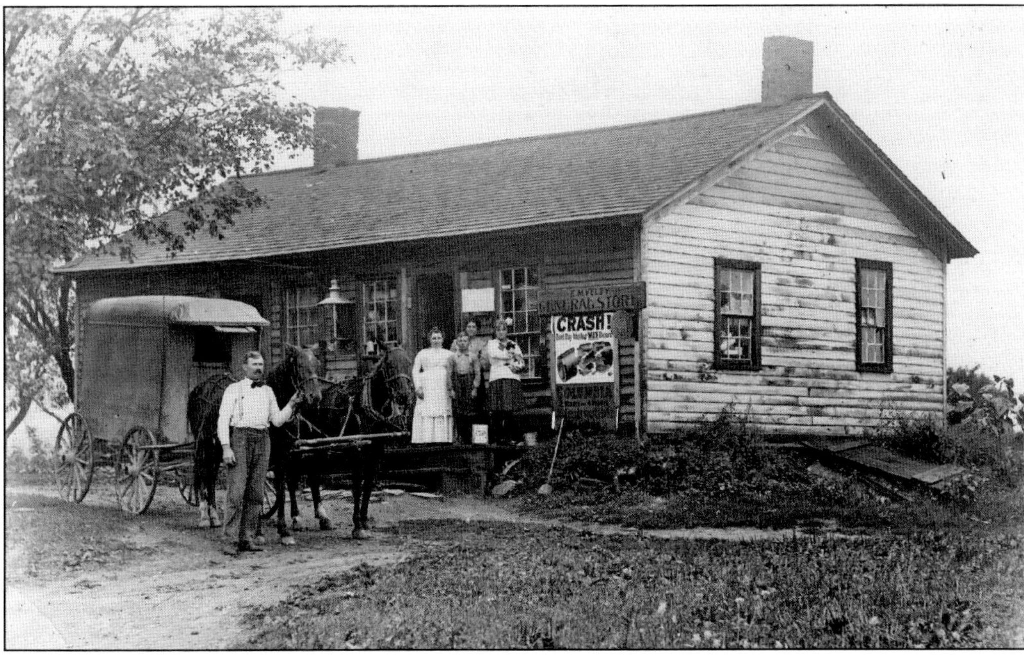

This store, which had a bar, was located on Sisson Highway at Kromer's. Farmers would wait in this store while their grain was being processed at the mill. It seems they would often spend their money on drink, and Kromer did not get paid. He solved that problem by buying the building and moving it elsewhere on his property for use as a shed. (As told by Marvin Cohoon.)

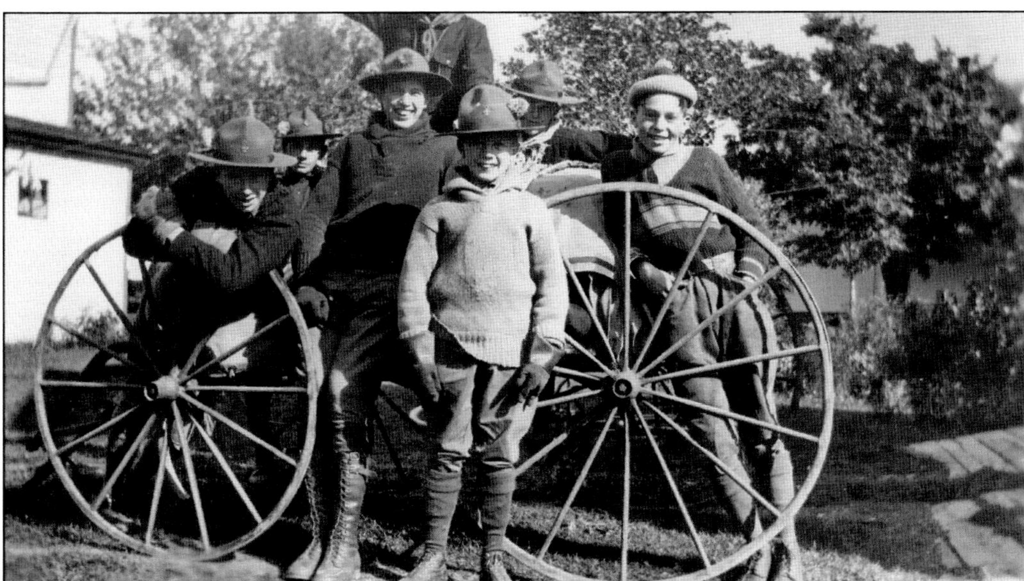

These fresh-faced young men were members of Eden Boy Scout Troop No. 7, organized in 1921. Howard Nobbs is the boy in the light sweater. In 1913, the first Boy Scout camp was on the Kromer's Toad Hollow property on East Church Street. After the number of campers grew too large to meet there, the Buffalo Boy Scout Council purchased property a few miles north on Sisson Highway that they named Toad Hollow Camp. (Courtesy of Gary Nobbs.)

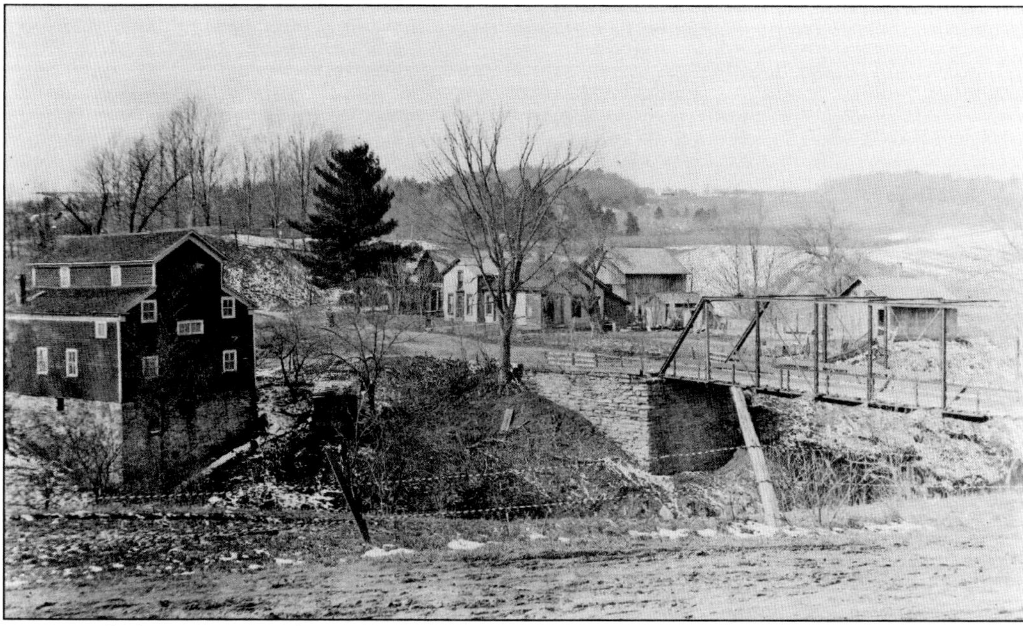

Simeon Clark, a spinning wheel maker, settled the creekside community at Clarksburg along New Oregon Road in 1819. The next year, he built a gristmill and a sawmill. The gristmill is shown here around 1900 when twin brothers Heman and Herman Wightman owned it. They lived with their families in the home across the road. The far building, under the pine tree, was a store and post office. Today the mill is a private club.

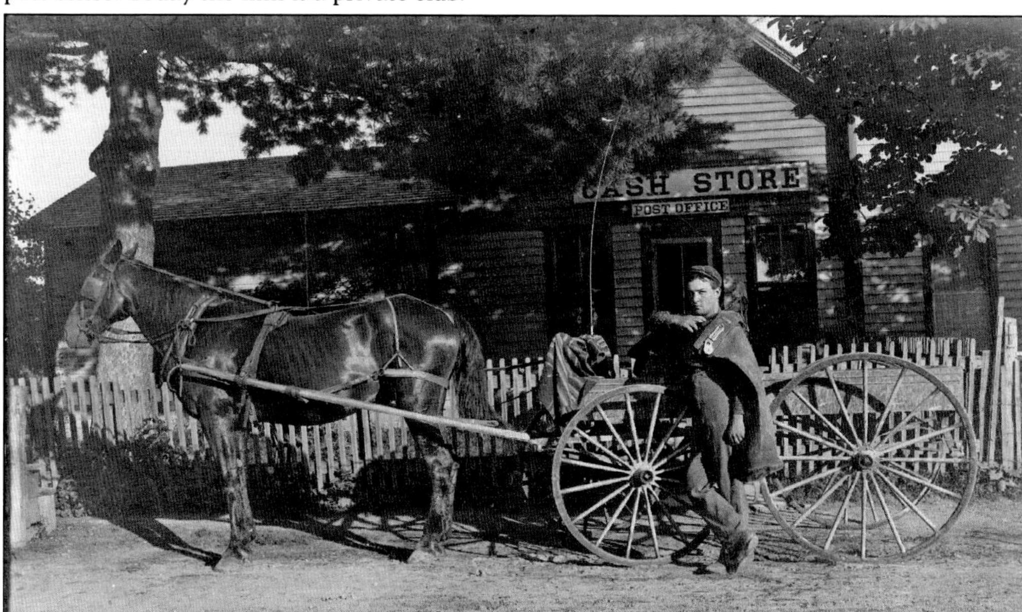

Rural postal carrier Martin Stinson poses with Old Salty in front of the Clarksburg Post Office about 1900. During the times when the dirt roads turned to deep mud, Stinson would release Salty at the top of Schuster Road, which then connected Sisson Highway and East Eden Road. While Stinson finished on foot, the horse would retrace the easier steps of the route alone, stopping at George Haier's barn on Sisson Highway.

Four

On the Farm

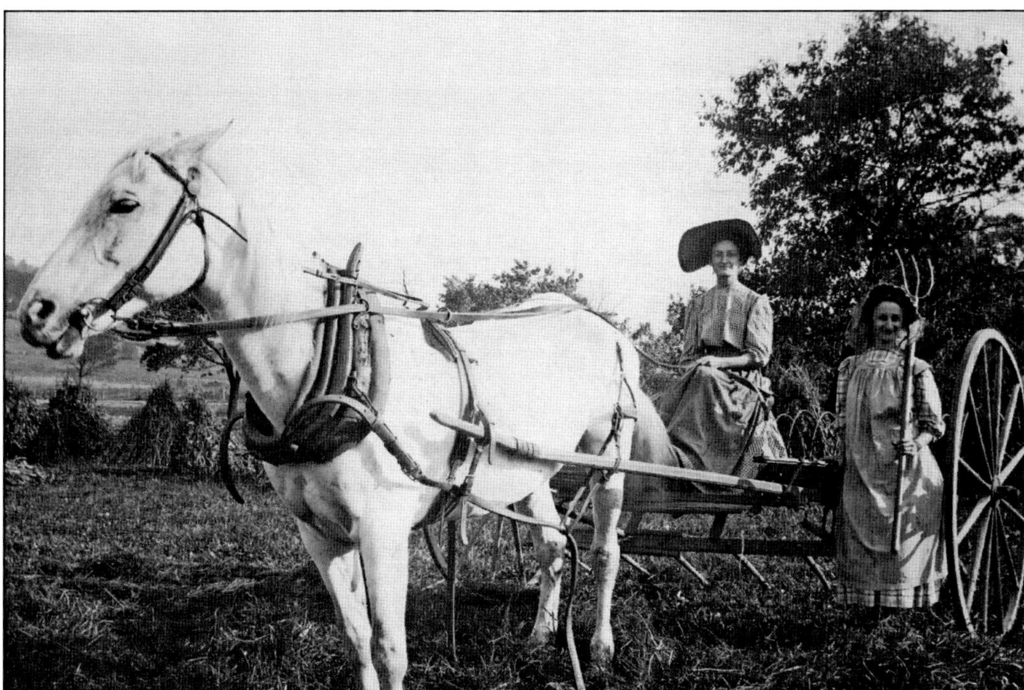

One might get the impression from this photograph that life on the farm was like a walk in the park. The reality was far different, especially in the earliest days, when thick forests had to be cleared. Oxen and draft horses were key to accomplishing the most grueling work, but the need for human muscle power cannot be underestimated. Life was hard, and everyone in the family worked to ensure their livelihood and survival.

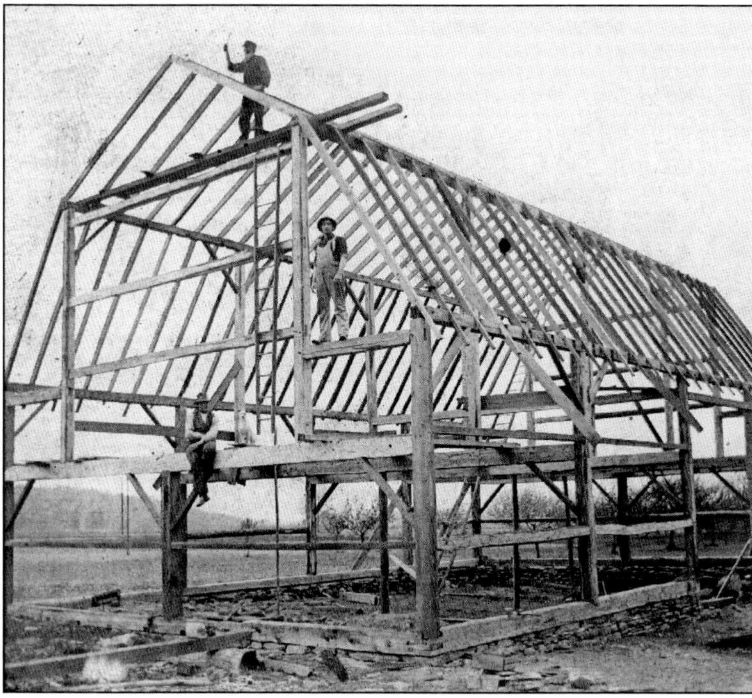

Next to shelter for humans, the barn was the most important building on any farm. This c. 1900 photograph shows a typical barn raising at the Georgi (now Rizzo) farm on West Church Street. Neighbors from miles around gathered to help build the barn. Children helped as they could, and women prepared food for the whole group. The raising was mostly work but also a social occasion. The structure was usually completed in a few days.

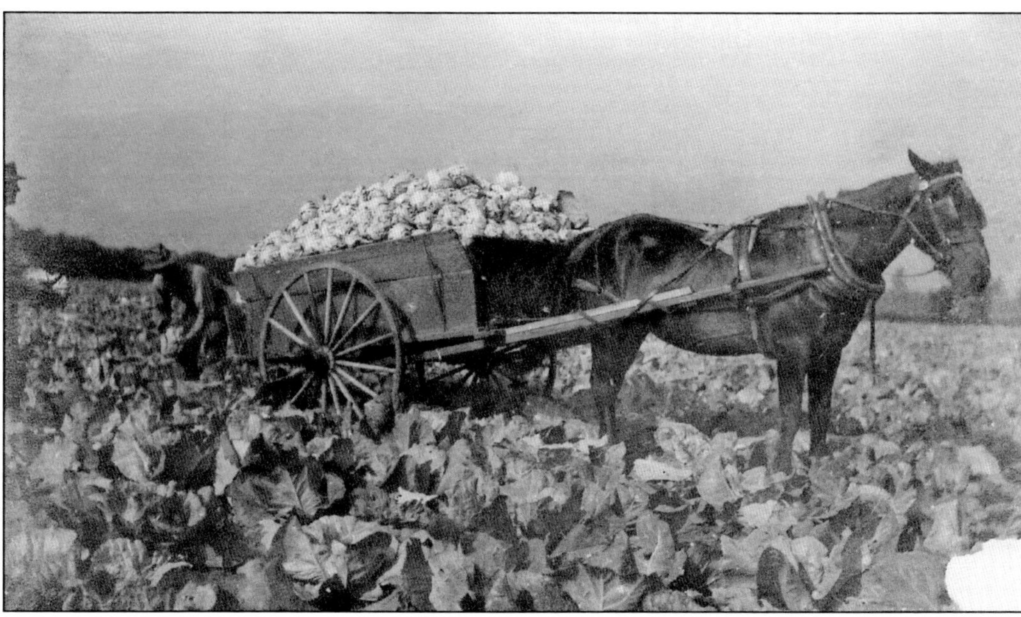

Horsepower was an essential part of farm life well into the 20th century, even after the advent of steam- and gasoline-powered machinery. It is likely that the horse pulling the wagon of ripe cabbages also pulled the plow that prepared the field at the beginning of the growing season.

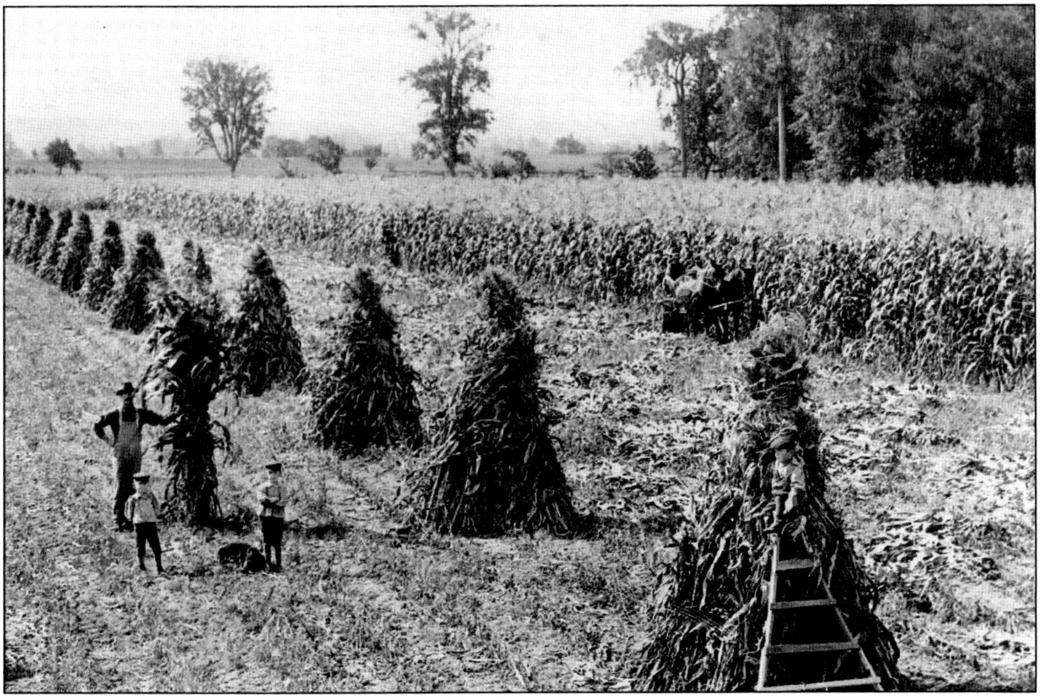

Some sights in Eden never change. Cornfields today are just as prominent as this one on William Henry's farm in 1895. This picture, featured on the Milsom Fertilizer Company's calendar, shows how their product helped produce 12-foot-high cornstalks. Henry is shown in the distance operating the corn binder. His three sons, (from left to right) Clarence, Frank, and Walter, are seen in the foreground with Jake Machmer. (Courtesy of Walter J. Henry.)

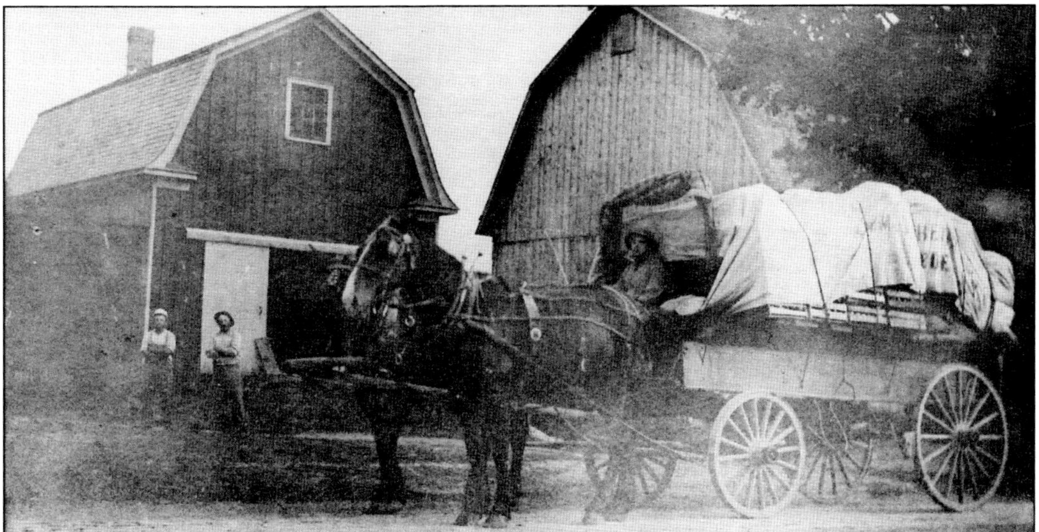

By 1915, the boys pictured above had grown into more responsible jobs. Clarence Henry's wagon is loaded and ready to make the trip to the Elk Street market in Buffalo. He would drive into the city in the late afternoon. After sleeping in a barn overnight, Henry would sell his produce the next morning and then make the 15-mile trip back to Eden. Shown in the background are Henry's brother, Walter D., and their father, William D. (Courtesy of Walter J. Henry.)

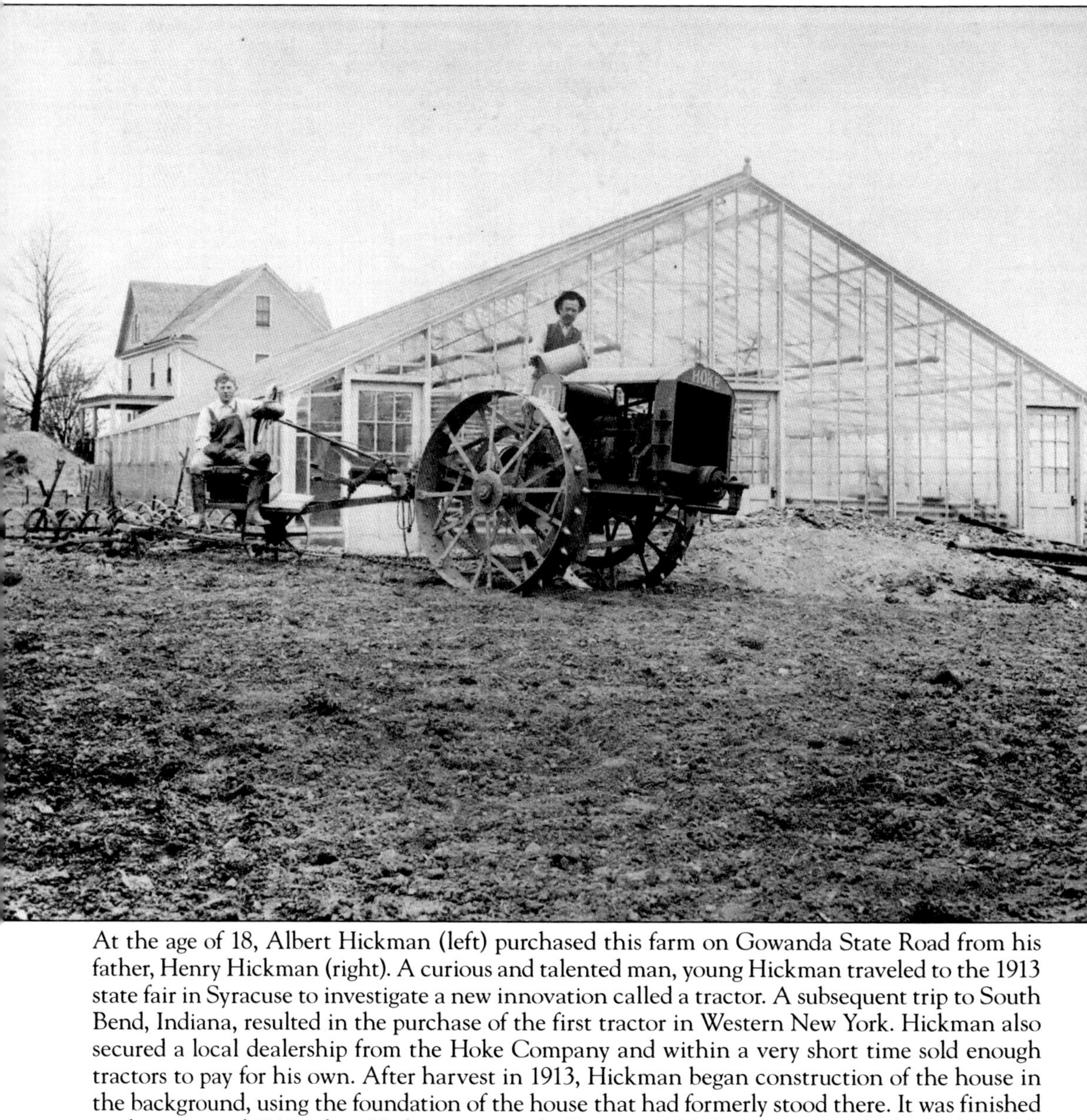

At the age of 18, Albert Hickman (left) purchased this farm on Gowanda State Road from his father, Henry Hickman (right). A curious and talented man, young Hickman traveled to the 1913 state fair in Syracuse to investigate a new innovation called a tractor. A subsequent trip to South Bend, Indiana, resulted in the purchase of the first tractor in Western New York. Hickman also secured a local dealership from the Hoke Company and within a very short time sold enough tractors to pay for his own. After harvest in 1913, Hickman began construction of the house in the background, using the foundation of the house that had formerly stood there. It was finished in the spring of 1914, when Hickman was only 20 years old. That same year, he built the steel-frame greenhouse seen in the photograph. It was another first for Western New York. Prior to then, greenhouses were temporary lean-to structures. Hickman's greenhouse measured 100 by 40 feet and was big enough to accommodate one horse and a plow. This young man was going places! (Courtesy of Warren Hickman.)

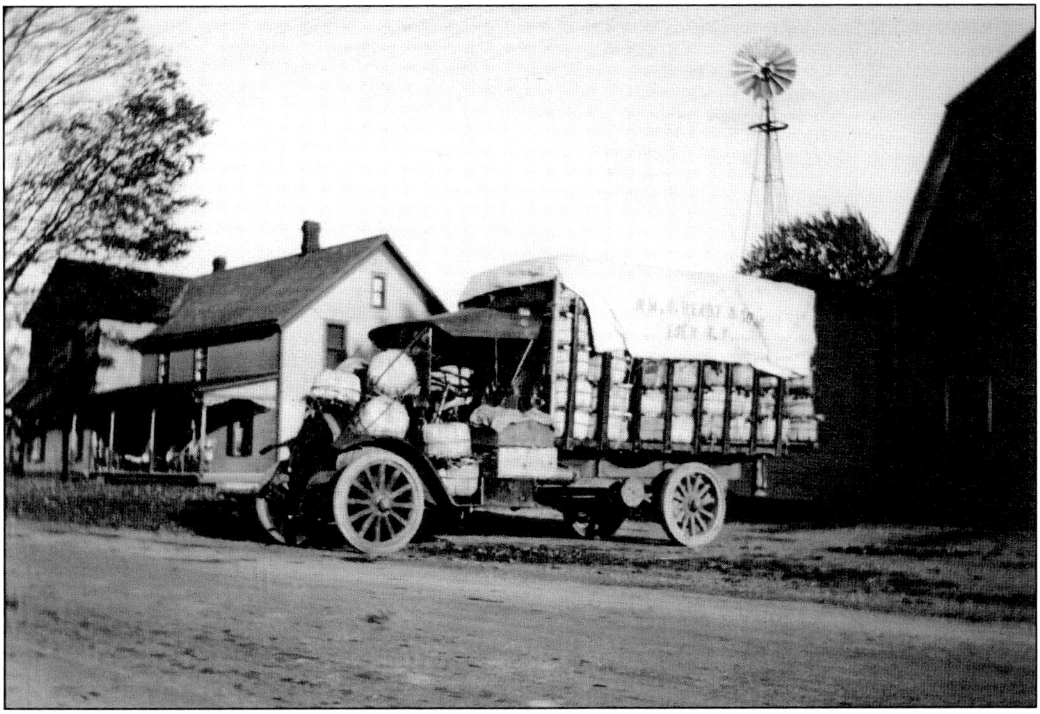

A very full load of spinach is packed and ready to go. Around 1920, the William D. Henry farm was using this chain-driven truck for market runs into Buffalo. It is parked on Route 62 in front of a still-existing barn with the Henry house in the background. In the 1860s, part of the home, which has since been remodeled, was a tavern owned by W. Stafford.

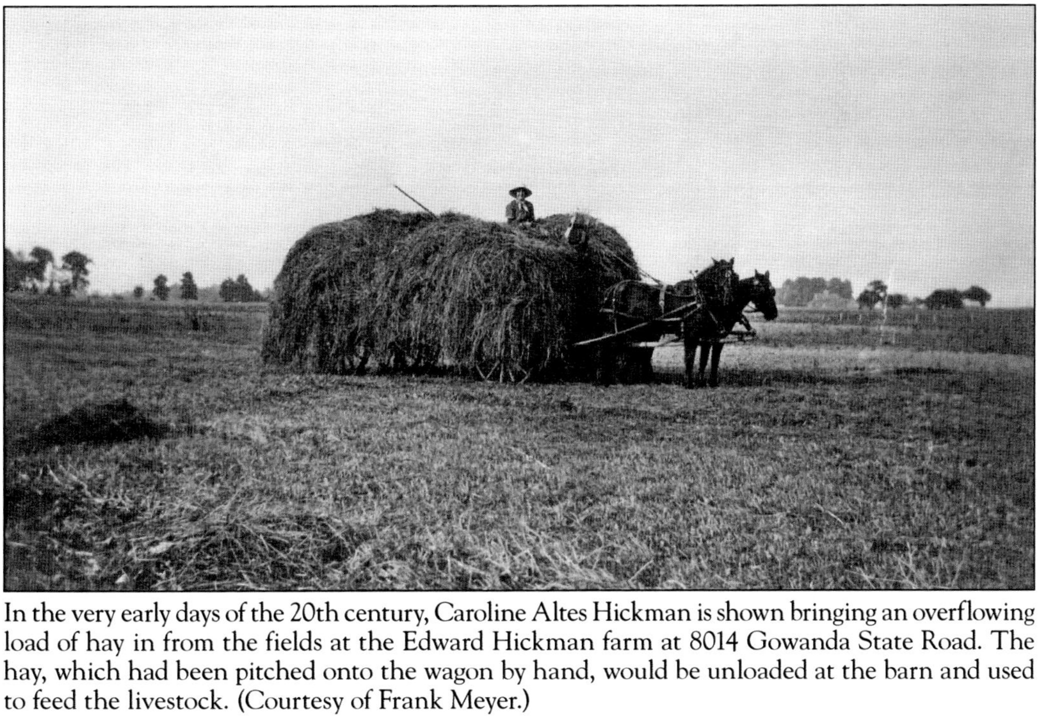

In the very early days of the 20th century, Caroline Altes Hickman is shown bringing an overflowing load of hay in from the fields at the Edward Hickman farm at 8014 Gowanda State Road. The hay, which had been pitched onto the wagon by hand, would be unloaded at the barn and used to feed the livestock. (Courtesy of Frank Meyer.)

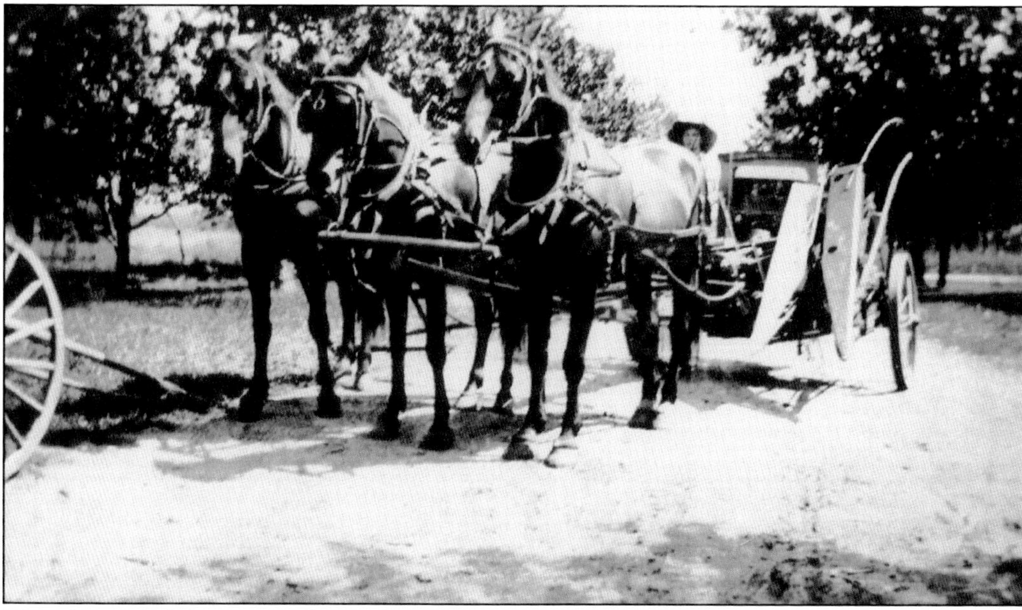

This photograph from around 1910 shows a three-horse team pulling a corn binder. It was designed to cut corn stalks, bundle and tie them together, and then drop them on the ground. Bundles were then hand stacked into conical-shaped "bucks" (see the top of page 51). Three horses were probably needed to pull the binder, which had a heavy, cleated "bull" wheel that transmitted the mechanical power necessary to make the cutter and binder operational. (Courtesy Frank Meyer.)

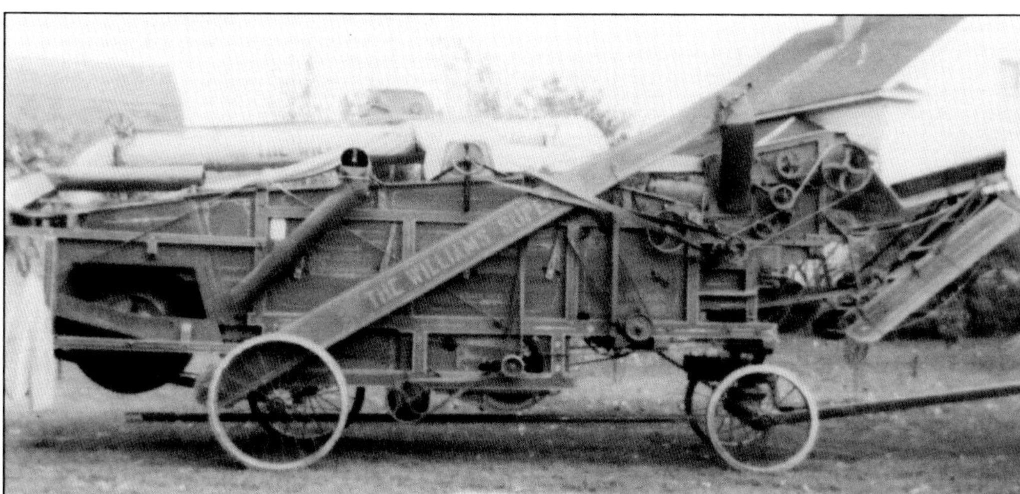

Mechanization was a great boon to the agricultural industry. The thrasher, or thresher, significantly reduced the drudgery of farm labor. Used to separate grain from husks and stalks, the thrasher was powered by a tractor engine. From the 1920s to the 1940s, Alwin Kehe worked as a custom thrasher, taking his machine to farms in the area as grain became ready for harvest. (Courtesy of Bob Kehe.)

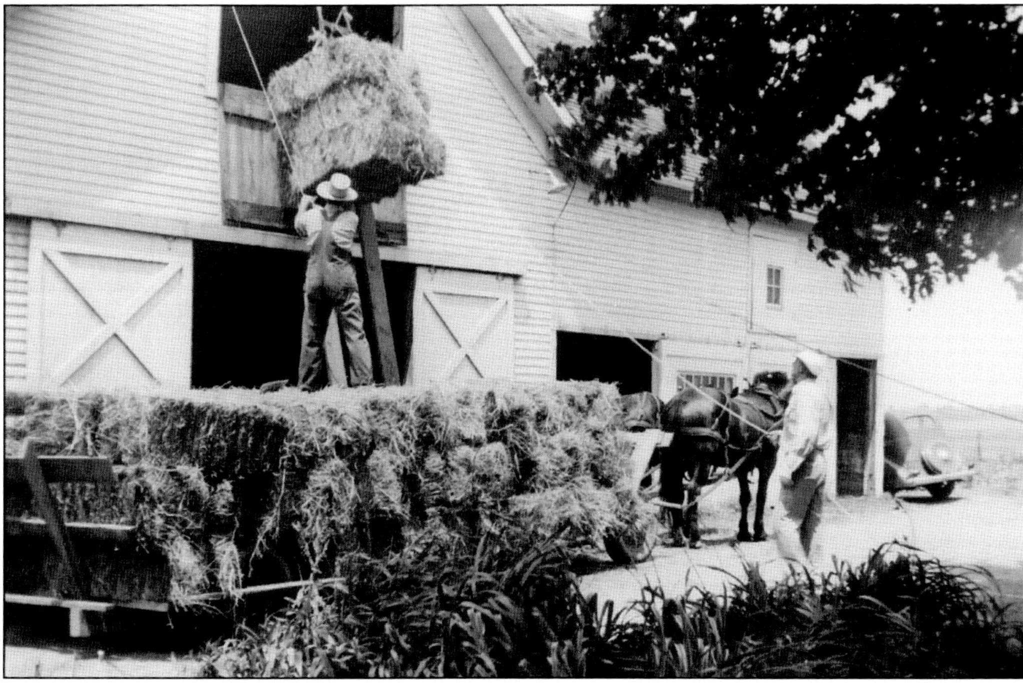

Throughout the 1920s and 1930s, most farms used both machinery and teams of horses. The use of horses for some tasks continued into the late 1940s or early 1950s. In the photograph above, hay bales are loaded into the loft the old-fashioned way, from a horse-drawn wagon using ropes, pulleys, and manpower. The unidentified men are working on Edward Hickman's farm, located at 8014 Gowanda State Road. Hickman's fine set of barns was destroyed by fire in 1951. In the lower picture, from the early 1940s, Alwin Kehe's thresher is shown transferring a load of hay from the wagon into the Oscar Brusehaber's barn on Bauer Road. The Frick thresher with a Hart self-feeder, described as "the Cadillac of threshing machines," replaced Kehe's original machine seen on the previous page. (Above courtesy of Frank Meyer; below, courtesy of Bob Kehe.)

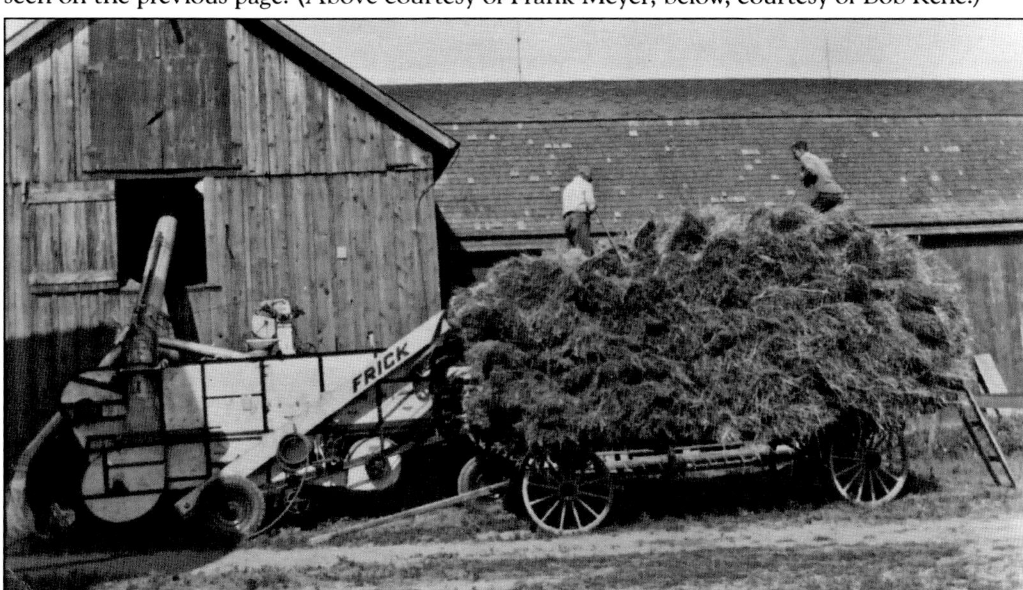

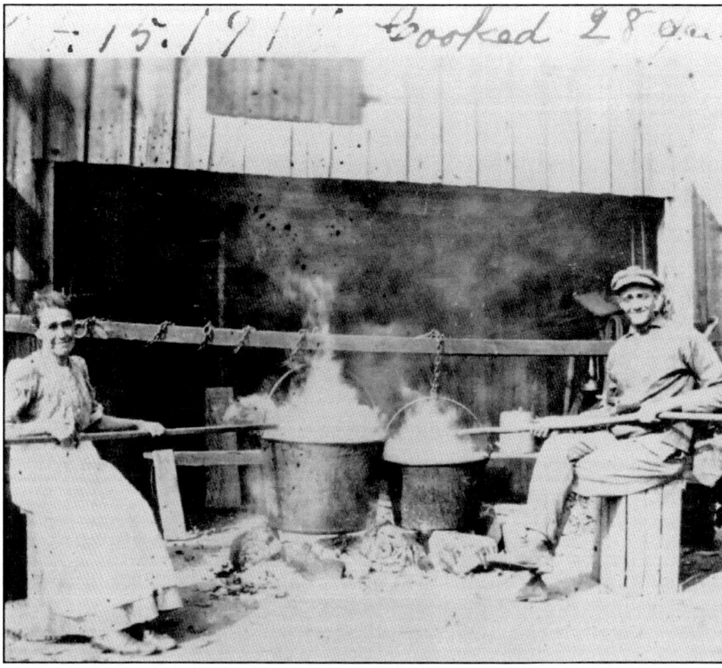

In 1918, Oscar Brusehaber and his mother, Katherine, are shown tending the kettles during the all-day fall ritual of making apple butter. Quantities of fresh apples were peeled, cut up, and combined with cider to cook down into apple butter. Constant stirring was required until the mixture was ready for canning, sometime in the late afternoon. The reward of the day was a supply of rich apple butter to be enjoyed all winter long. (Courtesy of Stirling and Jean Brusehaber Muck.)

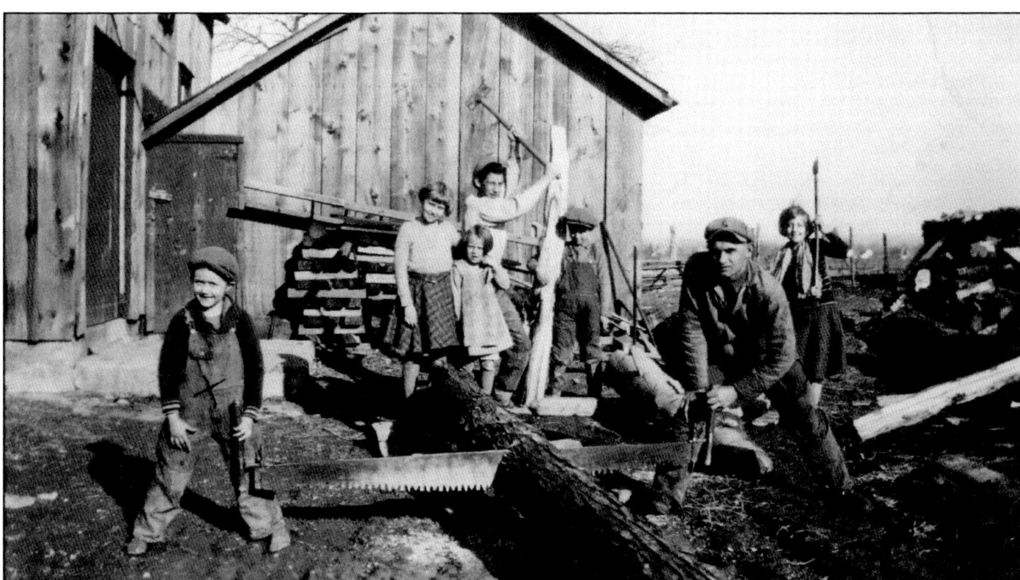

Skills that today's parents would never dream of teaching were learned by farm children, often at a young age. In the mid-1930s, a hired man shows Jean Brusehaber how to use a two-man crosscut saw. According to their age and ability, every member of the family helped with farm chores. The women and daughters shouldered not just the household tasks but also worked in the barns and fields. (Courtesy of Stirling and Jean Brusehaber Muck.)

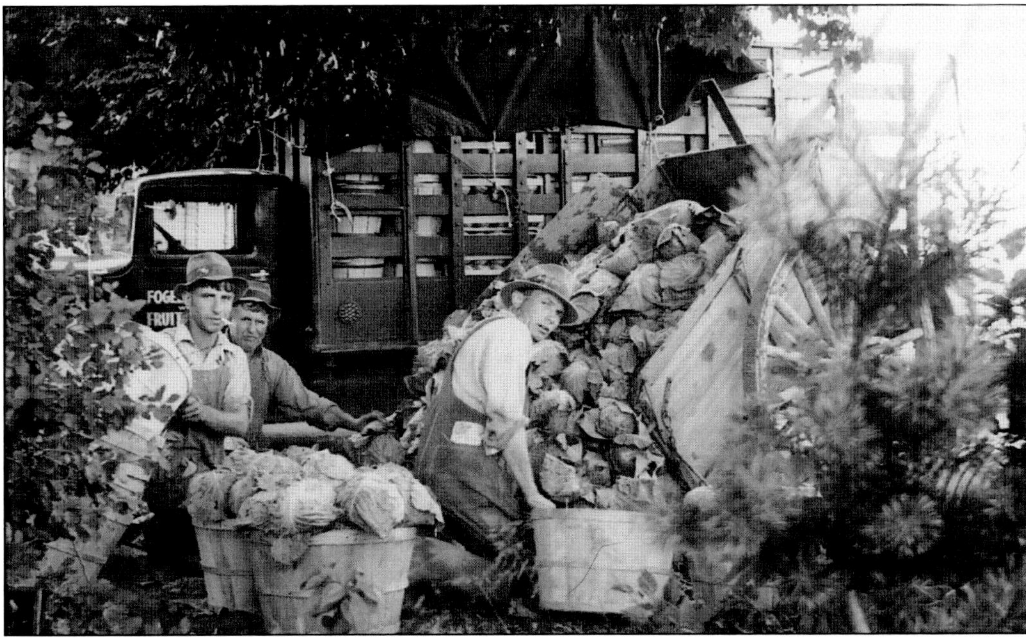

With a large tree to provide shade, sorting and packing produce offered a respite from the sun in the fields. The scene was repeated with many other crops, such as corn, beans, cauliflower, melons, broccoli, and peppers. Shown here in 1937 are Will Agle (center) and two of his sons, Henry (left) and Allen (right), as they prepare a wagonload of cabbage for market. (Courtesy of Jim and Pat Agle.)

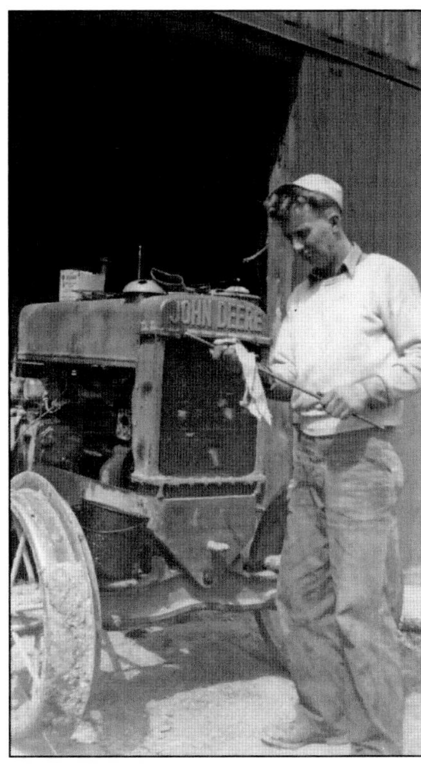

Maintaining a tractor was far different from maintaining a horse, so farmers needed to learn a new set of skills to keep their labor-saving machines in working order. Seen here in 1946 is Richard Brusehaber attending to his John Deere tractor. (Courtesy of Stirling and Jean Brusehaber Muck.)

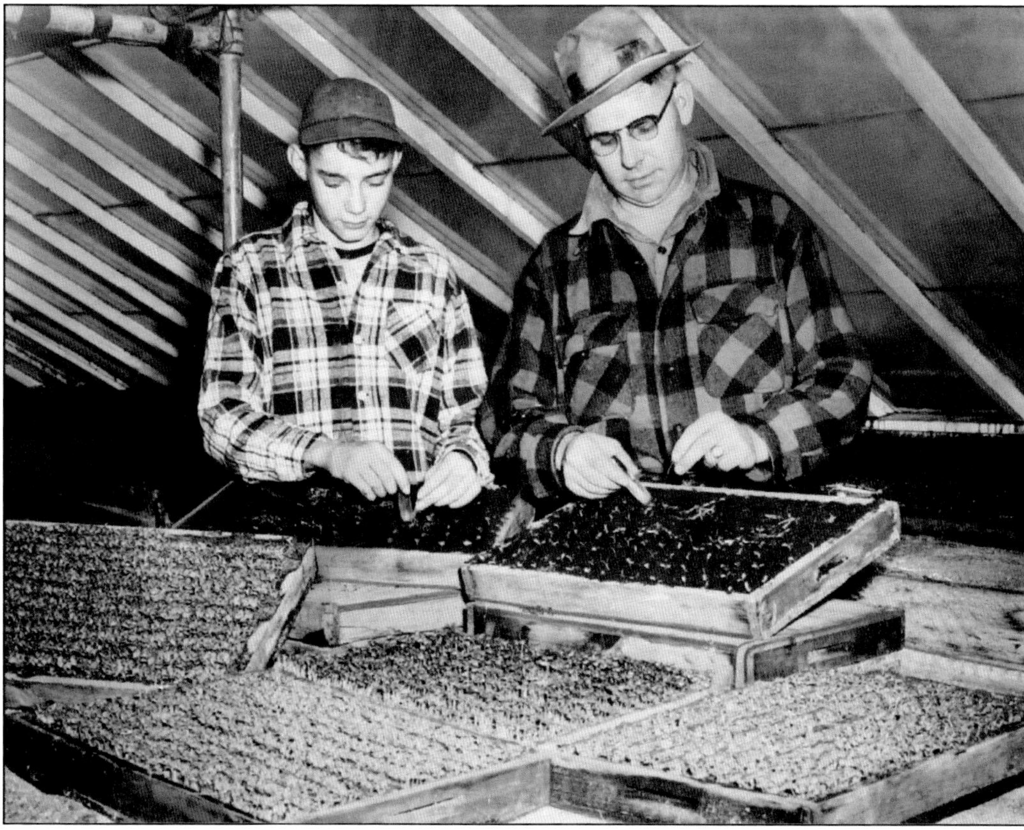

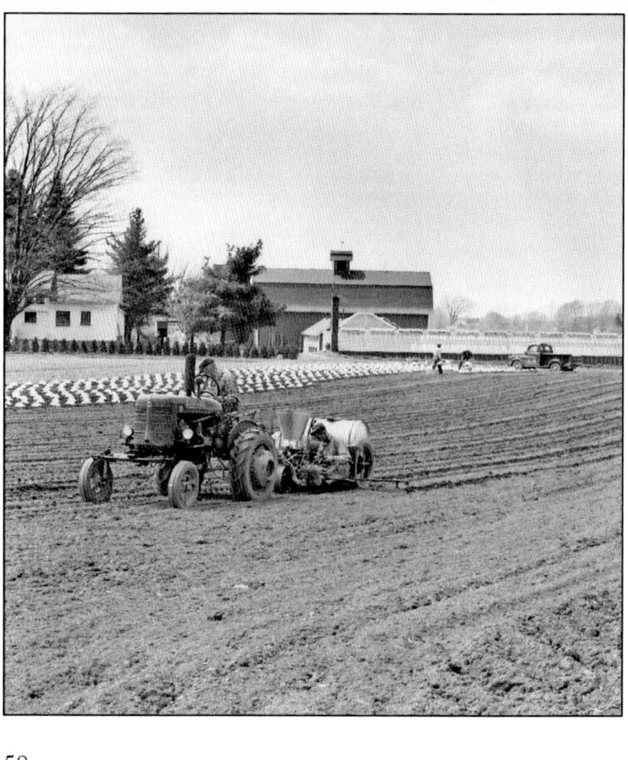

Farming duties were not limited to the months of the growing season. The above photograph from the early 1950s shows George Zittel and his father, Amos, transplanting lettuce seedlings. The tiny plants were nurtured in the greenhouse during the winter months until early spring, when they were planted in the fields. The picture at left illustrates how individual tomato plants were placed in the ground using a single-row transplanter. Wax paper caps, seen in the background, were placed over each plant, creating a mini-greenhouse effect. Covering the plants allowed crops to go into the ground sooner, thus extending the growing season. Art Beattie drives the tractor as Chuck Benkleman does the planting on the Amos Zittel farm in 1954. (Both, courtesy of George Zittel.)

Walter and Adeline Feasley established Feasley's Dairy on West Church Street in 1947. Their sons, Bill and Bob, joined them in partnership in 1955. Bob was in charge of the cows and outside operations, and Bill ran the dairy, where milk was pasteurized and bottled. Milk and Feasley's own ice cream were sold for many years in the outlet store adjacent to their home. Nothing tasted better than milk from a cold glass bottle, which one returned for a refill. In the photograph at right, Adeline Feasley and son Bob appear to be asking Bill Feasley, "Got milk?" Why else would the glasses be empty? The 1962 picture below shows Bill at work in the dairy, accompanied by his sister, Barbara Fisher, and her son, David. The other children, from left to right, are Feasley's niece Karen, son Albert, daughter Lynn, and nephew Keith. (Both, courtesy of Bill Feasley.)

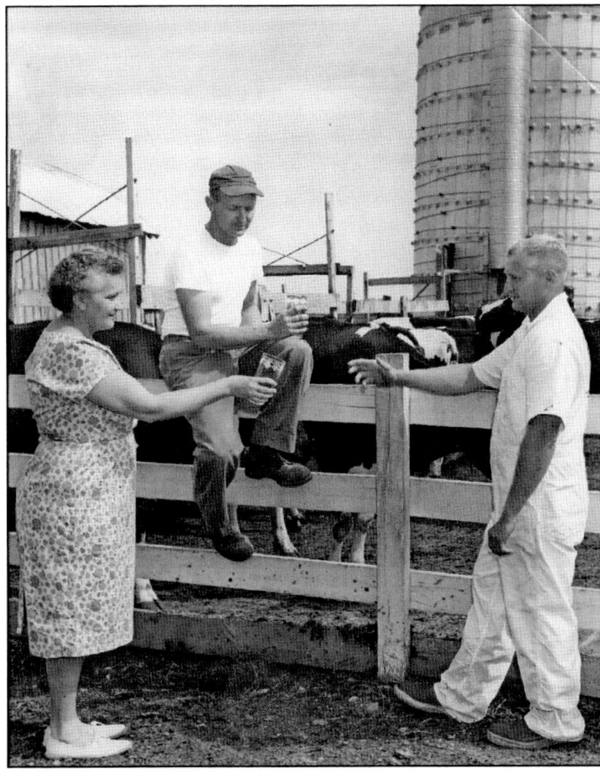

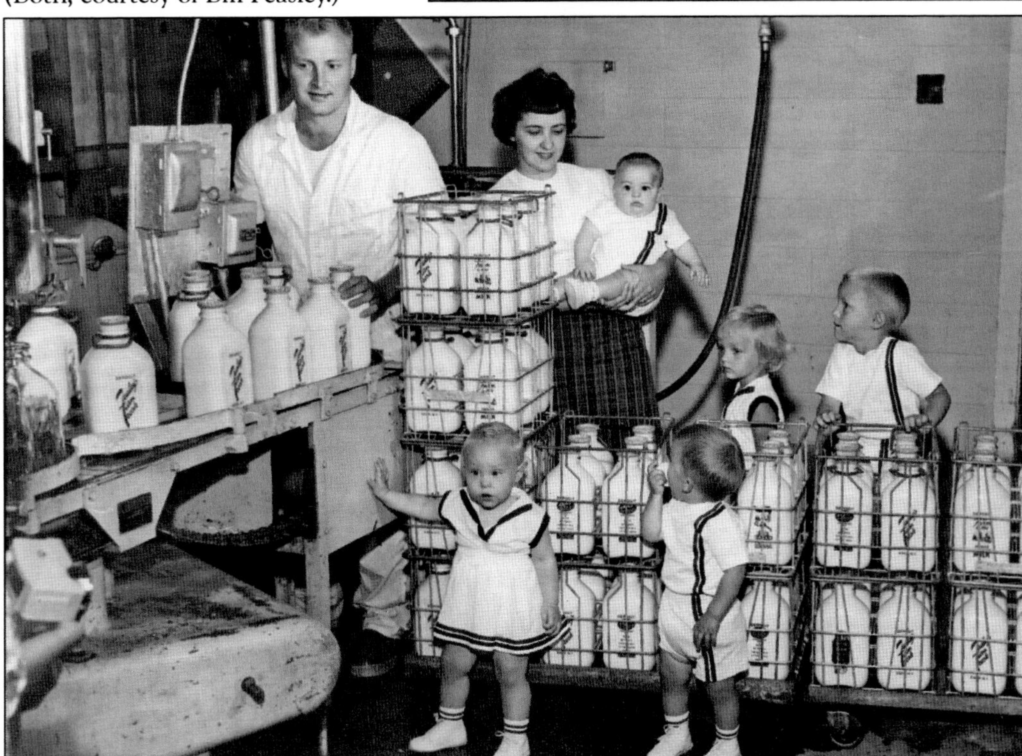

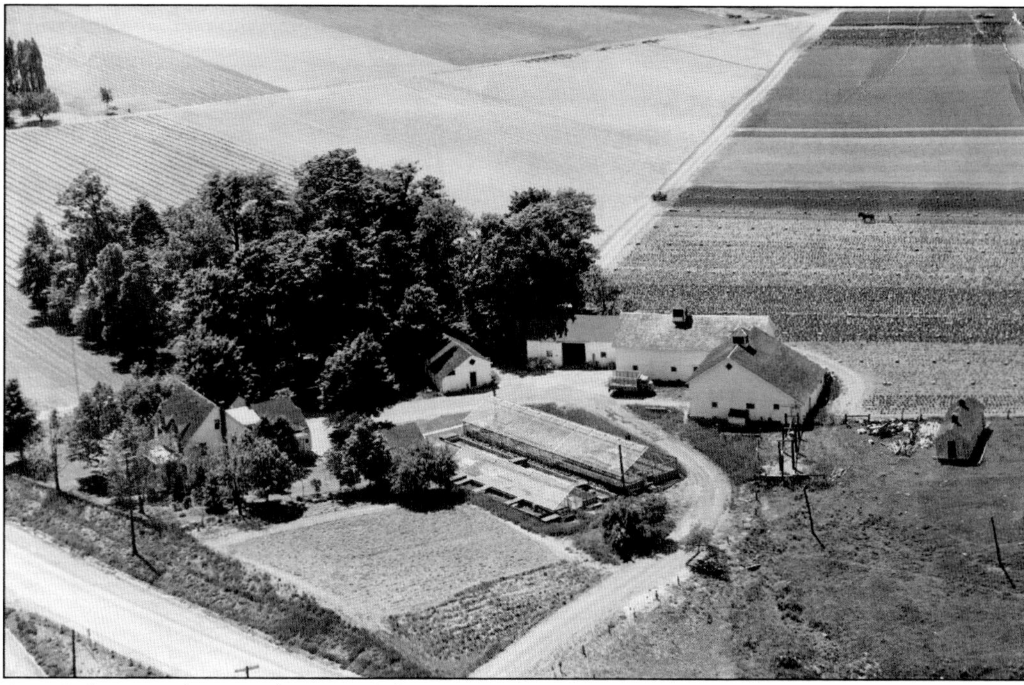

Aerial photography provides a good illustration of the barns, greenhouses, and other outbuildings that are an integral part of a working farm. This picture from 1949 shows the George H. Agle farm on Route 62 at the south end of the bridge. Another branch of the Agle family now owns the property. When the new bridge was constructed in 1990, the house was moved to the grove of trees at the left in the picture.

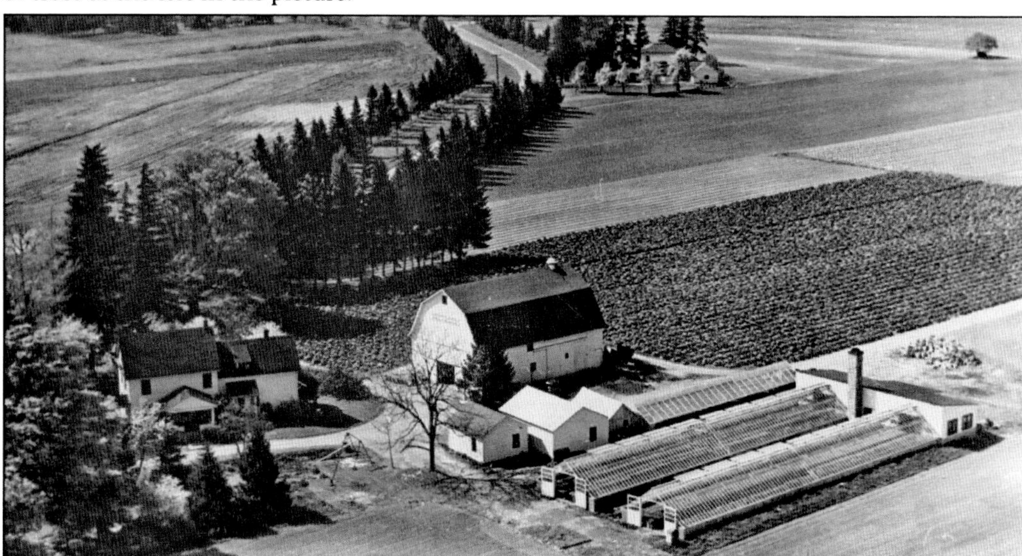

Unique to Edwin and Dorothy Minekime's West Church Street farm was their large crop of rhubarb. It was the year's first fresh vegetable, as seen in this picture from 1950, and many regarded it as a spring tonic. At its largest, the field covered 20 acres, with most of the product going to the Lawton's canning factory for processing. Some in Eden will remember the days of "U-Pick," when the Minekime children earned college funds by being responsible for the picking operation.

Five

COMMERCE AND BUSINESS

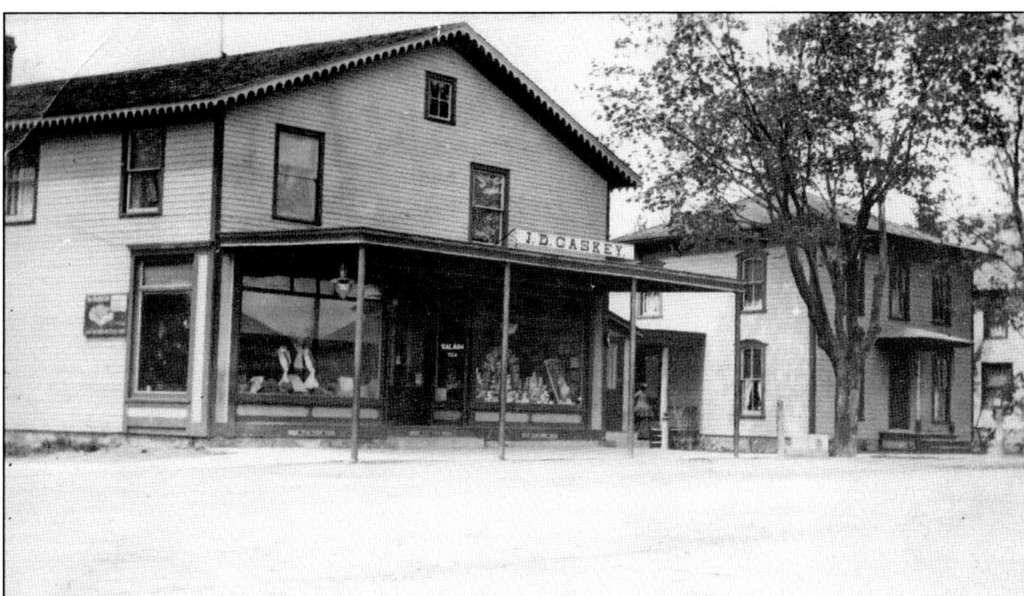

In 1813, a Mr. Harris established Eden's first store on a shelf in John Hill's kitchen. For sale were such articles as red cotton handkerchiefs, pigtail tobacco, and rum in a keg. Business was good, and in 1816, Harris built a small log structure on the corner of Main and Church Streets. On the same site, this 1824 frame building was J.D. Caskey's Store from 1876 to 1911. The Caskey home is seen on the right. The store building burned in 1974.

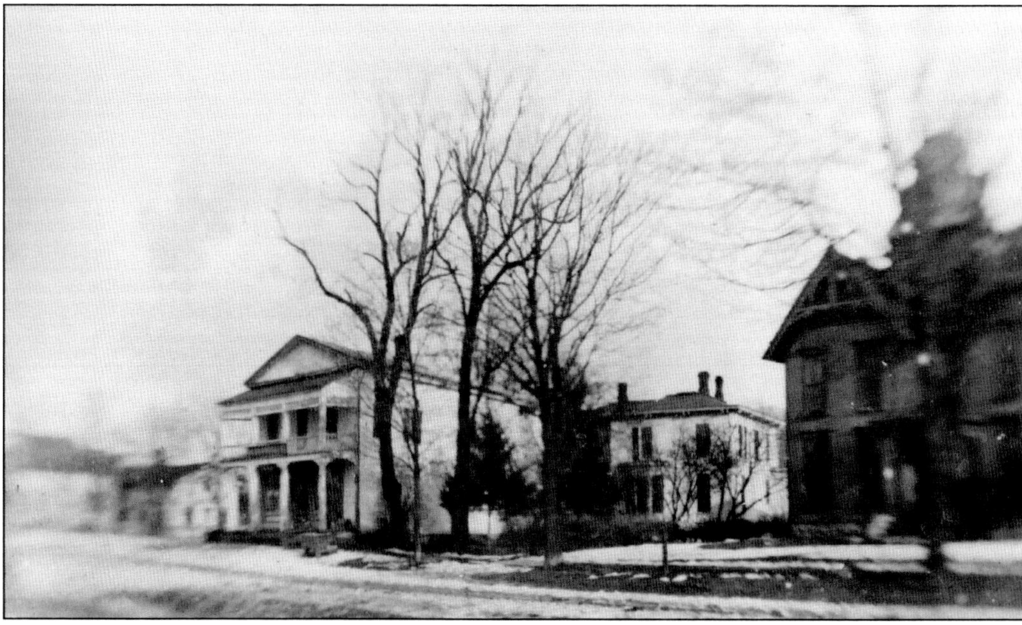

The HSBC Bank now occupies the corner where Lyman Pratt's store (left) stood for nearly 70 years. Beginning in the 1830s, Pratt and later his son-in-law, Harrison Parker, ran a thriving business. They offered almost unlimited credit to their customers, often accepting produce as payment. Pratt also kept a post office in the store. His home can be seen at center, and the Shaw house is on the right. The store burned in 1905.

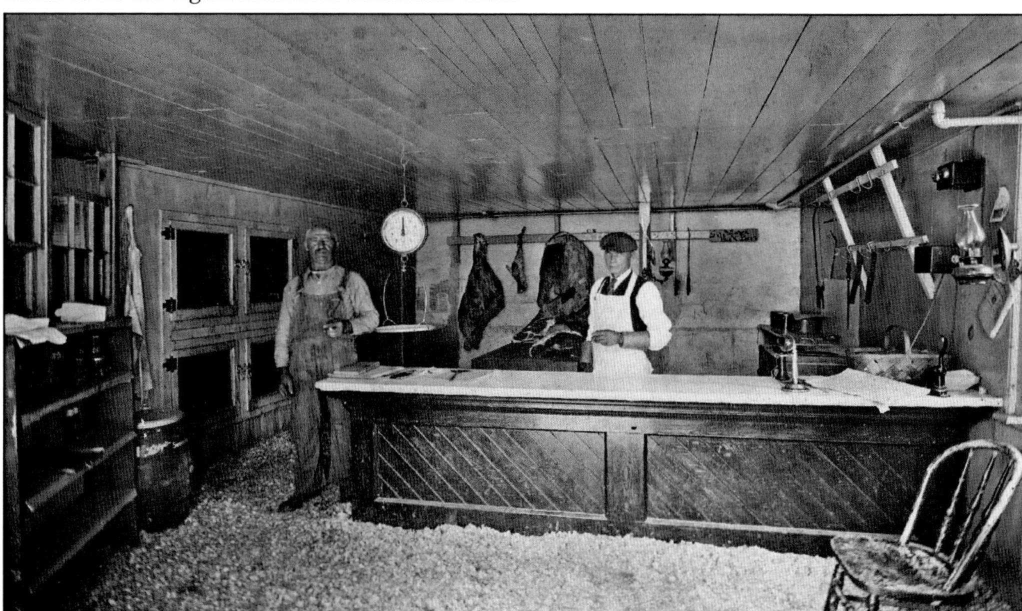

Over the years, there have been several meat markets in Eden. Marion Webster (right) operated one in the basement of the Ellicott Square Building. Lockers to the left indicate that there was probably some sort of refrigeration, though some meat was left to hang in the open. Wood shavings on the floor soaked up anything wet and perhaps some of the odor as well. This photograph dates from around 1910 to 1915.

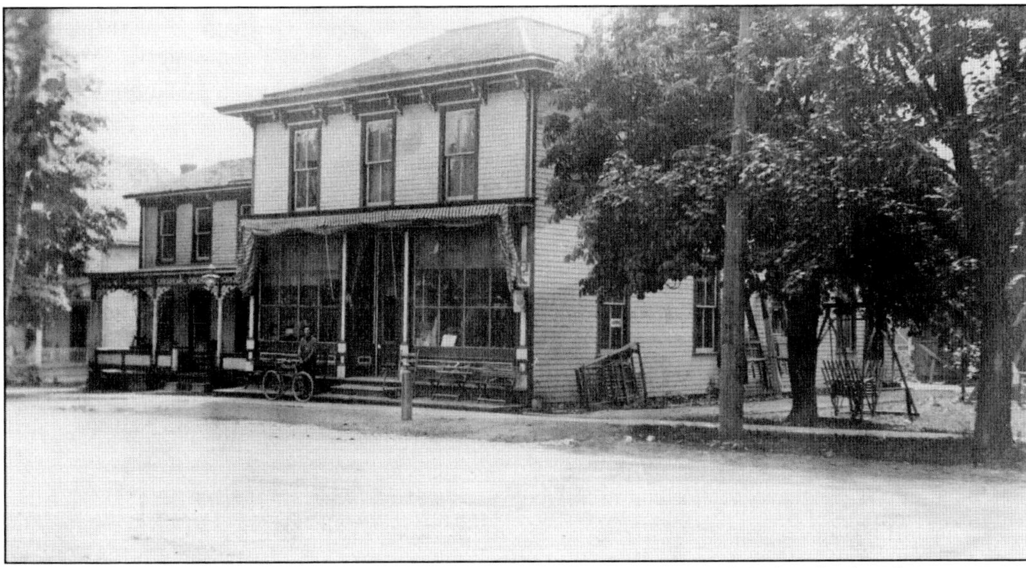

Eric Bloomquist bought this pre-1866 building in 1880 and remodeled it for his furniture and funeral business. However, he did not allow enough space for turning the hearse around on his property, so he built a turntable in his barn. From 1925 to 1956, the Nowaks operated a shoe and dry goods business in the building. During the 1930s, delivery boys picked up their newspapers from the store at 8606 Main Street.

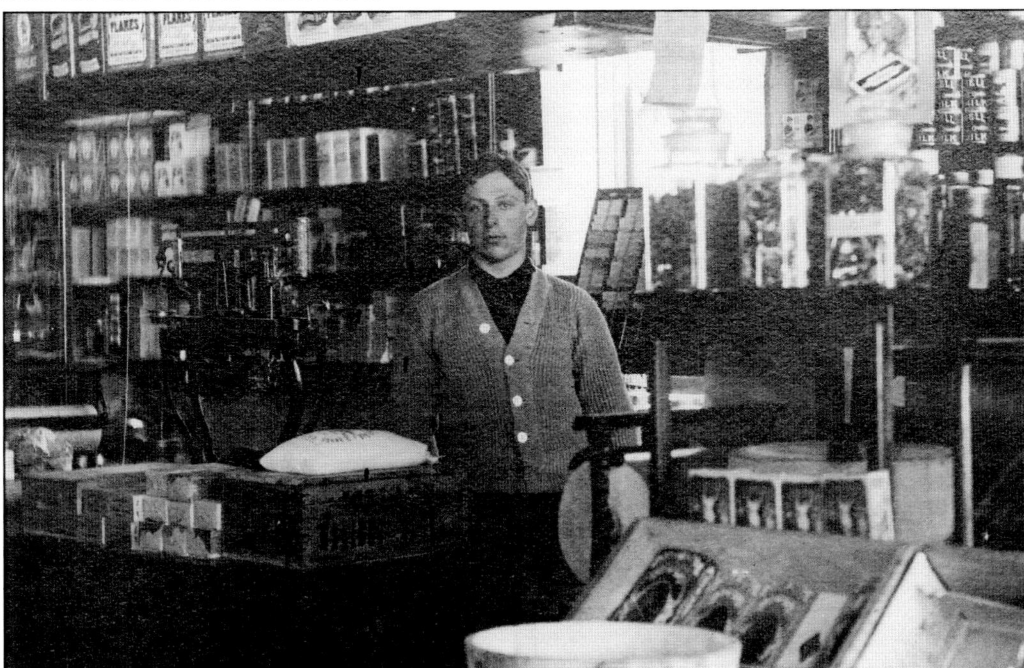

George Pyritz is the man behind the counter in Vellum's Store at 2763 West Church Street. The fact that Kellogg's Corn Flakes are available dates this picture to some time after 1895. Also seen on the shelves are Mother's Oats, canned milk, and jars of penny candy. A scale was used to weigh products such as flour and sugar. Cloth bags held beans and other dried products. A wooden box of dried Icelandic halibut is on the counter.

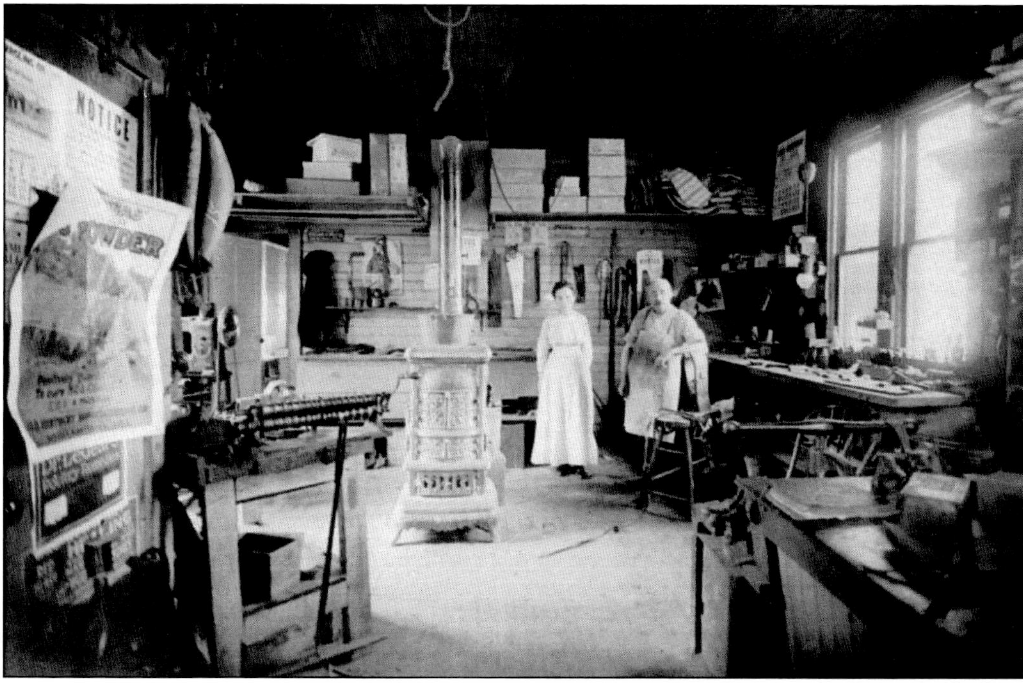

Mary and Jerome Grosjean are shown in the harness shop they built and operated from 1898 until 1923. A wood-burning stove in the center of the room provide heat during the winter. When demand for horse and buggy accessories waned, Grosjean added shoes, leather goods, and luggage to his inventory. Most recently, the Main Street building was Smith Hardware.

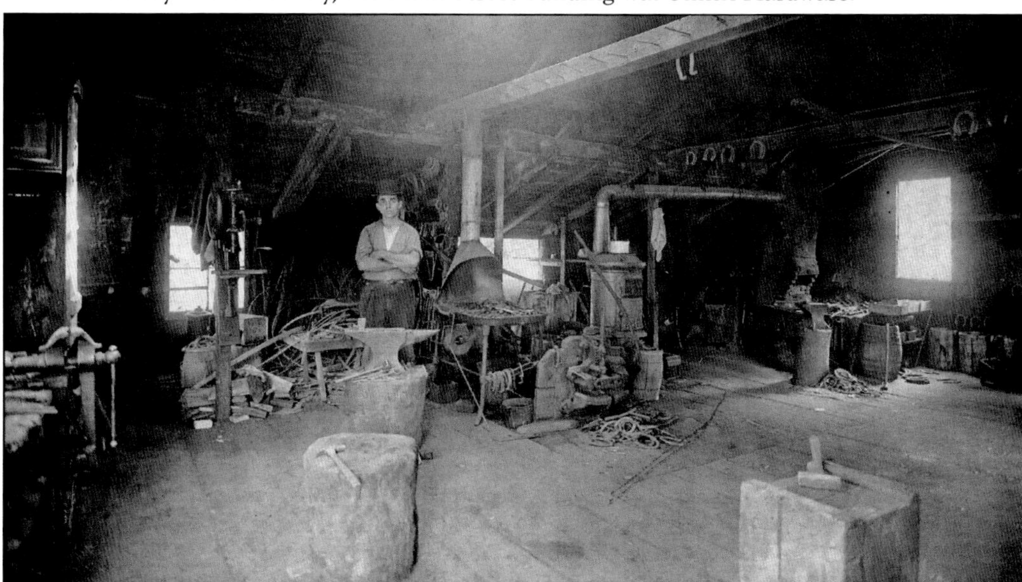

Newton Ryther is shown in the blacksmith shop built by his father, Solon B. Ryther. The shop, which straddled the creek, was next to their home at 8625 Main Street. The elder Ryther was son-in-law to Asa Warren. From the mid-1830s on, three generations of Rythers ran the business, shoeing horses and repairing farm tools and wagons. The shop building burned in 1937, but the home is still a residence.

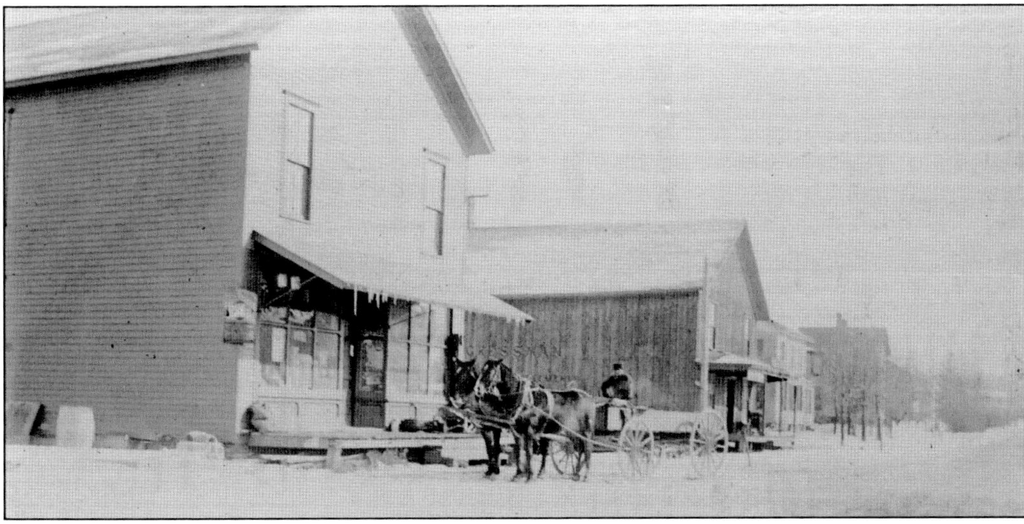

Redfield and Davis Hardware, established in 1889, was the biggest hardware business in the area. They owned a complex of five buildings, including this one, which still stands on the corner of Green and Depot Streets. As demand for indoor plumbing increased, they went into that business also. In more recent years, the building was George "Pop" Willet's second-hand shop and Sam Haney's Auction Gallery. Present owner Adam Henrich operates his gunsmithing business in the building.

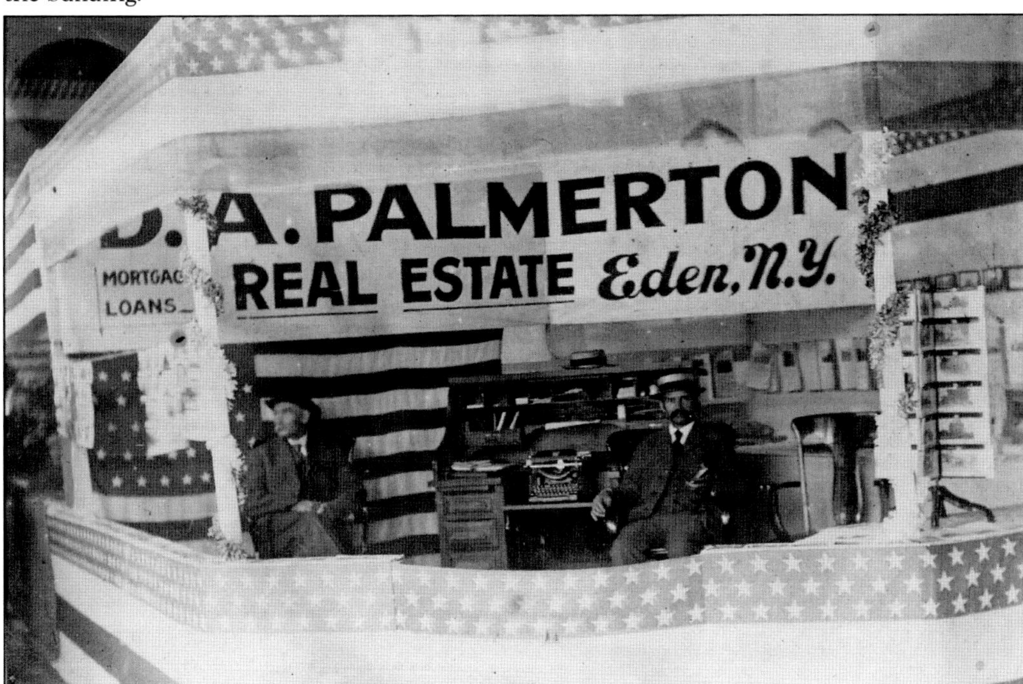

A long-standing Eden business began with Duran A. Palmerton (right) when he established his real estate business in 1896. He is seen showcasing his services at the Erie County Fair around 1909. Palmerton's son Jay added an insurance agency to the business in 1915. When Elton Palmerton returned from Navy duty in 1946, he became the third generation to join the business. He continued to run the Palmerton Agency until 1995.

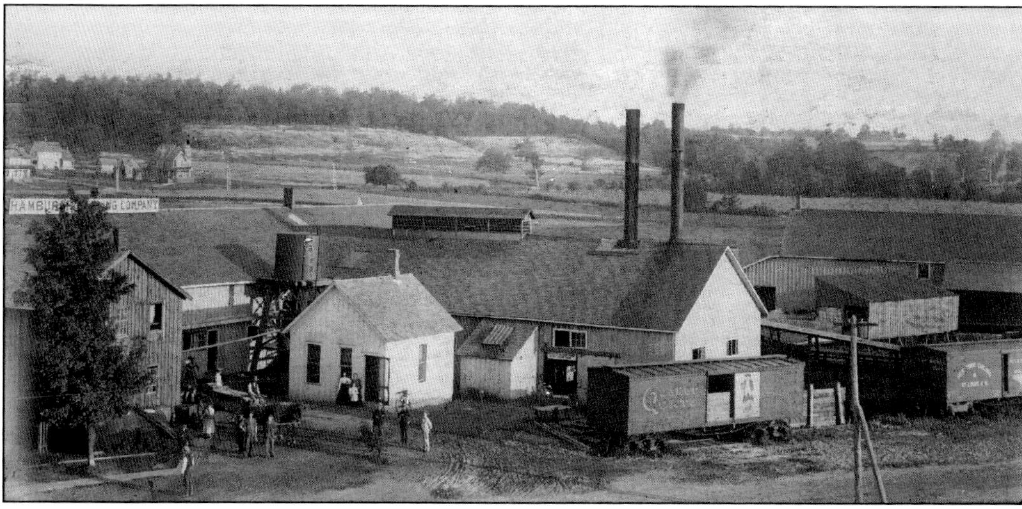

The Eden Center Preserving Company was founded and built in 1882 by a group of men from Eden and Hamburg. The proximity of the processing facility greatly increased the market for produce farmers. In 1891, Hamburg Canning Company purchased the Eden plant, which remained operational until the mid-1960s. The canning industry was an important economic factor in Eden for over 100 years, first in this facility and then in a newer factory on Gowanda State Road.

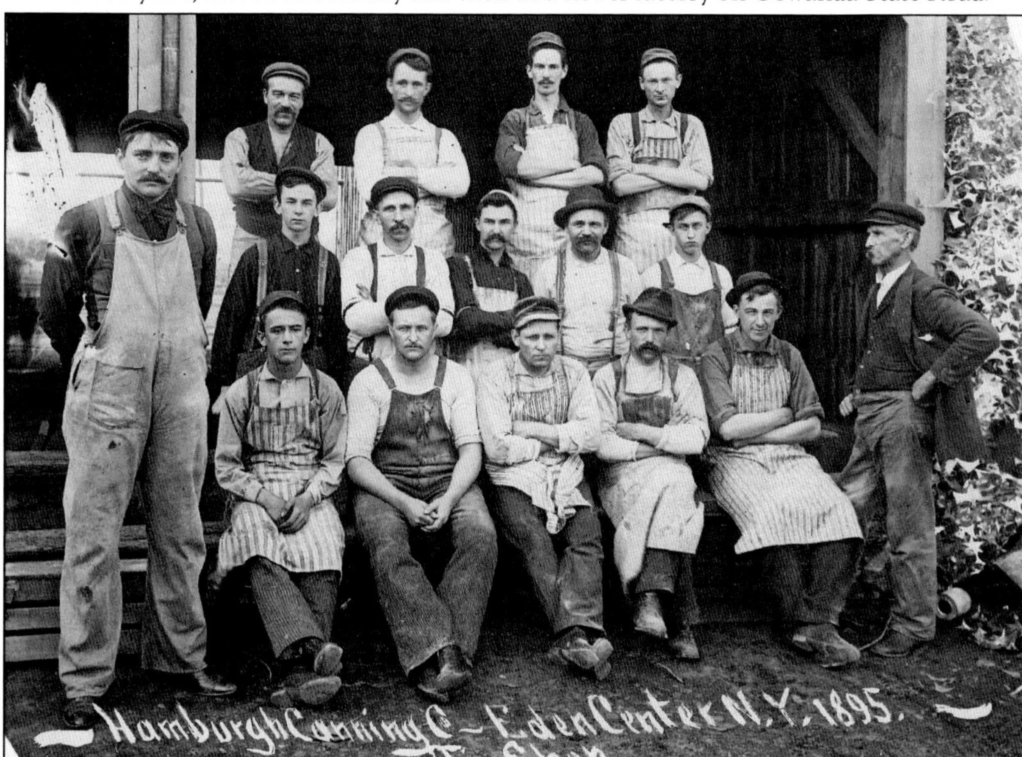

The canning factory provided employment for many men, women, and children. Among the workers were the men from the tin shop. They made the cans and sealed them after they were filled. Labels were applied by hand. Standing to the left is Daniel Pierce, who was the manger and principal stockholder of the company from 1891 until 1923.

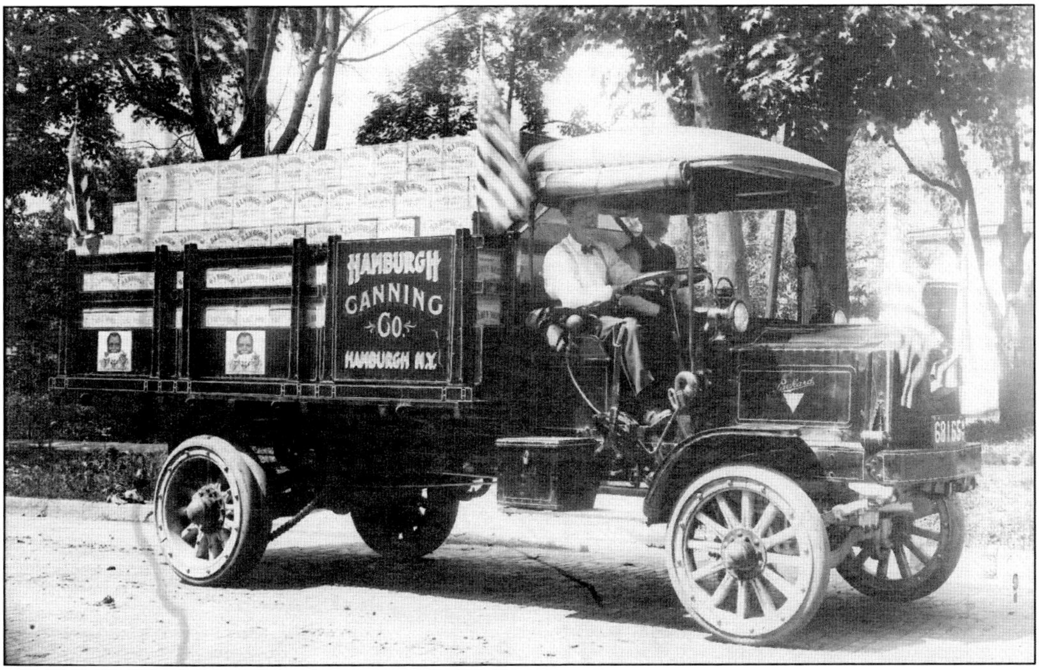

With flags flying, crates labeled "Early June Peas" make up this shipment of freshly processed canned goods. The delivery truck is a 1908 Packard. Notice that the steering wheel is on the right side instead of the left. George Ziegelhofer accompanies driver William Lakely.

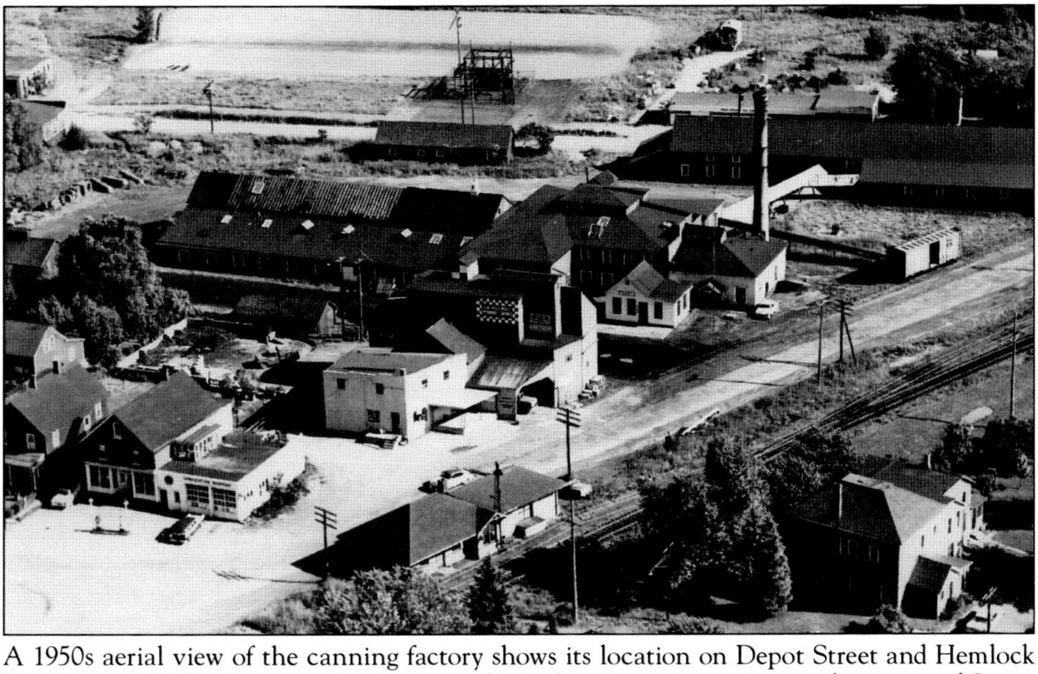
A 1950s aerial view of the canning factory shows its location on Depot Street and Hemlock Road. Laing's Mill is between the factory and Merchant's service station on the corner of Green Street. Most of the factory burned in 1969, but a few of the structures remain. The small white building with the peaked roof is now the office of Laing-Gro Fertilizers, which owns the old factory property.

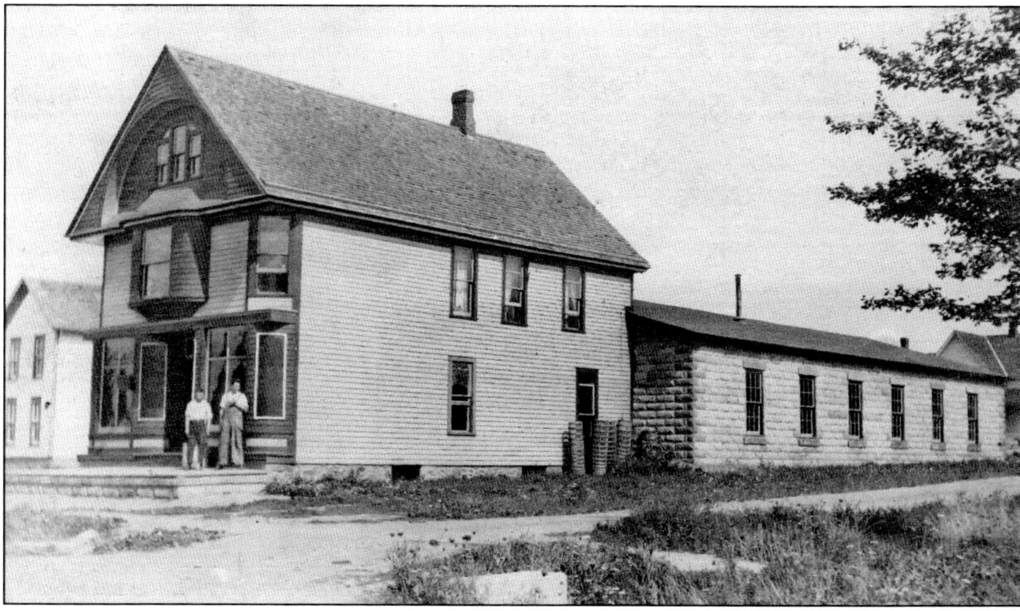

Before the familiar structure above became the Kazoo Company, it was the Eclipse Metal Manufacturing Company. Harry Richardson moved to Eden from Buffalo in 1907. He and Abram Lang erected this building, where they produced stove and furnace parts, peanut vending machines, and toys. The picture below shows workers in the earliest days of the plant. In 1915, a toy maker named Emil Sorg brought a wooden kazoo to Richardson to see if a metal one could be made. It could! Sorg and Michael McIntyre bought the building and toy business from Richardson in 1922, and the Kazoo Corporation was established. McIntyre's patent for a metal kazoo was approved in 1923.

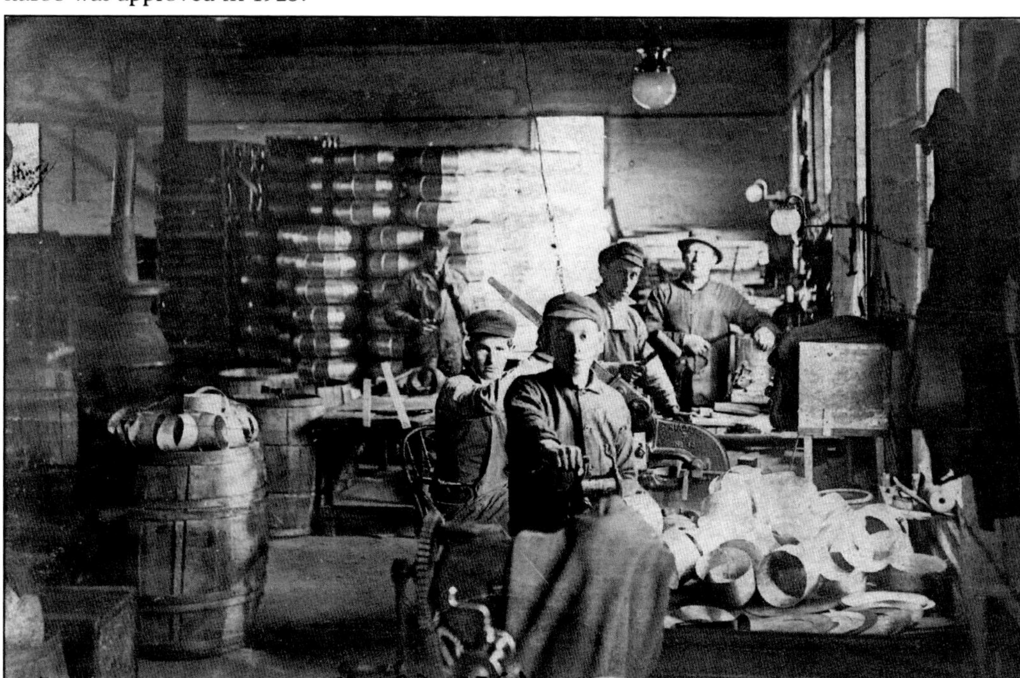

The schematic drawing for M.J. McIntyre's metal kazoo was filed with the US Patent Office in 1919. Where the earliest kazoo came from is a mystery, but it was a popular novelty in the early 20th century. In her *History of Eden, Volume II*, Doris Anderson described the instrument: "A kazoo, as every boy and girl should know, is a thingamajig you put in your mouth and hum into. Your hum comes out the other end fascinatingly different from when it went in." (Courtesy of SASi.)

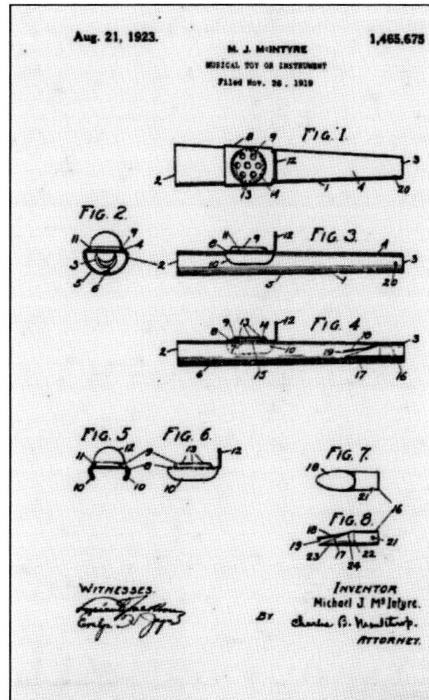

MICHAEL McINTYRE'S KAZOO PATENT - 1923

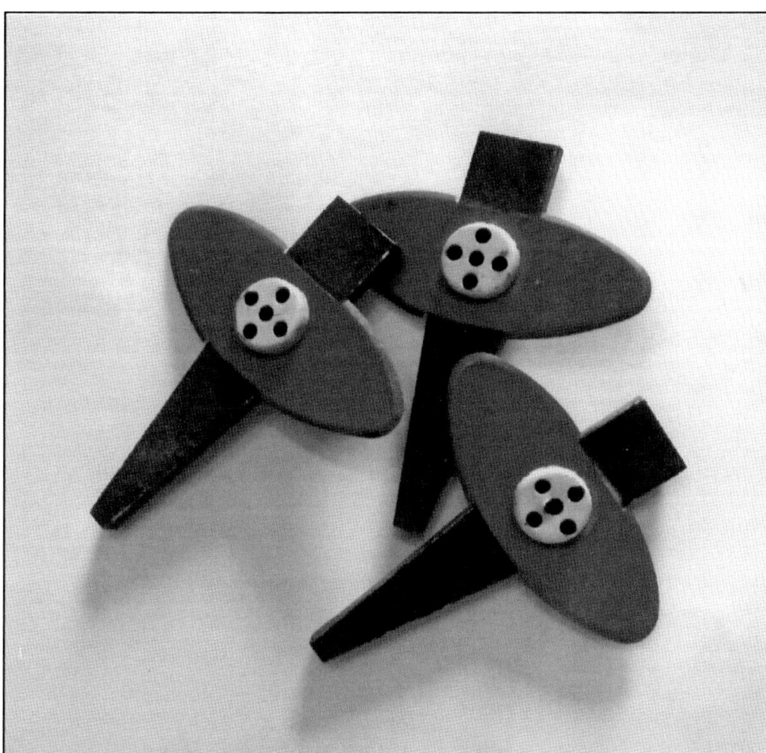

To celebrate the history-making flight of Charles Lindbergh across the Atlantic Ocean in 1927, the Kazoo Company fashioned these instruments. In addition to the standard kazoo, specialty items such as trumpets and trombones have always been made. In 1936, seventy-five employees turned out 10,000 items daily. In the mid-1960s, with production at nearly a million per year, Eden, New York, was the Kazoo Capital of the World. (Courtesy of Bob Maltby.)

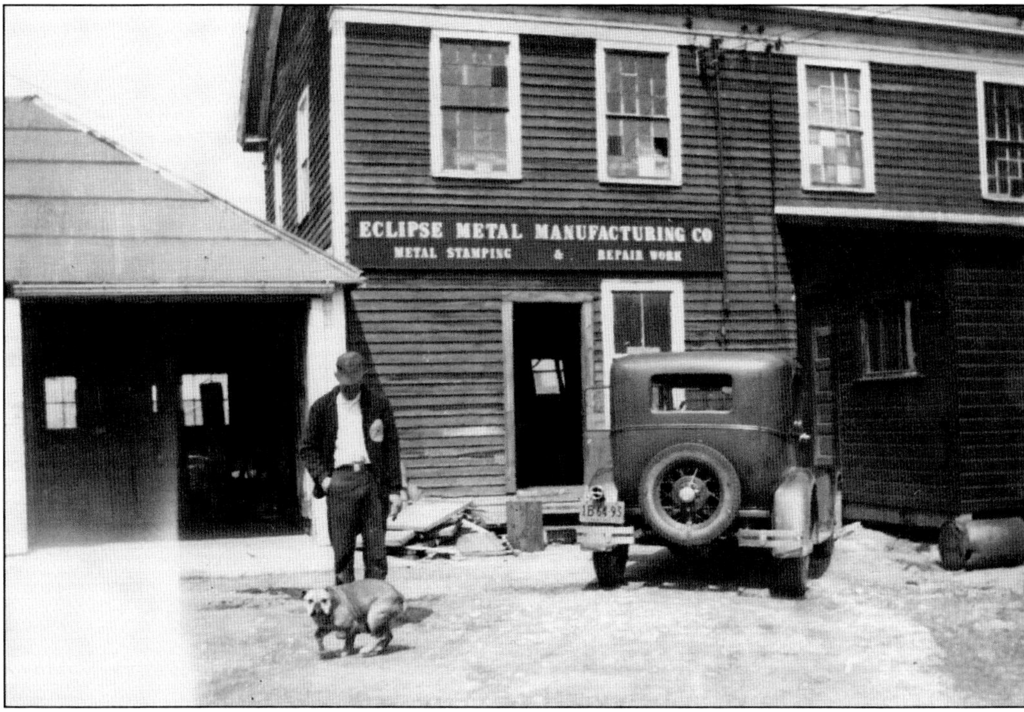

When Harry Richardson sold the Kazoo factory building to Emil Sorg and Michael McIntyre in 1922, he moved the Eclipse metal business across Main Street into what had been the Hines Blacksmith Shop. Taking his son Robert as a partner, Richardson continued to make furnace fittings and do sheet-metal work. The younger Richardson's invention of a portable picnic grill in 1932 probably saved the company during the Depression years. Around 1935, Ford Motor Company became interested in the grills and worked out a program to sell them through Ford dealers. A national interest was born, and the company grew. By 1951, production was up from 900 grills per day to 2,200. The metal shop area of the plant was destroyed by fire in late 1951. In just 30 days, a new, larger facility was built to replace it. The photograph below shows the plant in 1952.

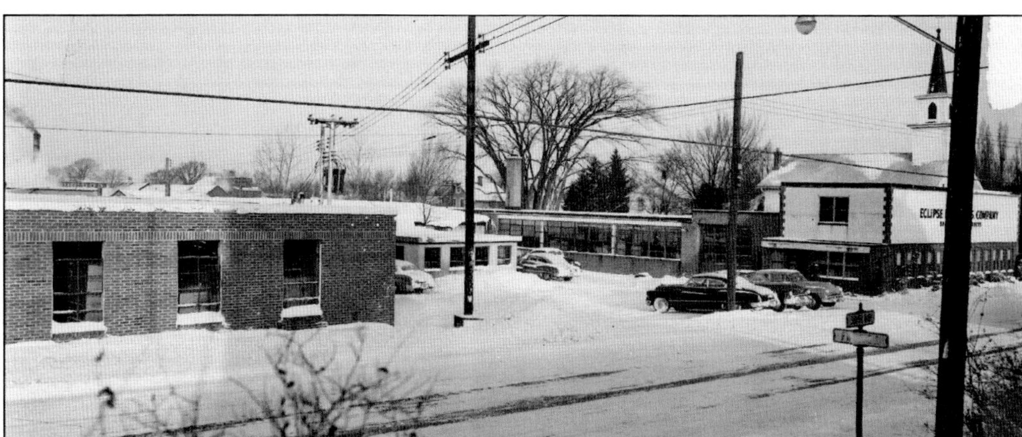

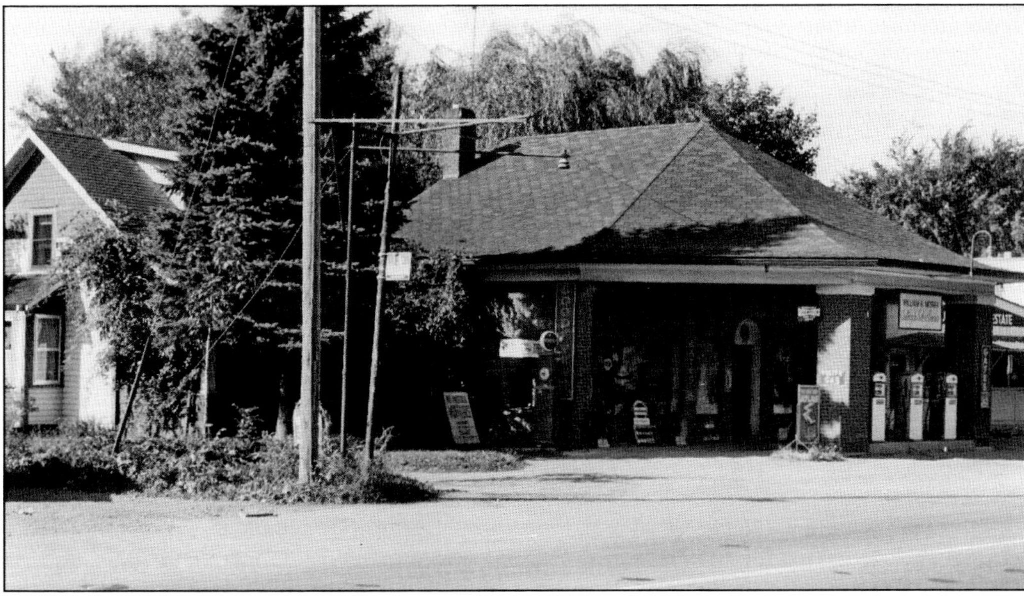

One of Eden's several service stations was Mosher's, shown here in the 1950s. Under two other owners, there had been a gas station at this North Main Street location since 1925. Unlike the gas stations of today, Mosher's offered a variety of automobile services, from oil changes to new wipers. An attendant pumped your gas, checked the oil level, and cleaned your windshield while the tank was filling.

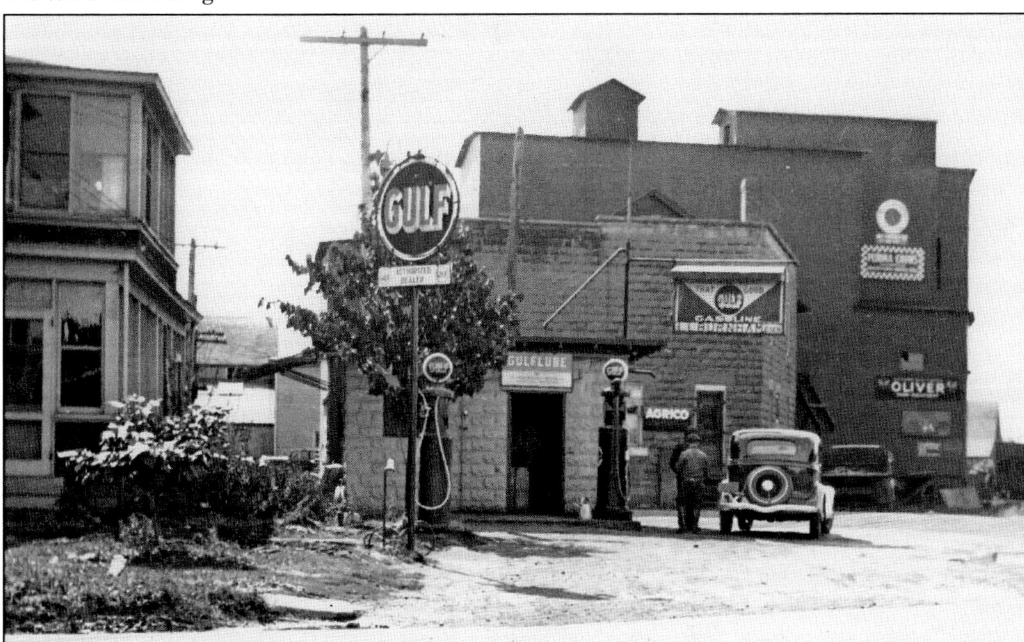

This 1934 photograph shows Howard Nobbs serving a customer at the first Gulf Oil gas station in Western New York. First owned by George Bartoo, it was purchased in 1924 by L.L. Burnham, who also established a wholesale business at the Green and Depot Street location. Upon Burnham's death in 1935, Nobbs and Silas Williams bought the retail outlet, and Robert Paige and Charles Harms acquired the wholesale division. (Courtesy of Gary Nobbs.)

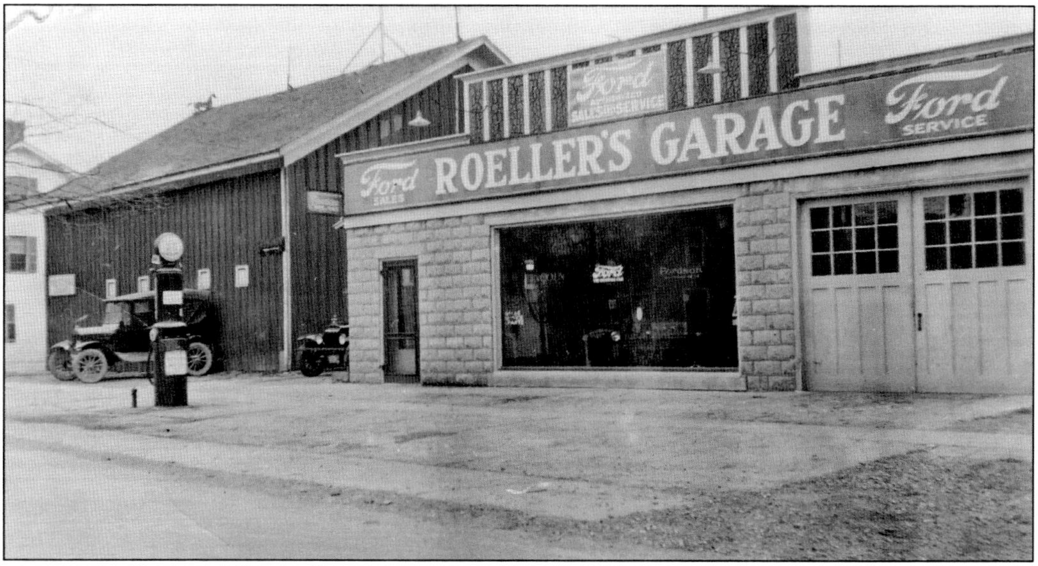

In 1917, William Roeller built this garage at 8550 North Main Street to sell and service Ford cars. He sold to Ernie Rice in 1936, and Rice in turn sold to Howard Nobbs and Silas Williams in 1944. They tore down the surrounding barns and sheds and added a large showroom. In 1952, they bought a small farm across Main Street. To free up space for their farm machinery and used cars, they moved the house on the property to Roswell Parkway. One year later, Williams took charge of the automobile division. Nobbs retained control over the farm implement portion of the business, which he operated until 1978. The partnership was dissolved in 1957, and Williams opened a new Ford dealership at Main Street and Legion Drive. The 1944 photograph below shows Willams sitting on a Model 9N tractor, with Nobbs standing to the side. (Above, courtesy of Jean Klug; below, courtesy of Gary Nobbs.)

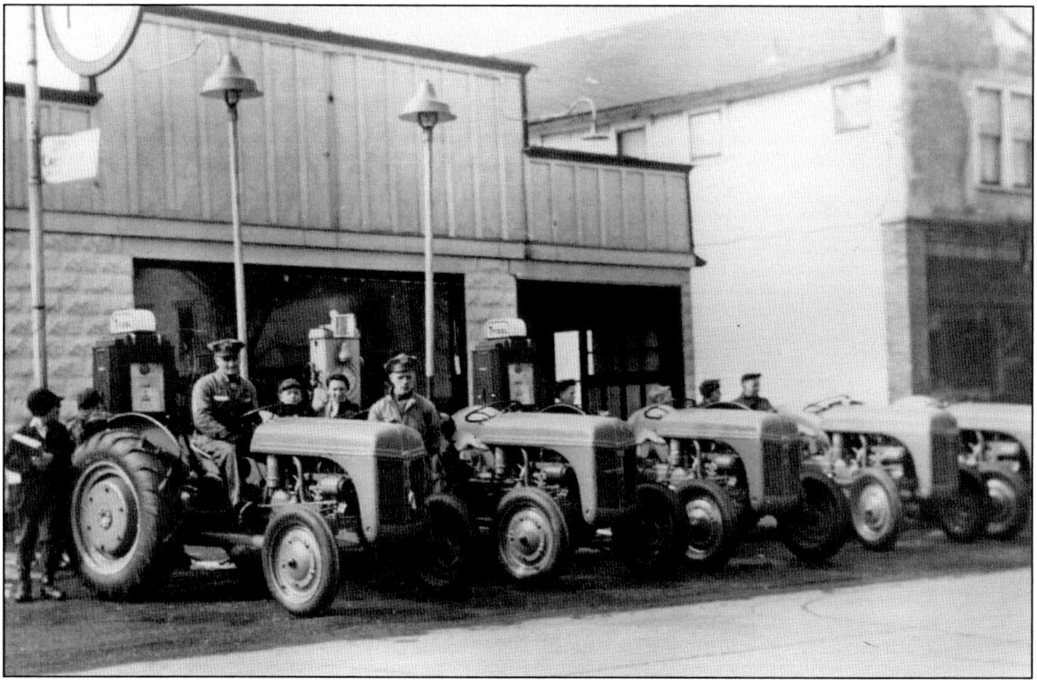

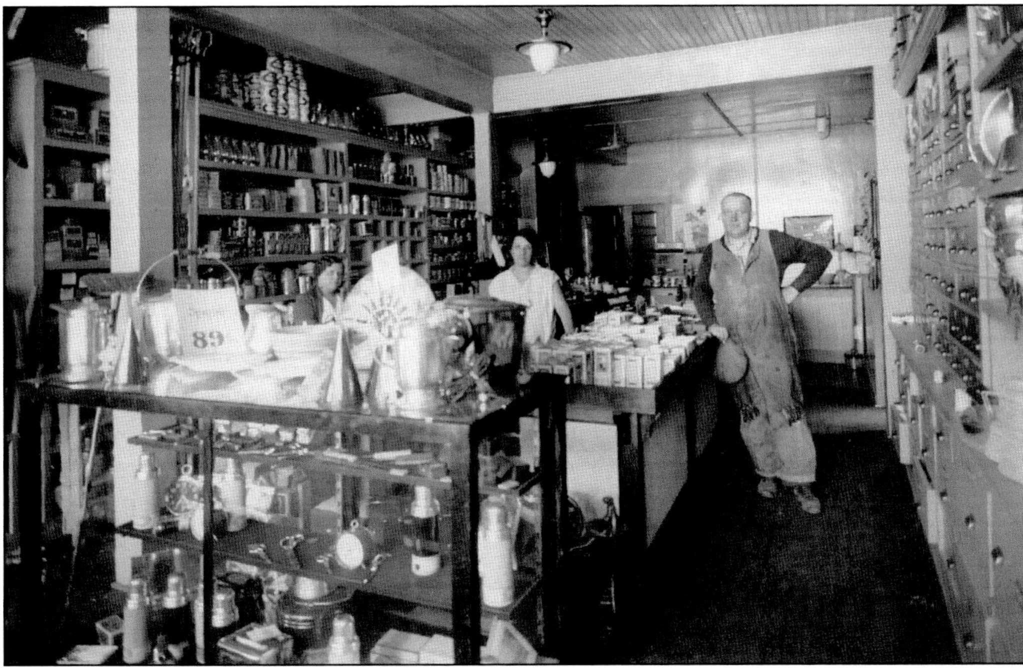

Over the years, there have been a number of hardware stores in town. What originally had been Grosjean's harness shop at 8544 Main Street became the hardware, plumbing, and heating business of Clarence Guenther in 1923. He used only half of the space and rented the other part to the Larkin Soap Company of Buffalo. Shown here in 1926 are Marie Jackson (left) and Emma and Clarence Guenther.

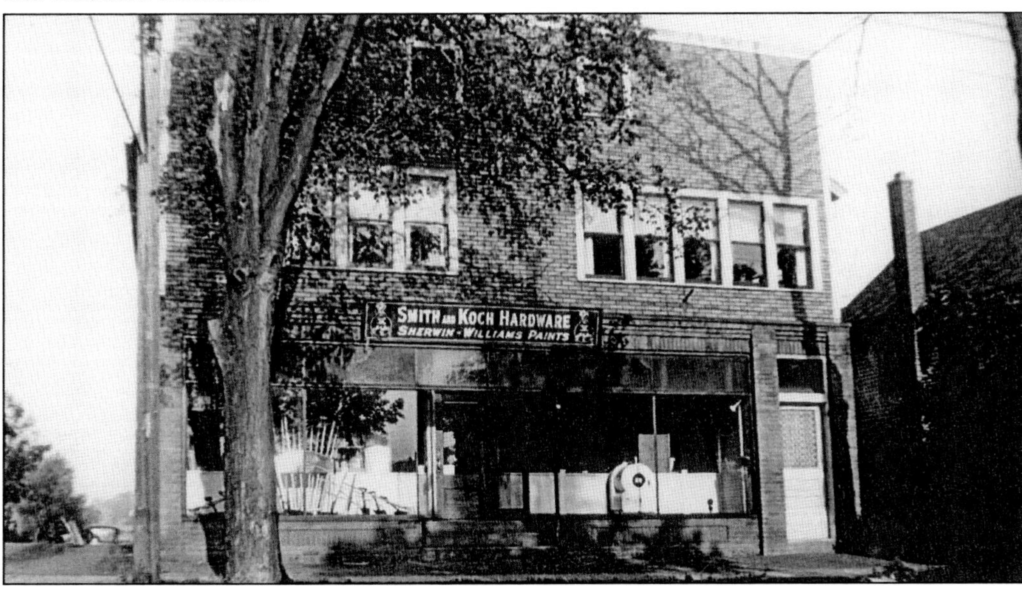

The hardware business succeeding the Guenthers' developed into a wonderful institution during the 20th century. In 1934, Smith and Koch Hardware, later Smith Hardware, was established by Clarence Smith and Walter Koch. Service from the friendly staff was excellent, and almost anything needed was available. After 72 years in business, it was a sad day in Eden when the store closed its doors in 2006. (Courtesy of Bettyann Smith Neifer.)

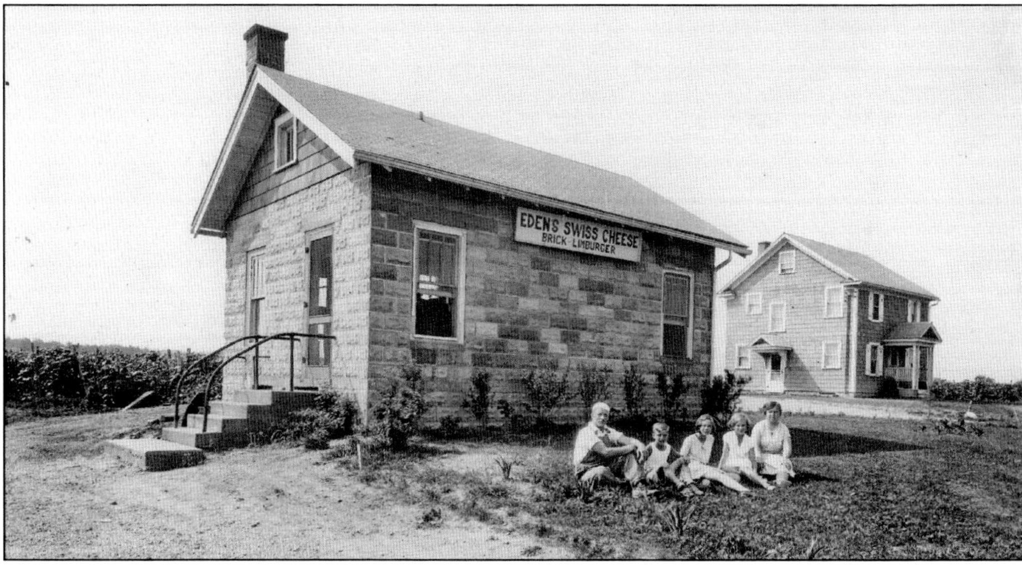

Another business that put the town on the map in the mid-20th century was the Eden Swiss Cheese Factory. Fred Rupp learned how to make Swiss cheese in his native Switzerland. Upon coming to the United States in 1914, he worked in the Eden plant of Buffalo's Hasselbeck Cheese Company. After further training, he became the first cheese maker in the state to use culture in the making of Swiss cheese. This skill led to his winning many prizes at the New York State Fair. In the picture above, Rupp is shown in 1930 with his wife and children in front of the factory he built on North Main Street. Grape vineyards border the factory and the family home, to the right. The lower photograph shows the interior of the factory and the cheese making equipment. Pictured from the left are Mildred Rupp Laing, Rose Rupp, Jeanette Rupp Van Note, Lester Rupp, and Fred Rupp. (Both, courtesy of Cheryl Laing Colvin.)

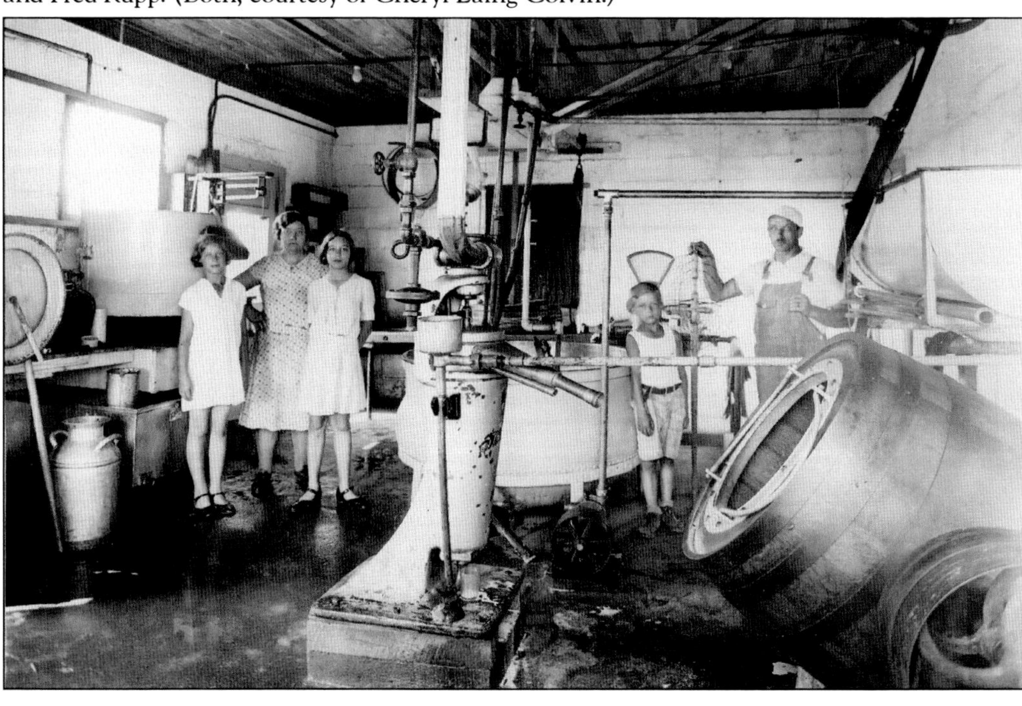

Lester Rupp successfully learned the art of cheese making from his father. Maintaining the standards set by his father, the business flourished in the decades following World War II. In addition to a variety of cheeses, gourmet specialty foods and candies were also available. During the Christmas season, the factory was exceptionally busy, and Rupp enlisted the help of family to assemble and prepare gift boxes for mailing all over the country. (Courtesy of Jennifer Rupp Soule.)

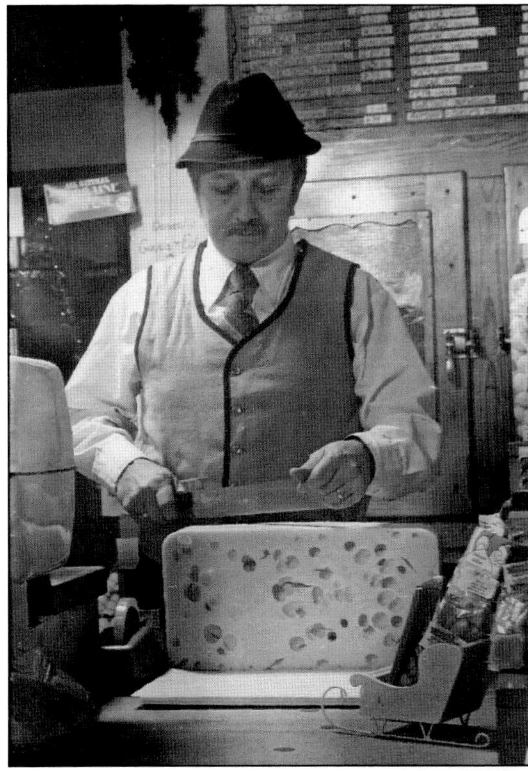

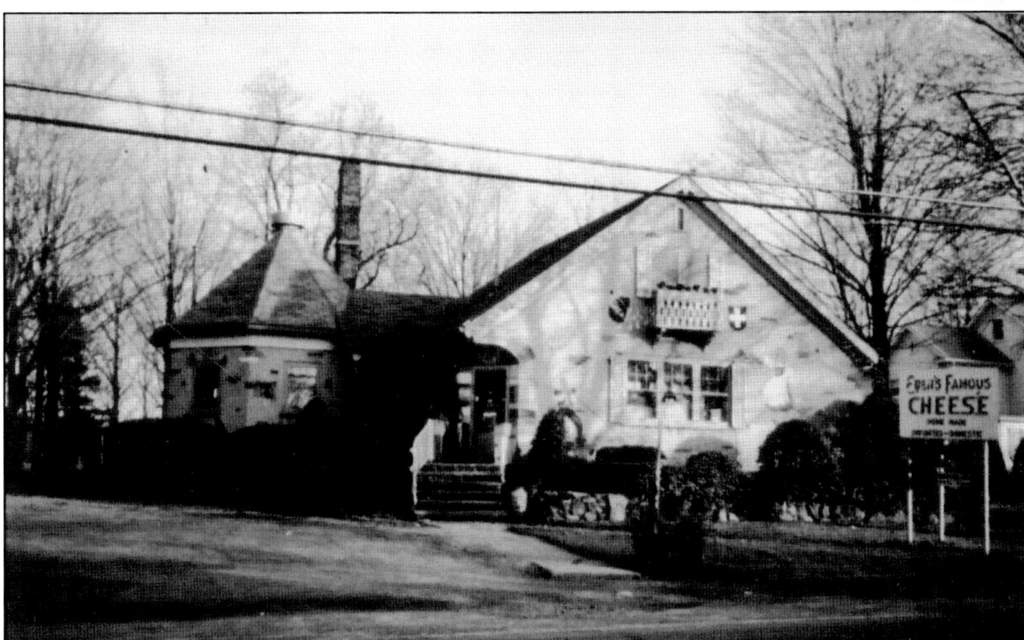

In a bow to her family's Swiss heritage, Lester Rupp's daughter Jane decorated the building to reflect a chalet. The building, though no longer a cheese factory, is still the recognizable landmark it came to be as Rupp enlarged and embellished the original simple structure that his father had built. (Courtesy Jane Rupp Gould-Badger.)

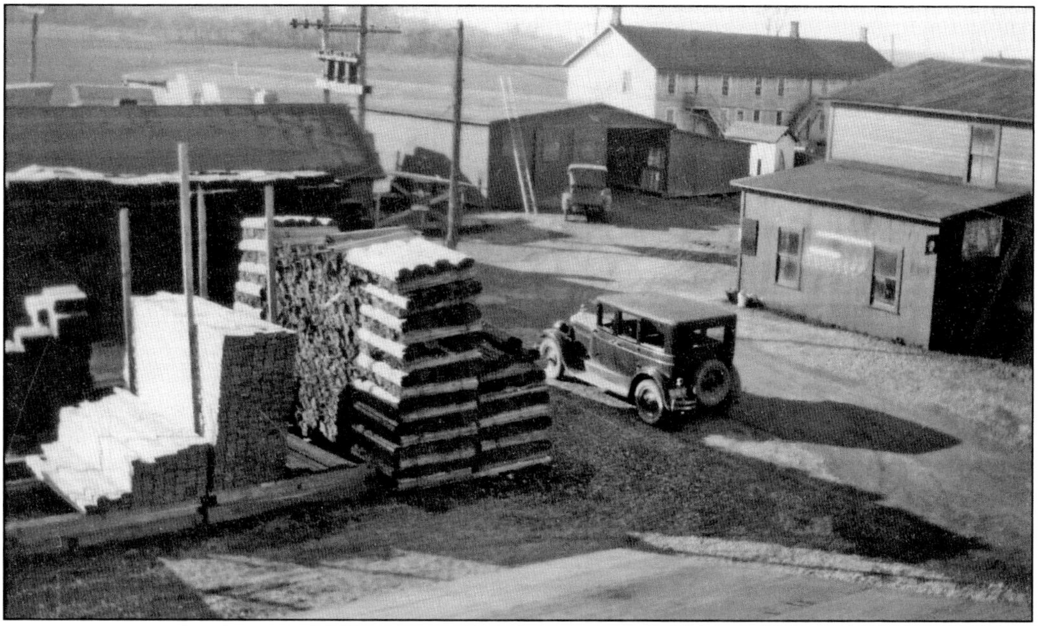

The vicinity of the railroad was a prime location for grain and lumber mills. Shown in this 1923 photograph is Herman Gumtow's lumber and planing mill, one of two located on Hemlock Road. George Dubois, who sold to Dan Dickman and Brothers in 1910, started the earliest mill on this site in the late 1800s. Gumtow purchased the business in 1920. He is remembered for building the original grandstand at the Erie County Fairgrounds.

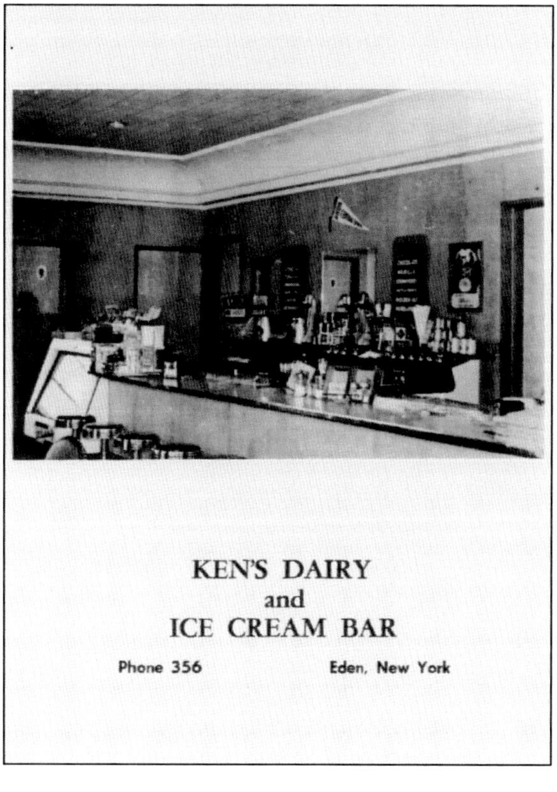

Ken Yager started in the dairy business in the early 1930s, while he was still in high school. In 1948, he built a dairy on North Main Street to process the milk for his home deliveries. In front of the dairy, there was an ice cream parlor. Its location directly across from the school made it a popular after-school destination in the 1950s and 1960s. Yager offered home milk delivery for nearly 50 years.

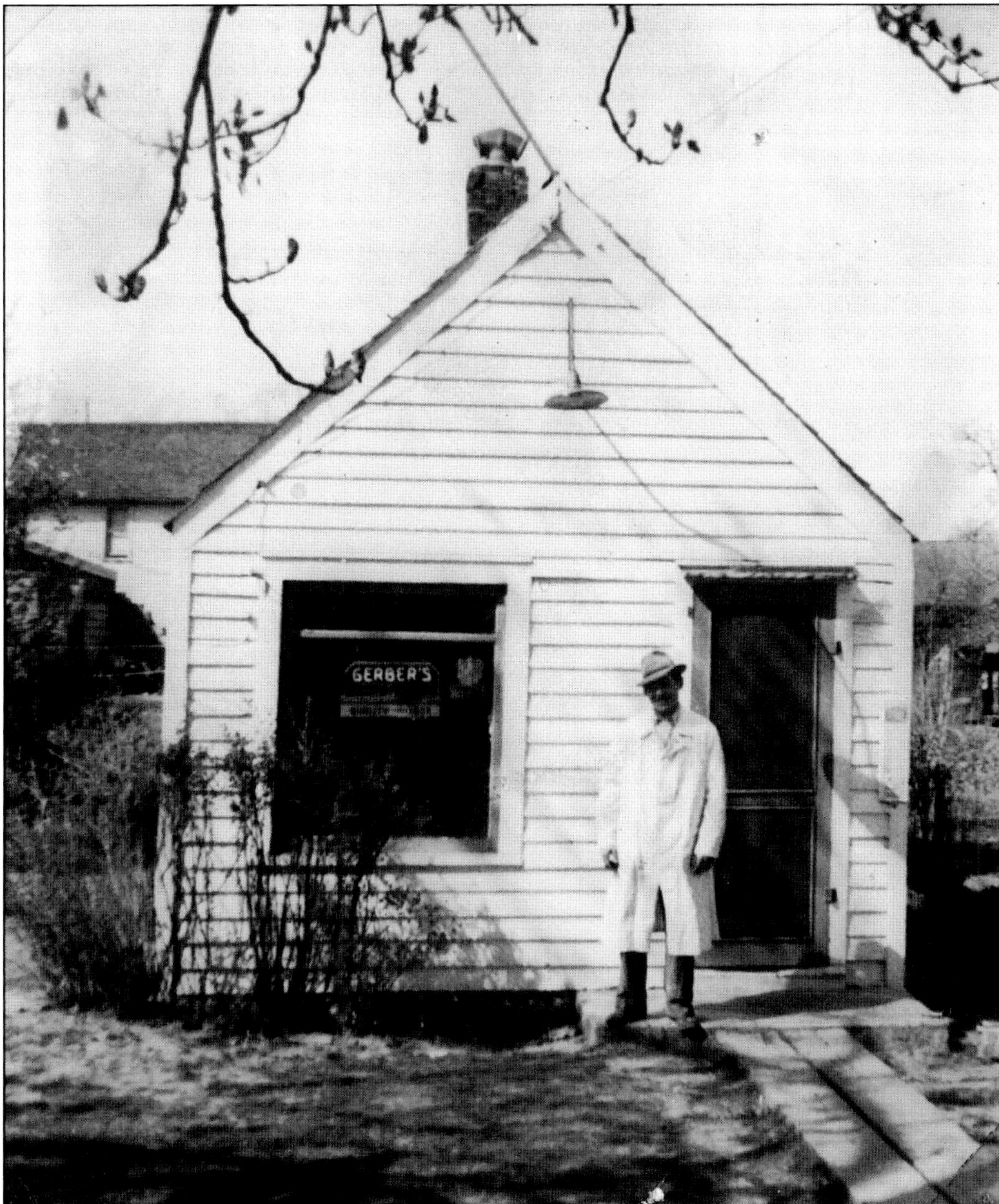

This small white structure has an interesting history. It was located in what is now the parking lot of the Four Corners Café. Originally a photographer's studio, it became Eden's first library and then a meat market under four owners. In 1941, George Guenther poses in front of his newly acquired business, Guenther's Choice Meats. He had recently purchased the business, including the stock from the Clayton Vellum Estate. Mary Demerly, to whom Guenther paid a monthly rent of $8, owned the building. There was an oil stove, but no running water or toilet, so it was necessary to access those facilities in the town hall across the street. Guenther operated his business in the little building for only a few years. After buying the original post office in 1943, he moved his business to West Church Street and later expanded it into a Red & White Store. The white frame building was eventually demolished for parking.

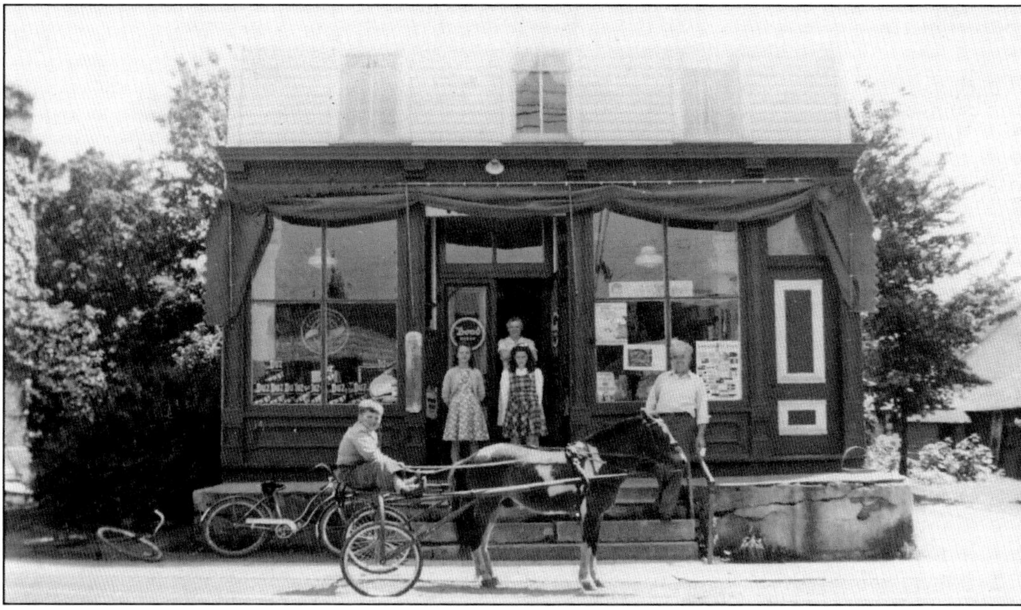

Running errands could be fun if one had a pony cart to travel in. In 1942, Paul Laing drove his pony to Vellum's Store at 2763 West Church Street. Glenn Vellum and his sisters Blanche and Pearl purchased the building in 1926 and ran a store there until 1954. The building, which dates from 1881, is now a dentist's office. It served as the post office from 1956 until 1982.

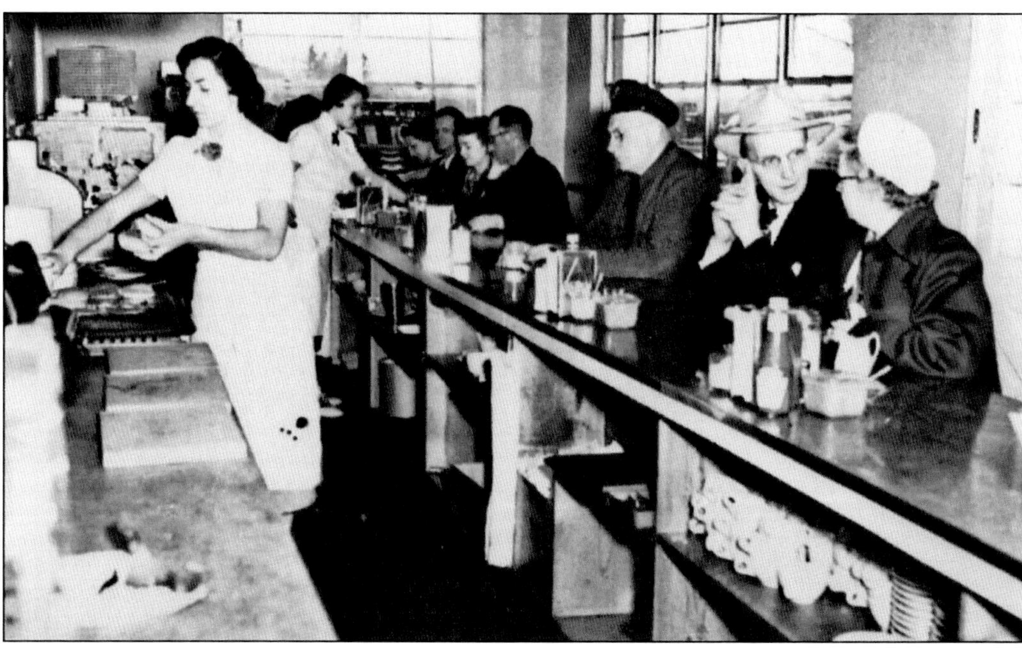

In the early 1950s, Renschler's Snack Bar was the place to go for breakfast or a great hamburger. Traveling south on Route 62, it was located just before Henry's Corners. There were no tables, just the counter where Constable Ken Shook waited for his lunch. Florence Mietlinski Rothaug tended the grill while Charlotte Renschler Dylon waited on customers.

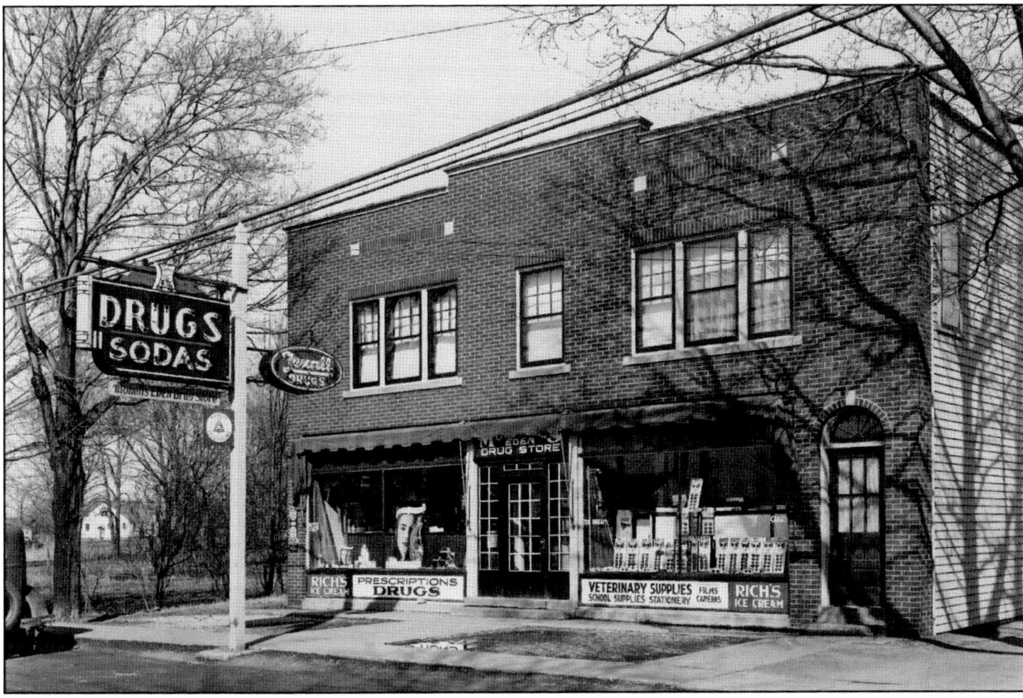

Many in Eden still remember Monell's Drugstore. Pharmacist Leon Monell, a 1911 graduate of Columbia University School of Pharmacy, operated his business at 8533 North Main Street from 1937 to 1966. Window advertising shows the variety of products available in 1947. In 1976, when it was La Via Pizzeria, a gas explosion caused a fire that destroyed the building.

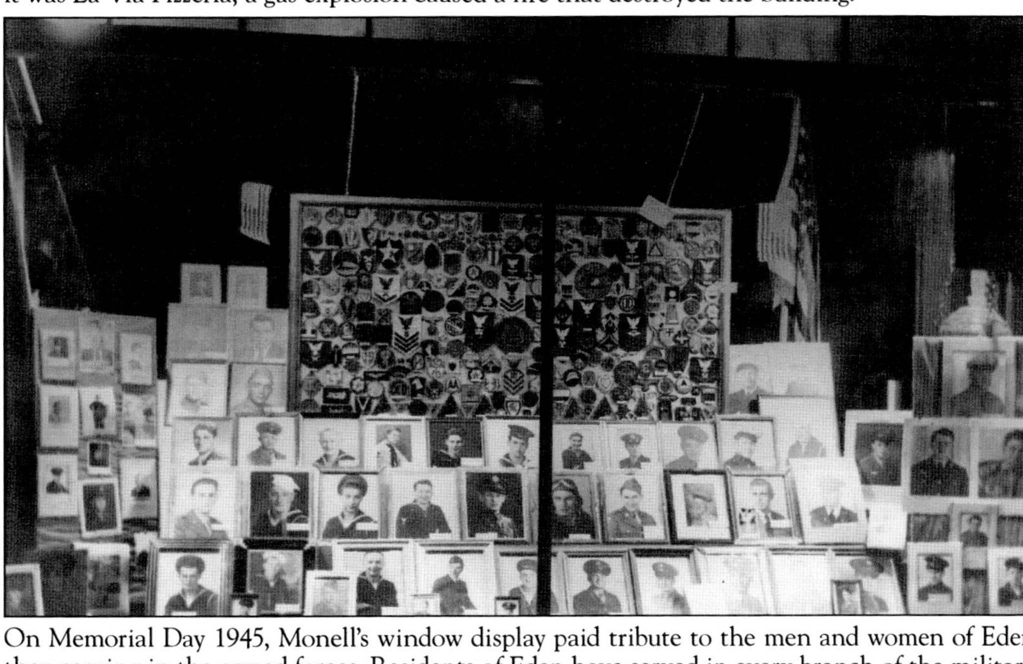

On Memorial Day 1945, Monell's window display paid tribute to the men and women of Eden then serving in the armed forces. Residents of Eden have served in every branch of the military since the Revolutionary War. They are honored every Memorial Day as the town gathers for ceremonies in Evergreen Cemetery.

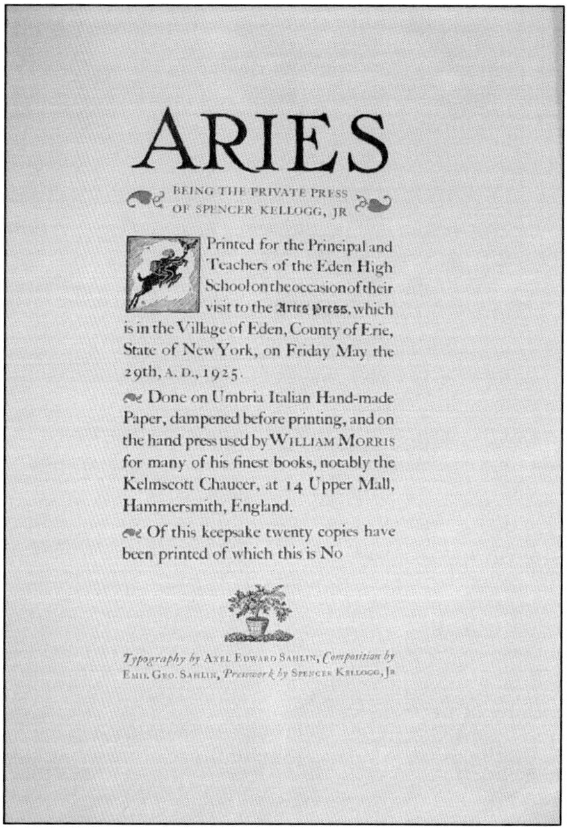

ARIES

BEING THE PRIVATE PRESS OF SPENCER KELLOGG, JR

Printed for the Principal and Teachers of the Eden High School on the occasion of their visit to the Aries Press, which is in the Village of Eden, County of Erie, State of New York, on Friday May the 29th, A. D., 1925.

Done on Umbria Italian Hand-made Paper, dampened before printing, and on the hand press used by WILLIAM MORRIS for many of his finest books, notably the Kelmscott Chaucer, at 14 Upper Mall, Hammersmith, England.

Of this keepsake twenty copies have been printed of which this is No

Typography by AXEL EDWARD SAHLIN, *Composition by* EMIL GEO. SAHLIN, *Presswork by* SPENCER KELLOGG, JR

A short-lived but interesting addition to the business community was the Aires Press, established in 1926 at 2804 East Church Street by Spencer Kellogg Jr. He hired a typographer, Emil Georg Sahlin, from the Roycrofters in East Aurora and commissioned preeminent type designer Frederic Goudy to design a typeface specifically for the Aires Press. The work produced during the press's three short years was limited but beautifully fine and unique. Shown here is a keepsake made just for Eden students. (Courtesy of Paradise Press.)

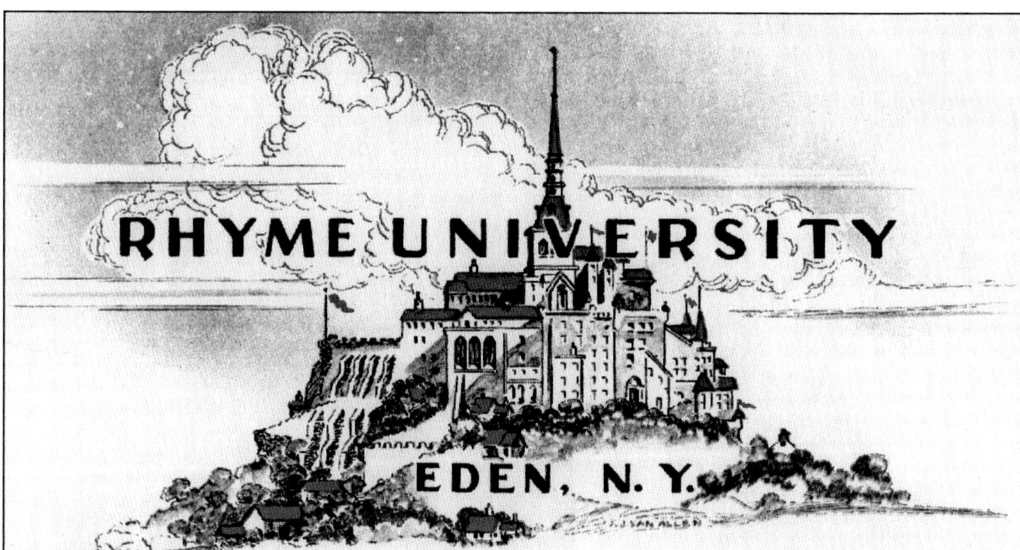

Leon Olsen ran a unique business from his home at 8492 Main Street. After being thoroughly unimpressed with the mimeographed kindergarten diploma of a neighbor's child, Olsen decided that something better was needed. He hired local artist John Van Allen to design a colorful certificate featuring Mother Goose characters as well as this letterhead. "Chancellor" Olsen successfully marketed the diplomas from 1952 to 1972, when he sold the business to a California company.

Six

Mind and Spirit

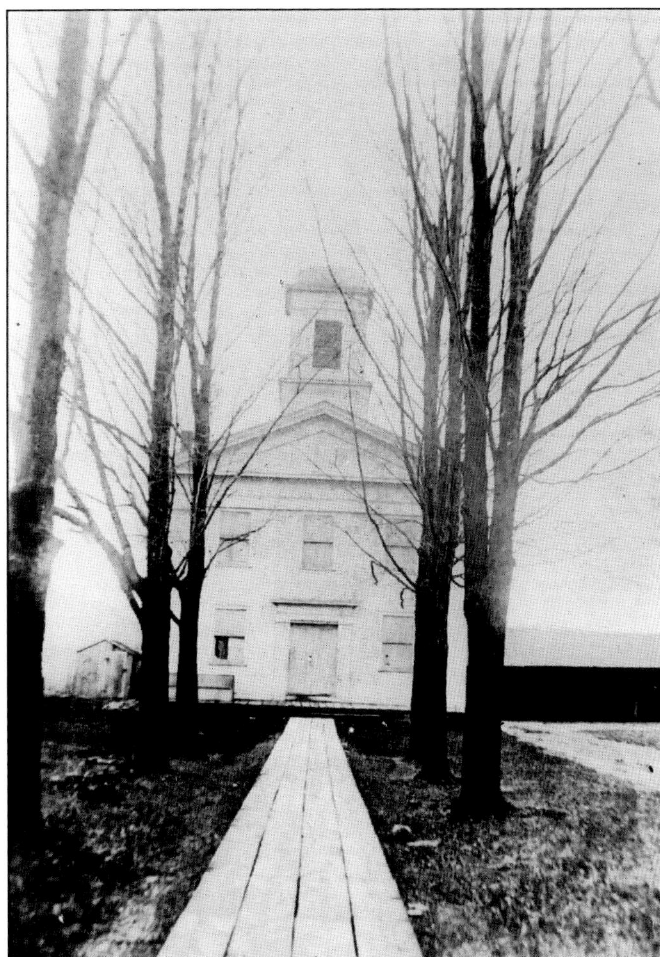

A plank walkway leads to a building where both mind and spirit were nurtured. It was built as the Eden Academy, a high school for which one had to pay tuition. The academy opened in 1842 but was not successful enough to sustain itself for more than a few years. The Baptist congregation purchased the building in 1848. It was sold and moved to Green Street in 1895 when the Baptists erected their current building on the East Church Street site.

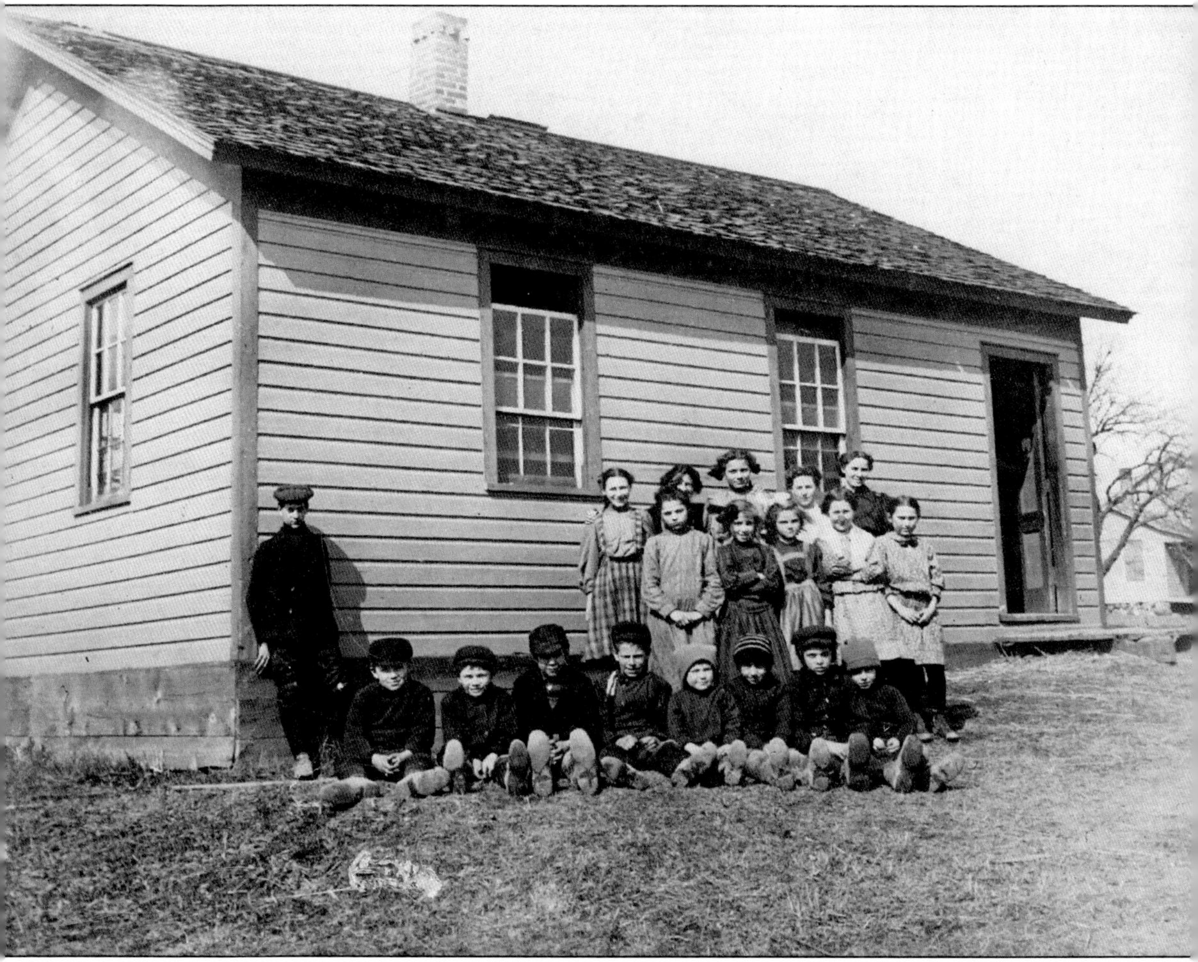

Education was a priority for Eden's settlers from the earliest years. Rowena Flack was teaching children at home in 1812. When residents gathered in 1814 to discuss building a school, a poor but enterprising man, Josiah Gale, promised to provide the nails. The War of 1812 was still being fought, and metal of any kind was a precious commodity, so people were astonished by his offer. True to his word, Gale produced nails to complete the project. It seems he had walked into Buffalo and salvaged nails from the structures ruined when the British burned the city. One-room district schools educated the town's youth for the next 125 years. Students from District School 13 (later 3), located on the corner of Shadagee and Ferrier Roads, pose with their teacher, Ella Decker, in 1906. One person taught grades one through eight. Most teachers were female, and they had to be unmarried. Throughout the school year, families took turns providing room and board for the teacher of their district. Furnishings were minimal, but all the schools had libraries, some with as many as 125 books.

Around 1854, the one-room school on East Church Street was reported to be overflowing. Space was rented in the Redfield Building until the frame structure, pictured at right, was built in 1881. It became the Eden Union Free School in 1896. The next year, state law required that all district pupils receive a high school education free of charge. For lack of a science lab, the school was not a fully accredited high school until 1925. The photograph below shows older students and their teachers in 1899. Some among this group made up the first graduating class that year. Graduation from high school was a tremendous honor and achievement. Ceremonies, filled with music and oratory, were quite elaborate, even if the class numbered only a few.

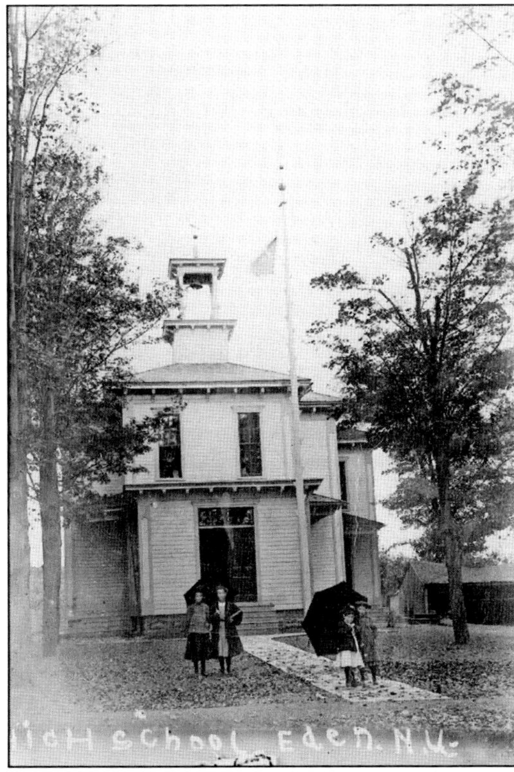

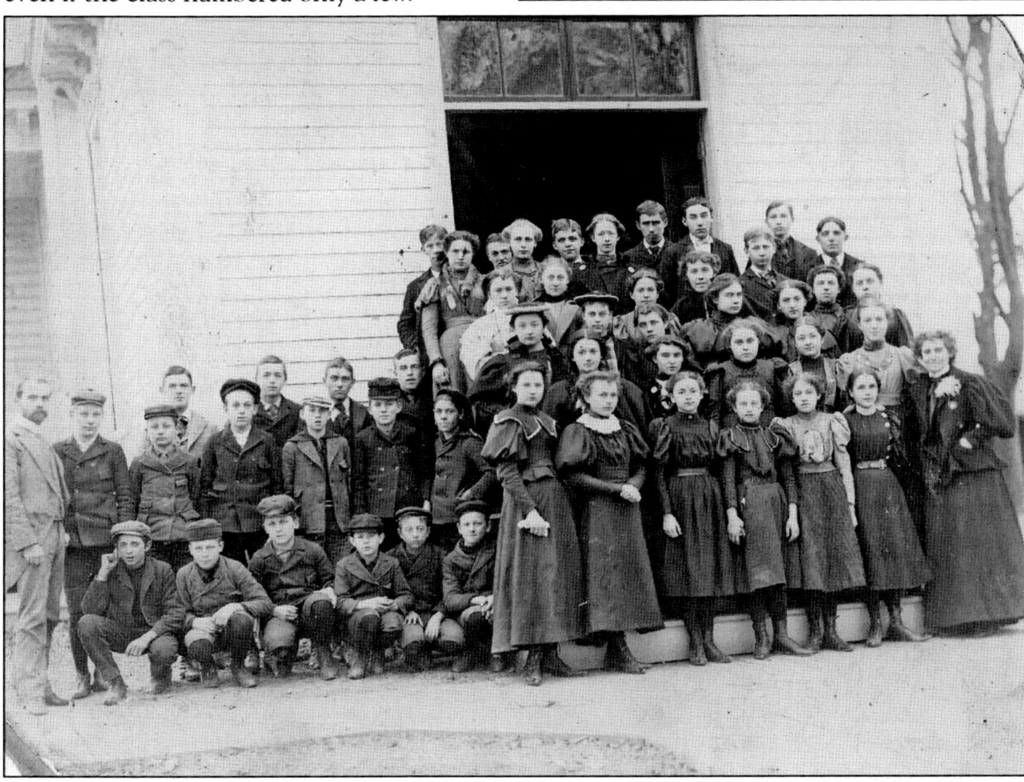

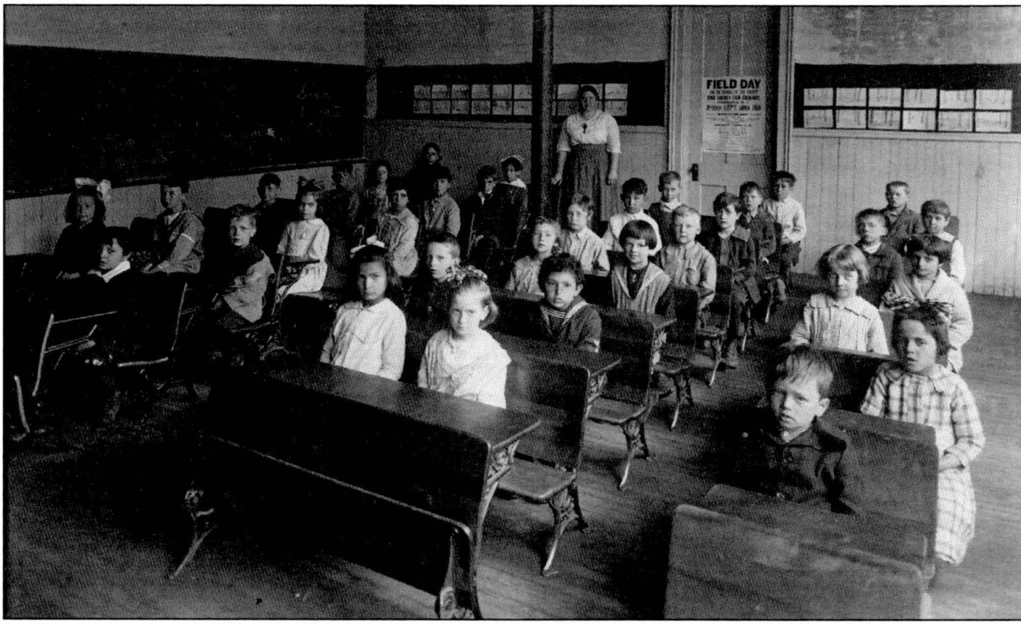

In September 1919, the first and second grades of the Union Free School pose for a class picture. The spare furnishings and the simplicity of the classroom were typical for the times. The teacher was the focal point, and she expected, and more often than not received, the attention and cooperation of her pupils. The poster on the door advertises a field day for all county school students at the Erie County Fair Grounds in Hamburg.

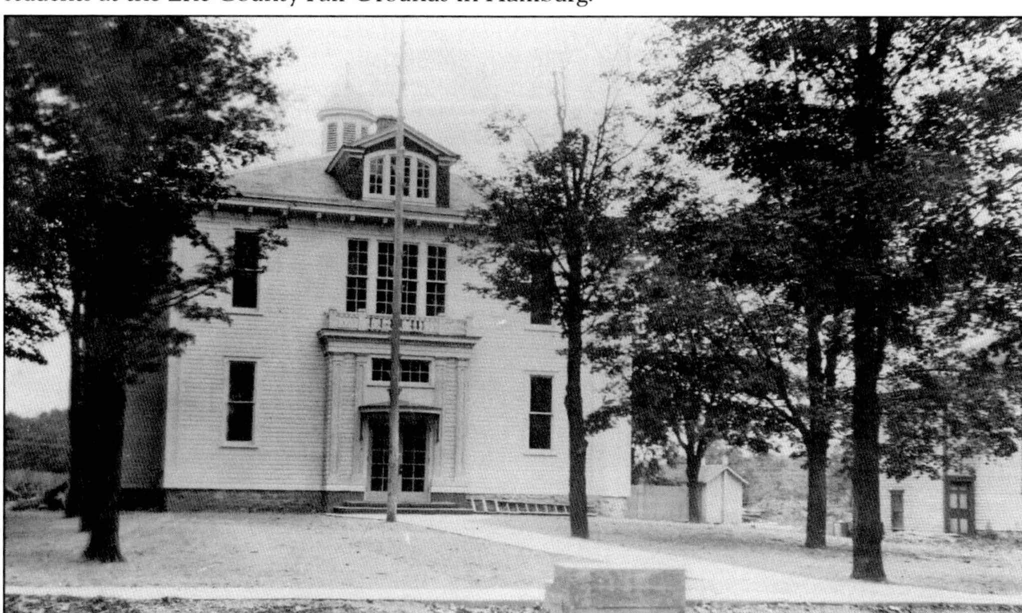

This 1922 photograph of the Union Free School shows one of three additions made to the structure over time. Extensive remodeling in 1927 included the brick addition of an auditorium/gymnasium onto the front. When the Eden Central School District was formed in 1939, a new school was erected on North Main Street. The old frame building and rear additions were torn down, and the school was remodeled for the Eden Town Hall, which it has been ever since.

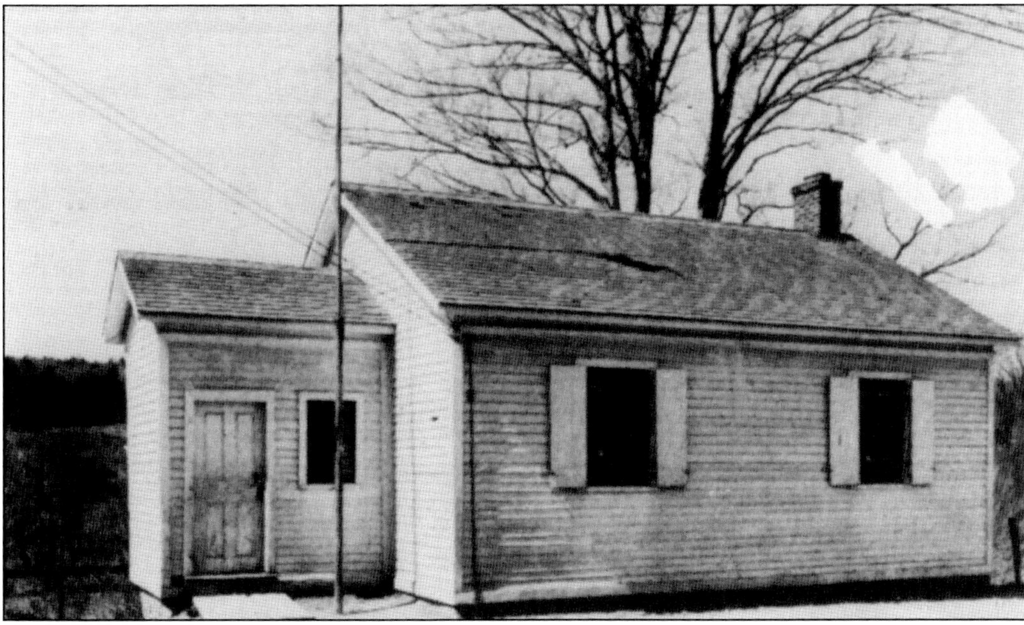

The district schoolhouse at Clarksburg is the only remaining one-room building still existing in its original state. The others have been demolished, moved, or renovated for a different use. This simple building, which dates from the late 1830s, sits alongside the creek near the corner of New Oregon and Clarksburg Roads. It is the intention of the current owner, Mike Hagelin, to donate the building to the Eden Historical Society.

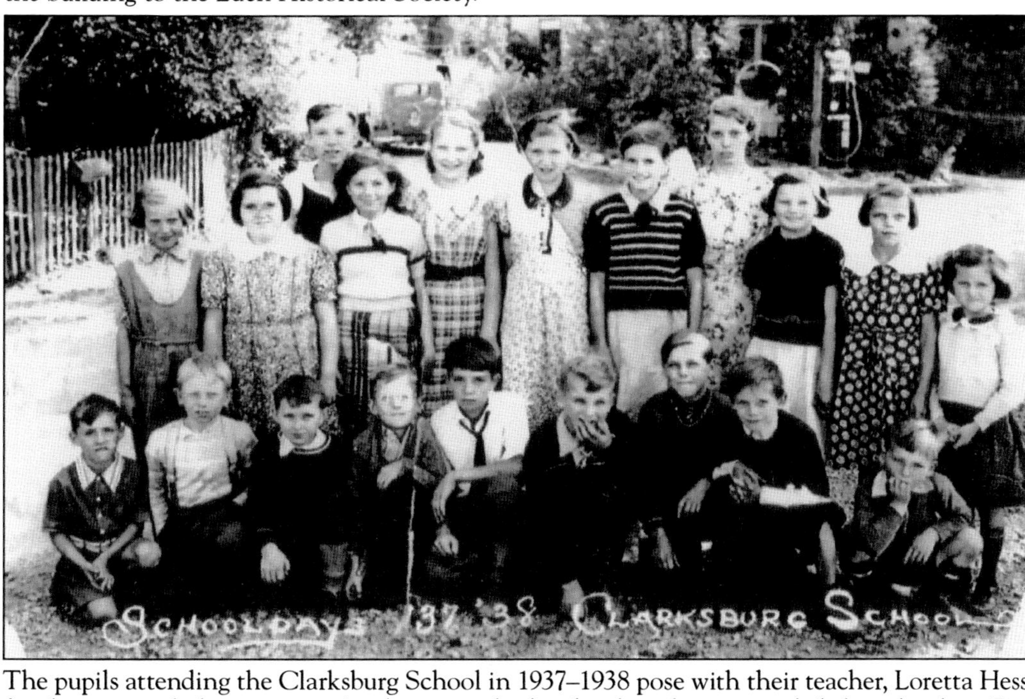

The pupils attending the Clarksburg School in 1937–1938 pose with their teacher, Loretta Hess, for their annual class picture. At that time, high school students attended the school on East Church Street. These children were among some of the last to attend the old school, because after centralization in 1939, all students in the district attended the new school on Main Street.

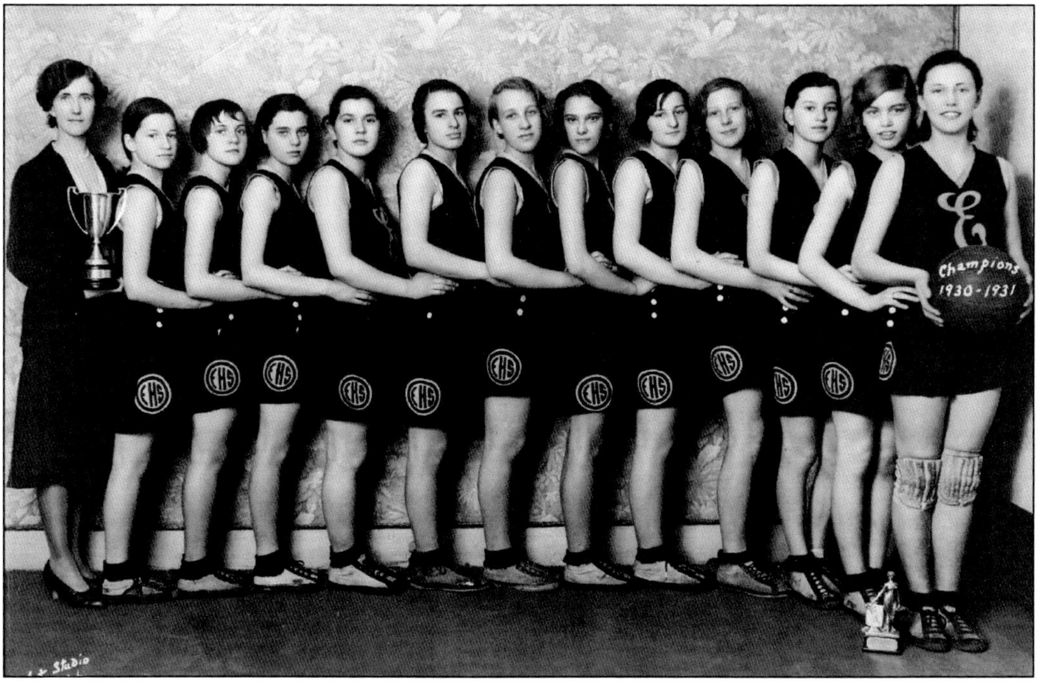

Yearbooks from the 1930s show that extracurricular activities were varied and numerous. Music and sports have always been among the most popular. Honors and championship teams are not just recent occurrences. The 1930–1931 girls varsity basketball team, shown above, was the Lake Shore League champion. The 12-member team is shown with their coach, Evelyn Meyers. In 1935, students in the school orchestra pose (below) on the east side of the school for their annual picture. A close look at the building shows where the 1927 brick addition merged with the original frame structure. The door and the rounded windows were covered over in 1955, when an addition for the Eden Free Library was constructed. It is now the police station.

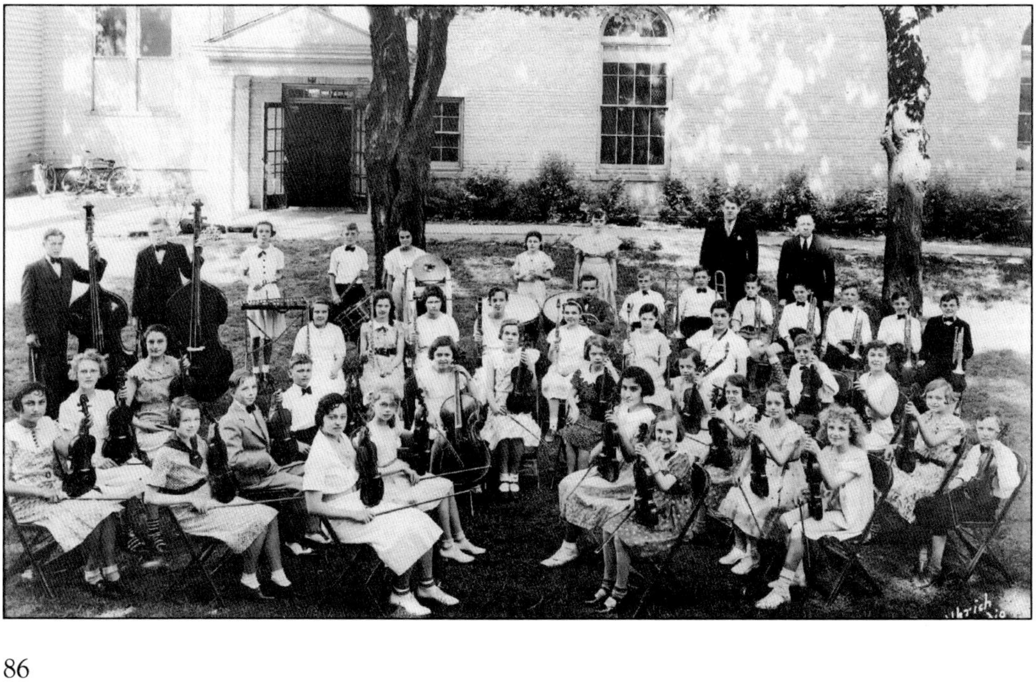

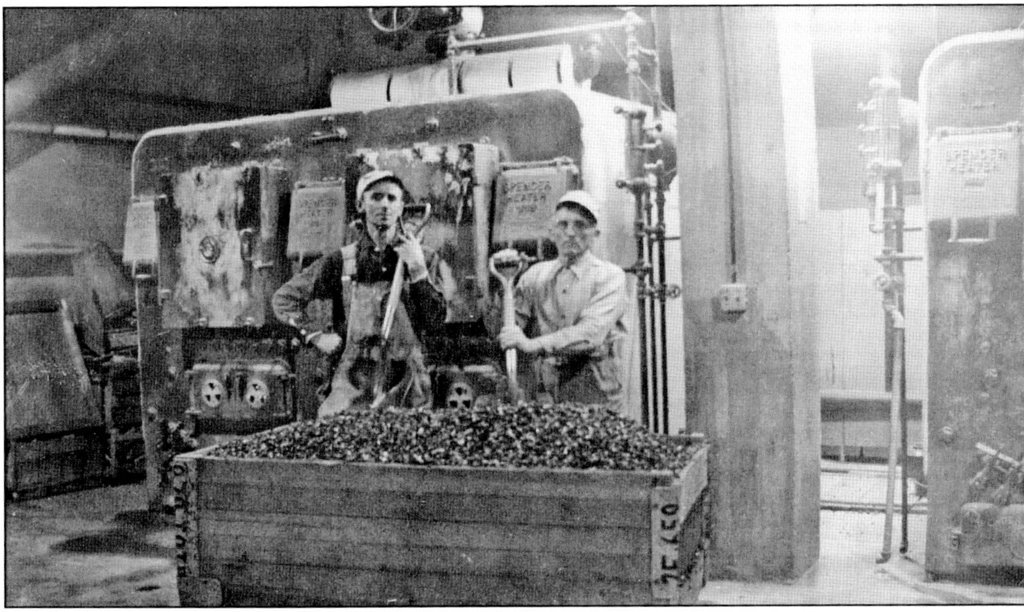

It took more than teachers to keep the school running. In addition to office staff, there was a clinic where the school nurse cared for the sick, tested hearing, and, aided by a local doctor, performed physical exams and gave immunizations. A dental hygienist cleaned teeth and checked for cavities. Maintenance of the building and grounds kept the custodial staff busy. In 1947, one of the harder and certainly less glamorous jobs fell to the janitors Len Shouldice (left) and Edwin Metz (right), as they stoked the furnaces with coal. Though many students carried their lunch to school, hot meals were always available in the cafeteria. All food was prepared on site and served by the cafeteria staff. A dietician created the menu, which was different every day, though certain items were repeated on a regular basis. "If it's Wednesday, it must be meatloaf," might have been the answer to "What's for lunch?" The cafeteria ladies in 1950 were, from left to right, ? Davis, Martha Nellis, Linnie Shook, Emile Keller, and Hilda Miller.

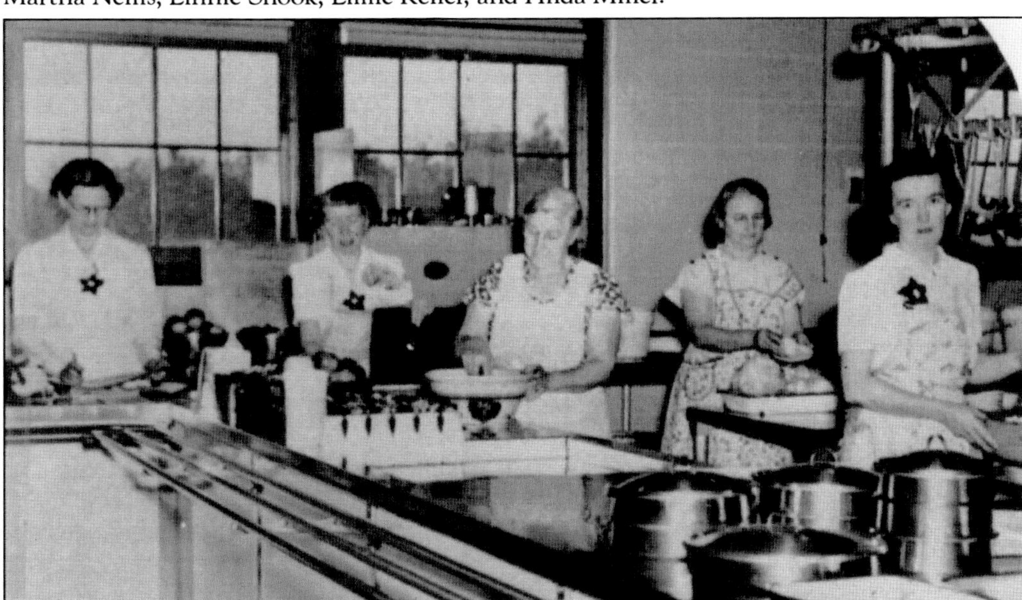

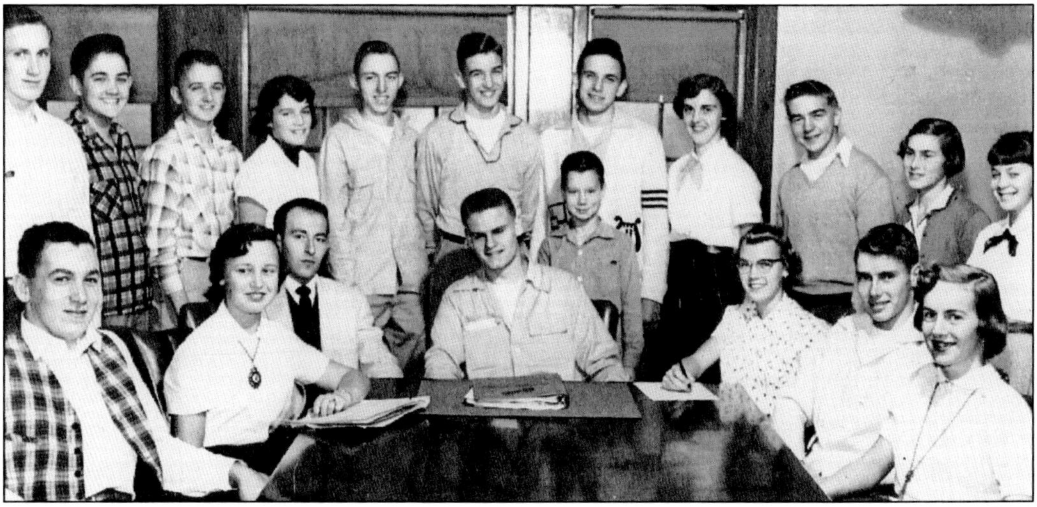

Service and special interest clubs presented students with a broad array of ways to pursue their interests and develop their talents. Groups such as Junior Red Cross, Safety Patrol, Railroad Club, Stage Crew, and Photography Club were represented in the 1955 *Embers*, the school yearbook. In addition to clubs, musical groups, and sports, students interested in the workings of government might serve on the student court or the student council, shown above.

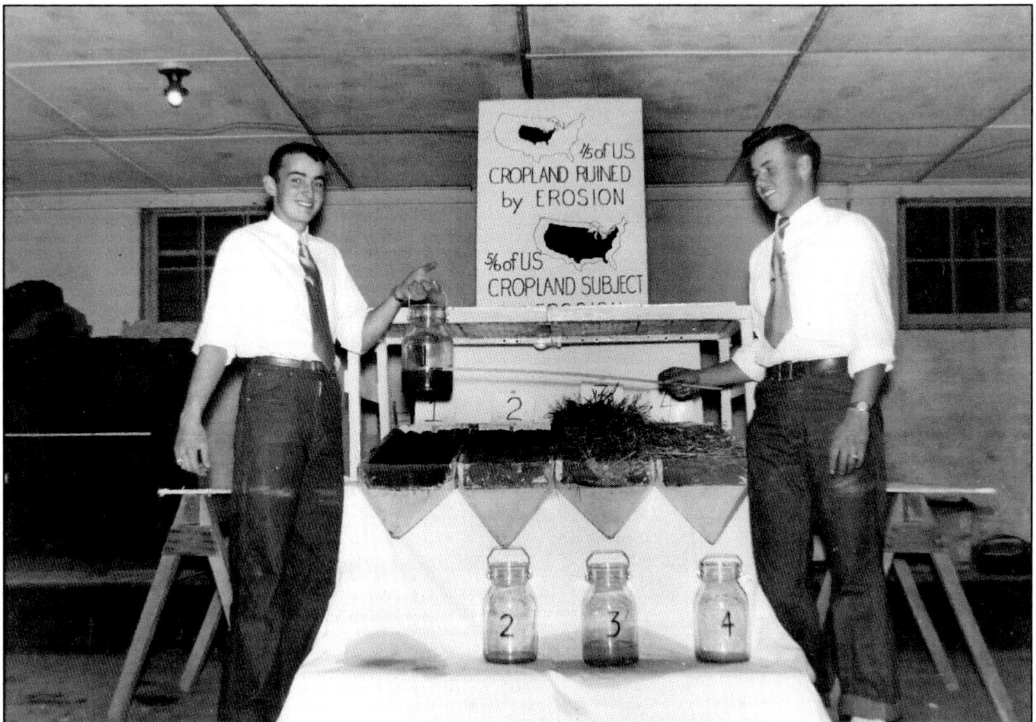

Scouting and 4-H clubs were popular activities for the young people of Eden. The 4-H motto was to "learn by doing," and its four-leaf clover emblem symbolized head, heart, hands, and health. Gerald Agle (left) and Harold Bley (right) were active members of Eden's 4-H Overalls Club. They are shown here in 1949 doing a demonstration for which they won national honors at the National Junior Vegetable Growers Convention in Cleveland. (Courtesy of Harold Bley.)

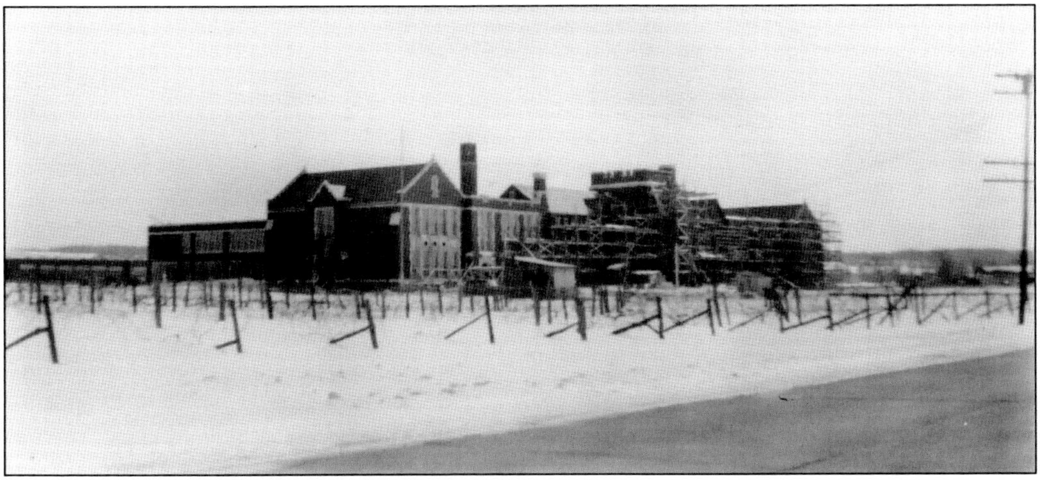

The proposal to consolidate the schools provoked much discussion and often heated debate right up to the final vote. In 1939, voters decided in favor of centralization and also approved a bond issue and the building site on North Main Street. The photograph above shows the new building during construction. With a faculty of 34, the new school opened in September 1940. Take note of the vineyards where Legion Drive now turns off of Main Street.

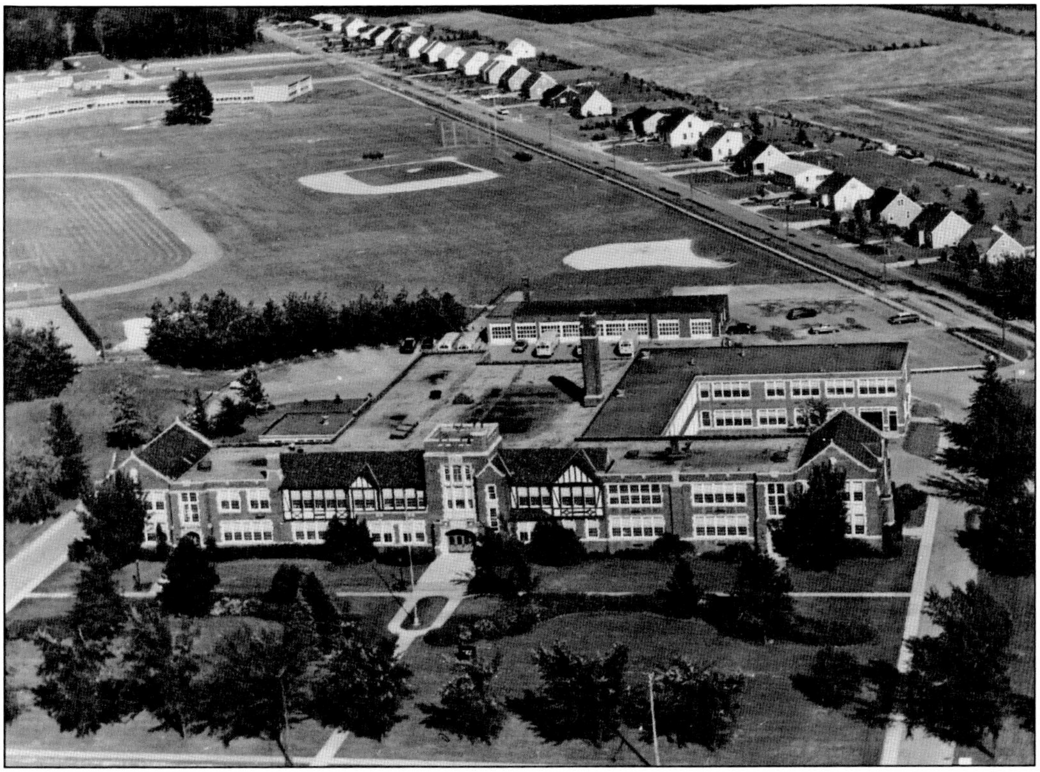

A growing population of students required additions and new buildings. An aerial view from the late 1950s shows an addition to the back of the school, sport fields, and the Grover L. Priess Elementary School, which opened in 1955. Another elementary school was built in East Eden on Hardt Road in 1964. New homes line Schoolview Road, which was later extended to Jennings Road when a new high school opened in 1970.

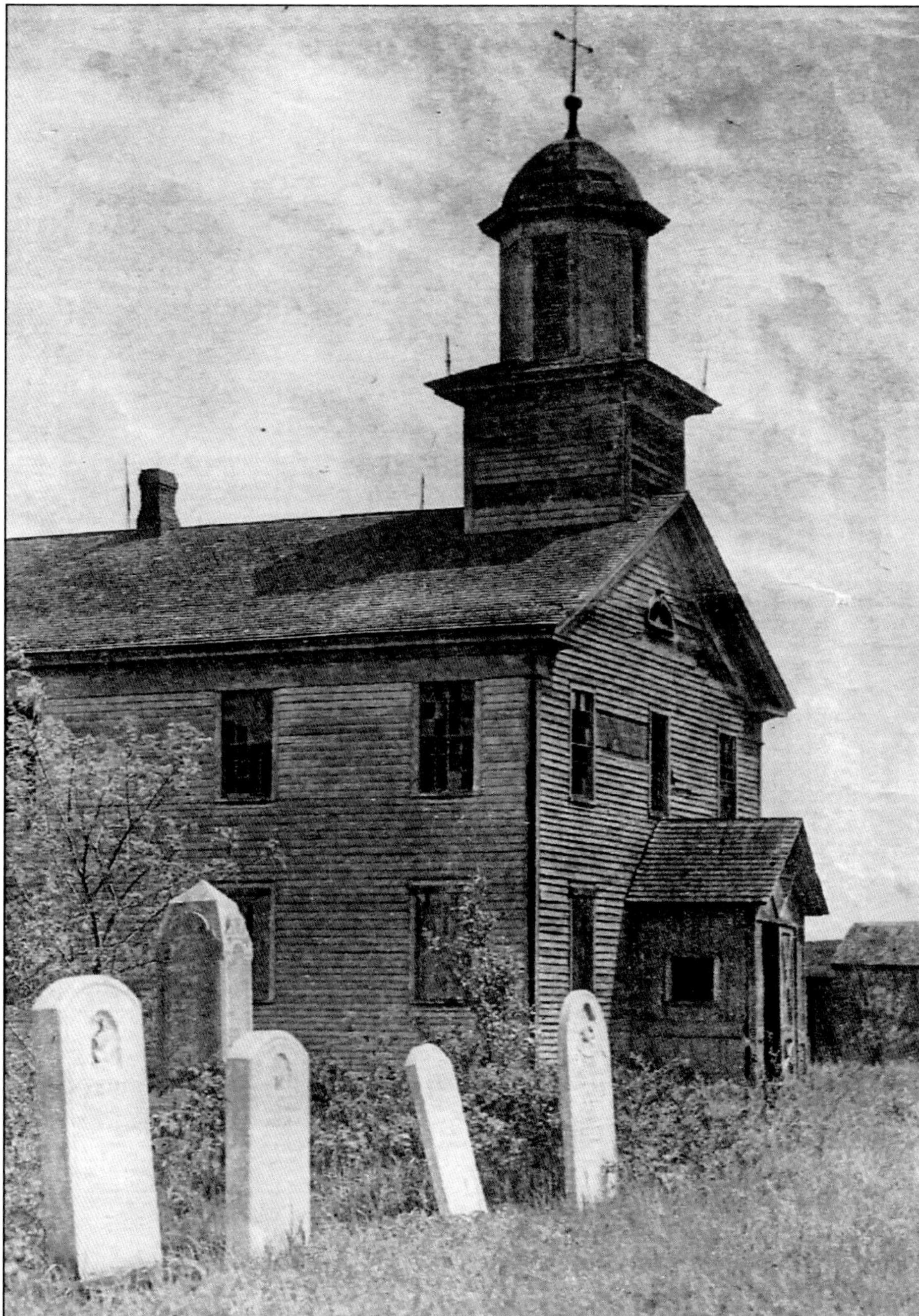

German immigrants, some Lutheran, some from the Reformed Church, built St. John's Church on East Eden Road near North Boston some time around 1830. The church was fated not to endure due to dissension between the two sects. In time, it became known as the "Mother Church" of the two parishes described on the next page. For decades, services were sparse, and the building deteriorated and was vandalized. It burned in 1958. Only the cemetery with its very early graves remains. (Photograph by W.H. Porterfield, c. 1940.)

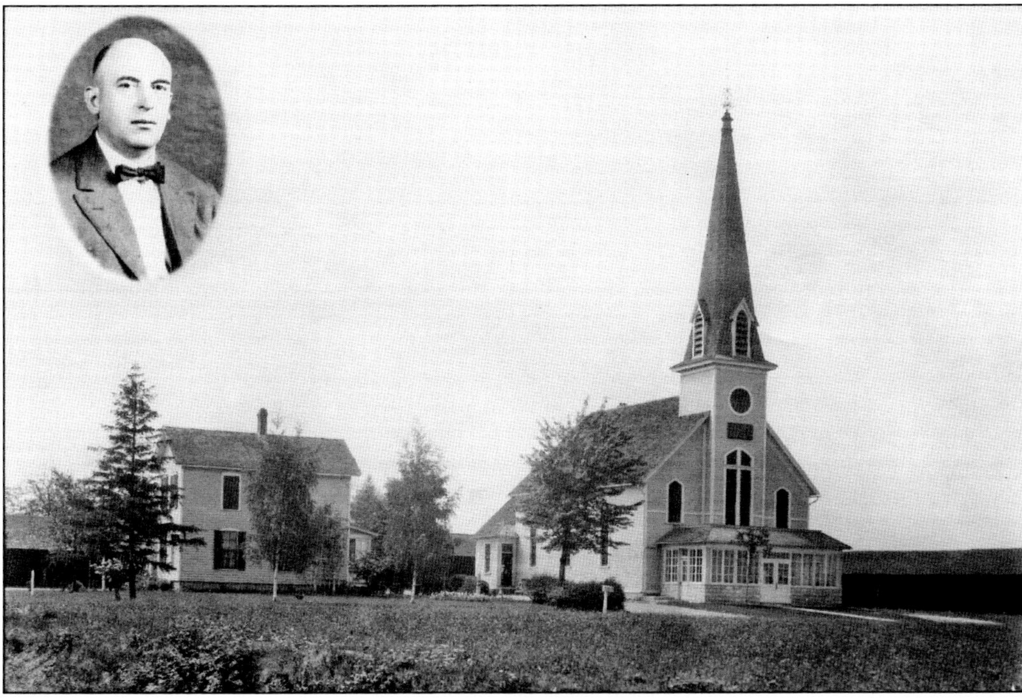

After separation from the "Mother Church" in East Eden, two more congregations of Lutherans were established before they reunited to establish the First Evangelical Lutheran St. Paul's Congregation in 1878. The church, with its soaring spire, was built in 1879. The church was demolished and the parsonage (right) was moved in 1930, when the current brick church was erected. Pastor Louis Zimmerman is shown in this 1915 photograph of the old St. Paul's. (Courtesy of Walter Henry.)

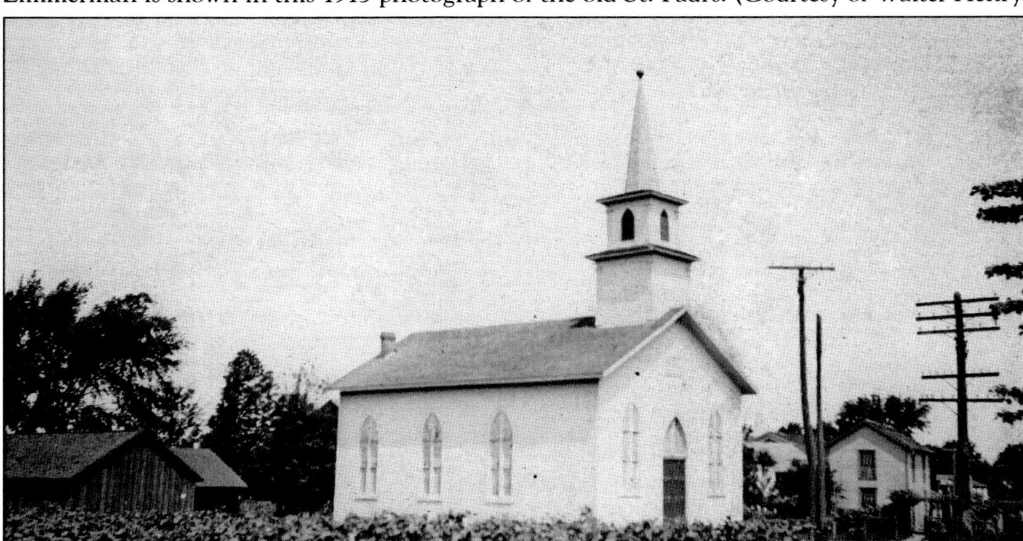

The Reformed Church congregants that remained at St. John's in East Eden eventually merged with the German Evangelicals in Eden Center in 1866. The joined congregations became St. John's Evangelical and Reformed Church and later still St. John's United Church of Christ. The church at the corner of Hemlock Road and Main Street was built in 1866 and is shown as it looked in 1910. In the 1970s, the parish moved to East Church Street, and this building was sold.

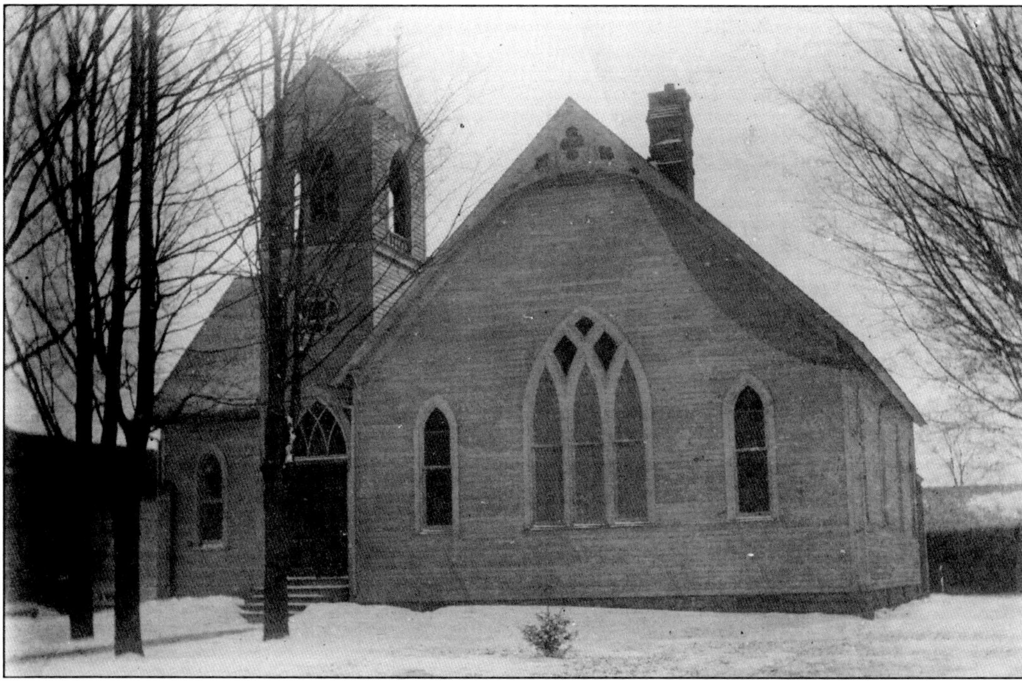

The Baptist church was the first formally organized congregation in Eden. Around 1816, the Holland Land Company offered what they called "gospel lots" to the first organized religious group in any town. One hundred acres in Eden were divided between the Baptists and the Congregationalists, who also claimed early status. That land on New Jerusalem Road was eventually sold, and each group purchased property on East Church Street. From 1848 to 1895, the Baptist church was located in what had been the Eden Academy building. It was moved and the structure, seen above, was erected on the same site. An early interior view of the building is seen below. Even though temperance societies discouraging the use of alcoholic beverages were not organized until several years later, the Baptist congregation adopted a resolution for temperance in 1820, after one of the church elders seemed to be intoxicated while he was shearing sheep.

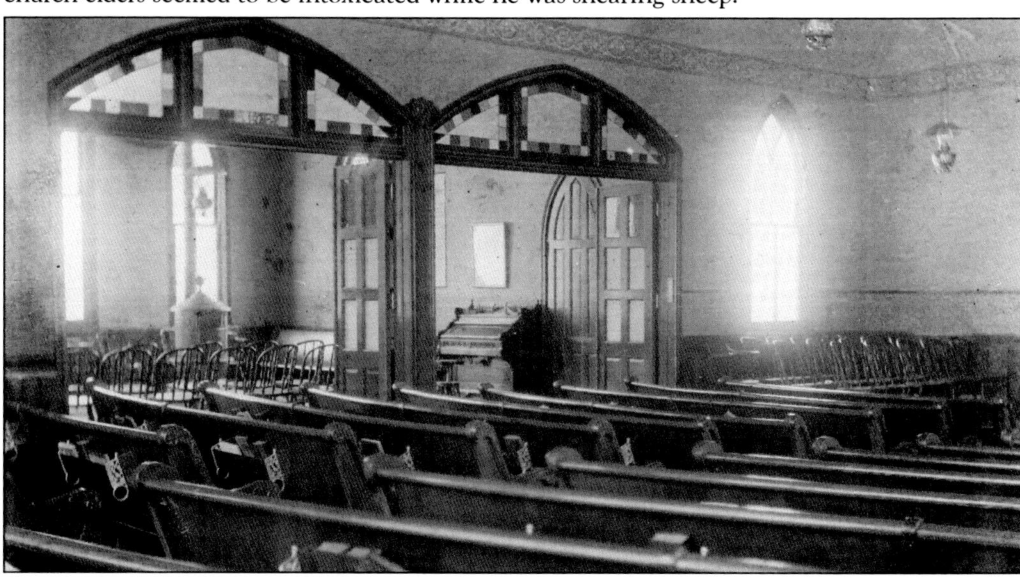

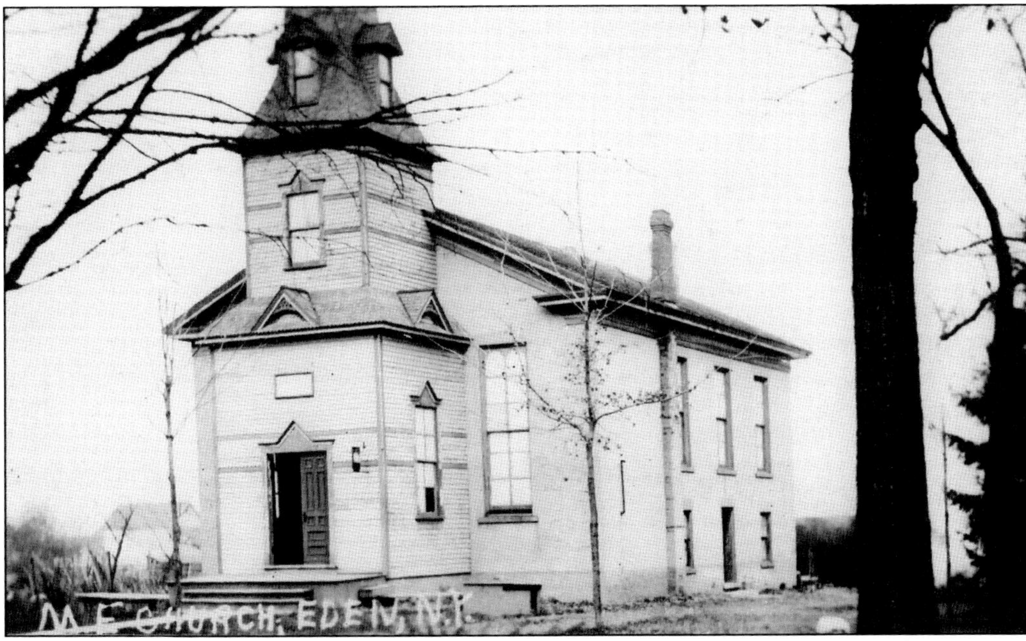

For several decades, beginning in 1811, Methodist worship services were held in homes, most often that of John and Jemima Hill. Circuit preachers, traveling on horseback along Indian trails and crude narrow roads, made the rounds of the new territory. The original church building was a simple, rather crude, box-like structure with spare furnishings. The brick and frame building seen above was completed in 1858 on the East Church Street site of the original church.

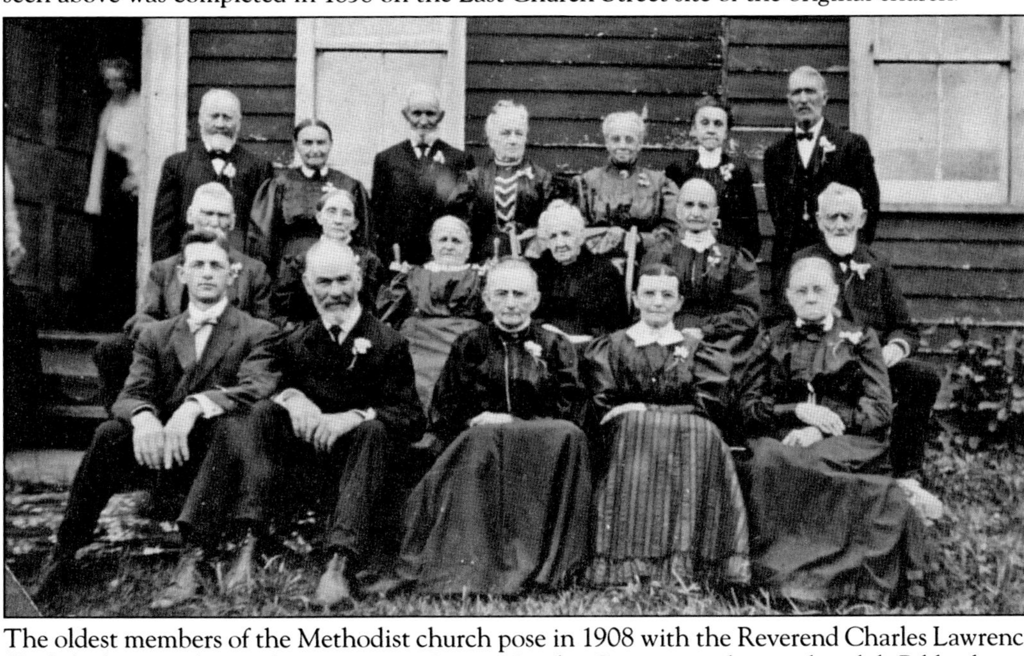

The oldest members of the Methodist church pose in 1908 with the Reverend Charles Lawrence (far left, front row). Beside Lawrence is James Hood, a Scotsman who taught adult Bible classes. An old parishioner recounted that Lawrence admitted to learning more about the Bible in Hood's classes than he had at seminary. Another of the Methodist ministers, the Reverend Howard Charles, became Eden's first town historian.

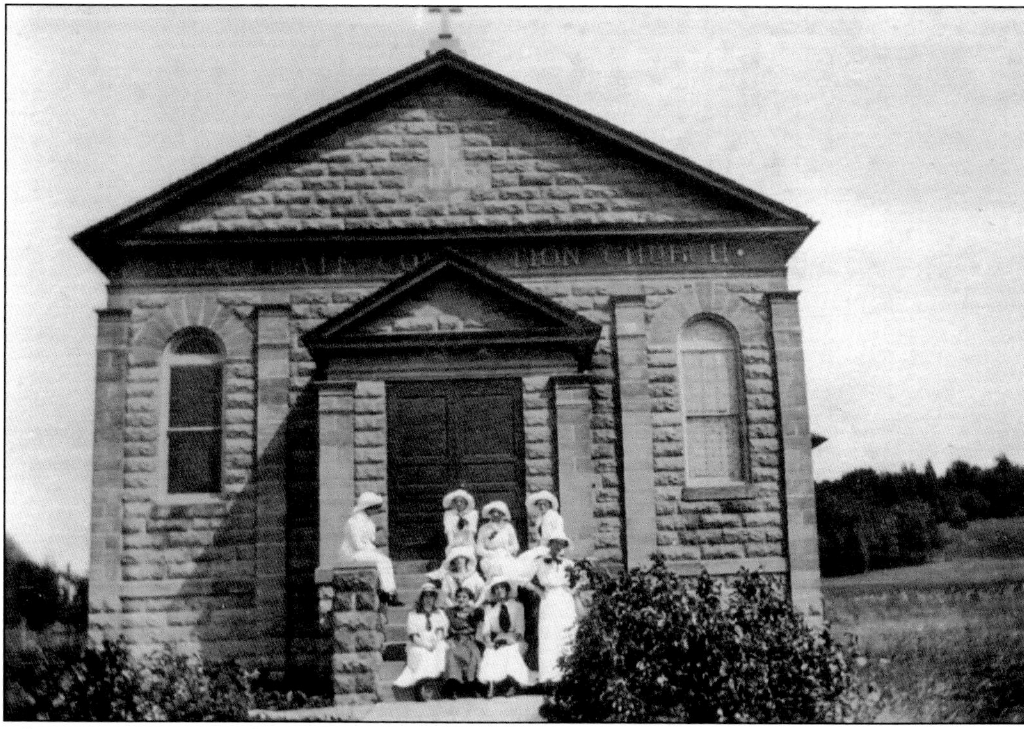

About 1910, a group of young women poses on the steps of the new Immaculate Conception Church. Until 1907, St. Mary's in East Eden was the only Roman Catholic congregation in the town. The faithful from Eden Center walked, rode horses, or drove buggies to East Eden to attend services. The first Catholic services in the hamlet were held in 1907 in an assembly hall above Taylor's Store on Green Street. The following year, the bishop of the Diocese of Buffalo ordered that a parish be established in Eden Center. A prominent Protestant resident, Abram Lang, donated property on Main, Park, and Second Streets for the church's use. Bishop Charles Colton dedicated the new church in December 1908. It served the parish until 1958, when the present Immaculate Conception Church and parochial school (below) were built across the road on Park Street.

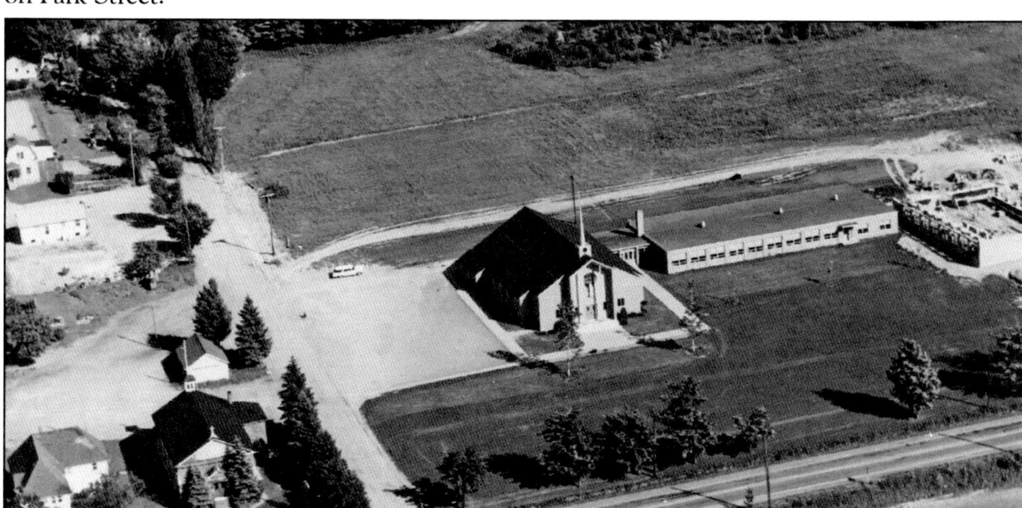

Seven

SERVING THE TOWN

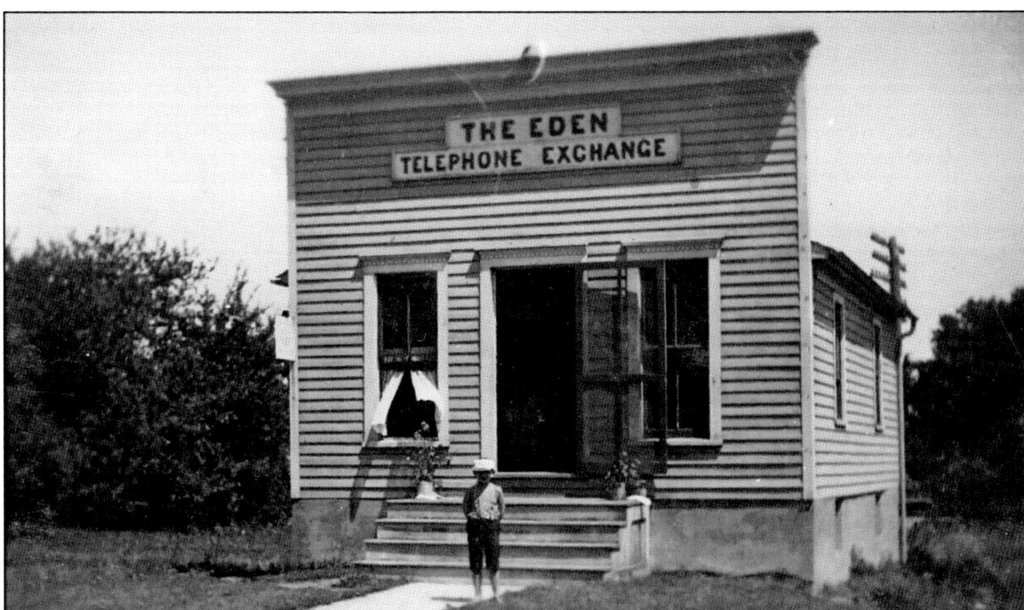

Though talked about as early as 1888, it was not until 1902 that privately owned telephone lines began to be installed in some of the businesses and a few residences. Roeller's Hotel and D.A. Palmerton installed Bell pay phones. Ward Wightman is credited with the idea of installing a telephone system in town. A corporation was formed in 1903, and poles and wires were installed. The Eden Telephone Exchange building on Green Street is shown in 1908.

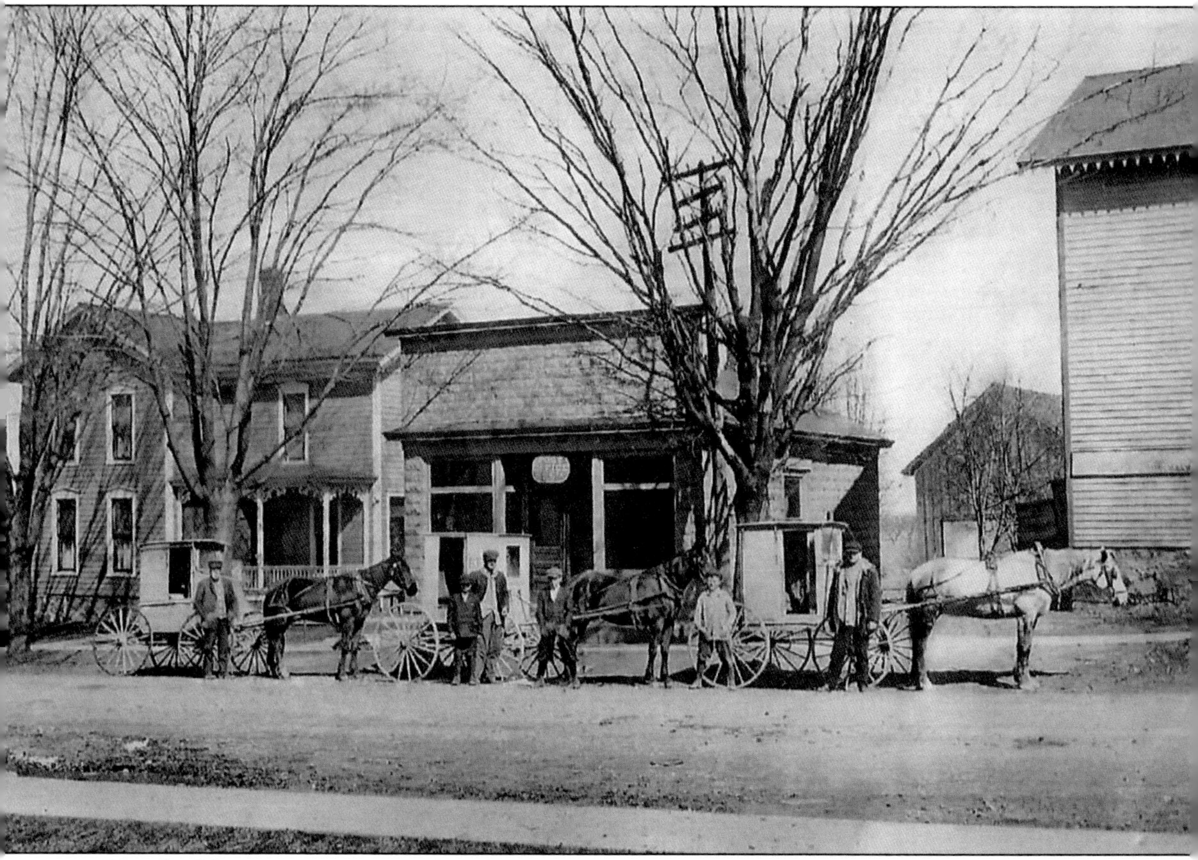

This building at 2764 West Church Street was the location of the first structure to be used exclusively as a post office. This 1917 photograph shows Eden's rural mail carriers in front of the US Post Office built by postmaster James Read in 1909. The wheels on the mail carts were switched to runners for winter delivery. The carriers are, from left to right, Francis Pound, Robert Beehler, and Martin Stinson and some unidentified helpers. Before Rural Free Delivery began in 1902, there were authorized offices in Eden Center, Eden Valley, Clarksburg, and East Eden. One of the first two carriers, Francis Pound, traveled 26 miles per day for the 18 years he held the job. The post office moved from this location around the corner to Main Street in 1943. In 1956, it returned to West Church Street as a first-class post office in the former Vellum's Store. In 1961, house to house or "city" delivery began in the hamlet.

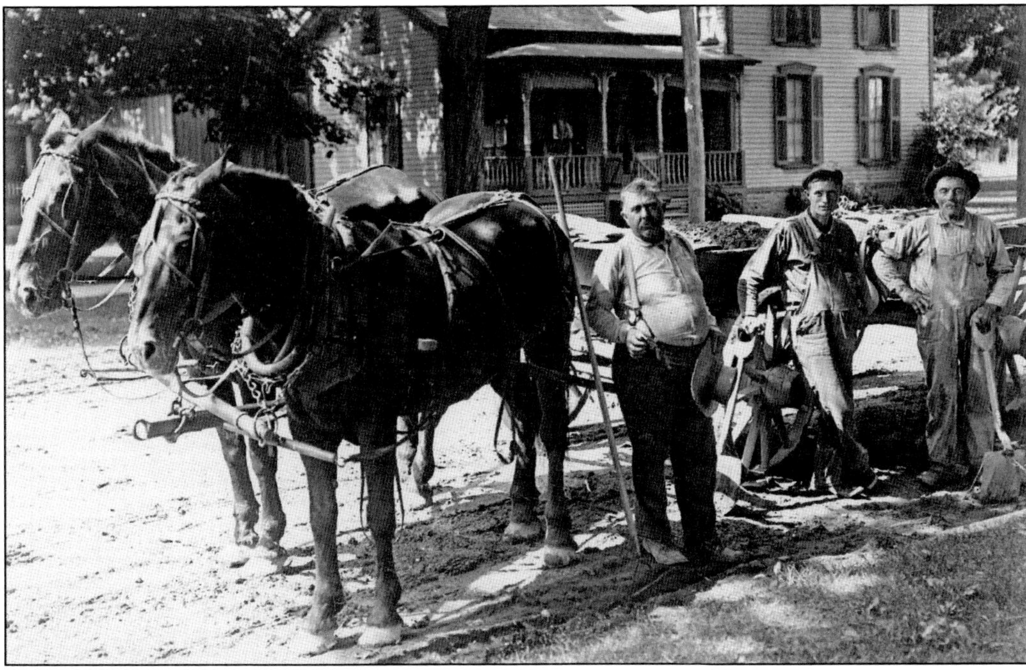

An essential service in any community has always been the building and maintenance of its roads. Those duties fell to highway superintendent Henry Eckhardt and his road crew in the early days of the 20th century. Challenging probably understates the nature of their job, when dirt roads were the order of the day. Manpower and horsepower provided the muscle necessary to create roads and keep them passable in all sorts of weather. Rainy periods had to be the worst. Pictured above are Eckhardt (center) and two of his men working on Main Street around 1910. The lower photograph shows the building of East Church Street between Jennings Road and Sisson Highway. The machine being used is from the Buffalo Steam Roller Company. A 1913 photograph of the same scene shows a team of horses pulling the roller. (Below, courtesy of Bob Maltby.)

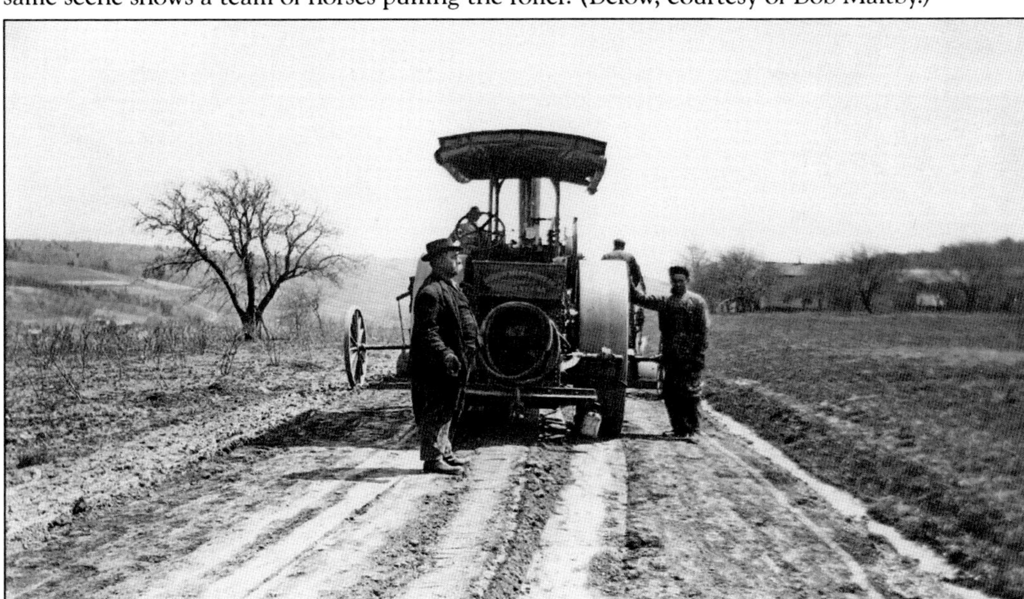

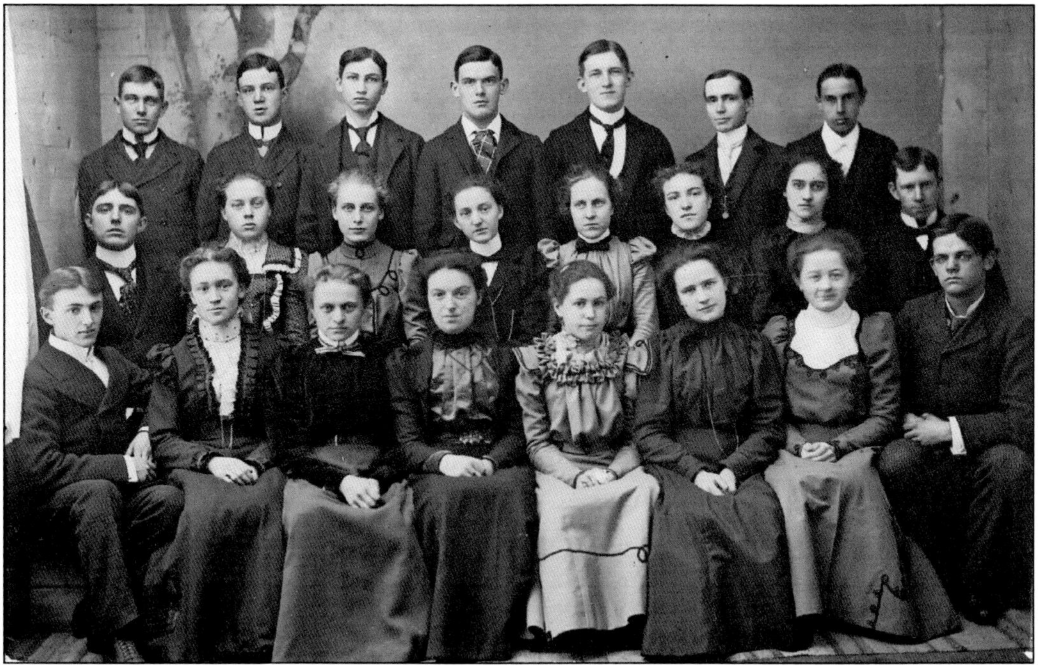

People from the 21st century might find the purpose of this group to be unique and perhaps somewhat odd. Pictured in 1899 are the flower girls and pallbearers from Frank Caskey's funeral business. Presumably their job was to solemnly follow the horse-drawn hearse to the cemetery, where the young men would carry the casket to the gravesite. Following the burial, the ladies would mound armloads of blooms upon the fresh grave.

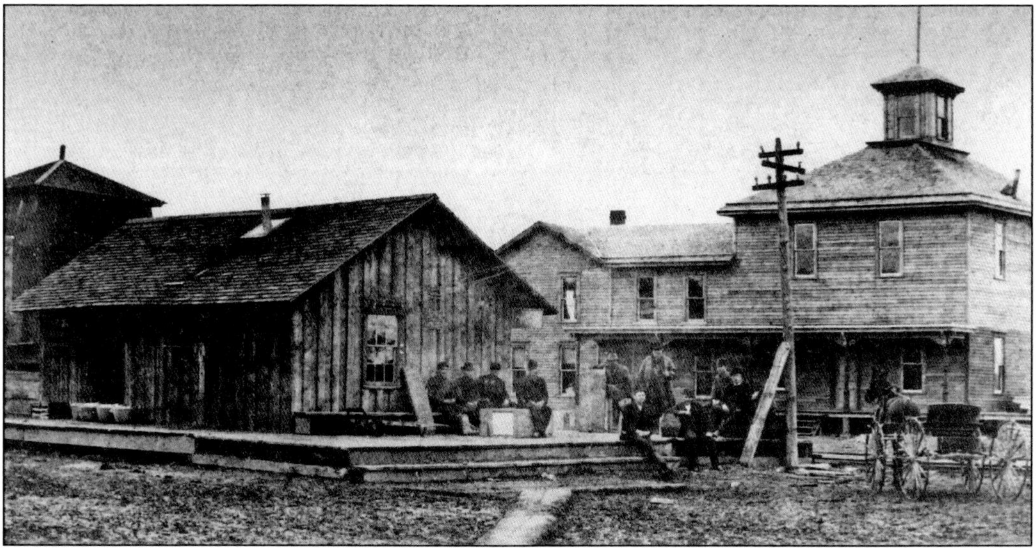

The coming of the railroad to Eden opened up a whole new world of possibilities for commerce and individuals. The Buffalo-to-Jamestown line, running through Eden and Gowanda, was completed in 1875. The crudely built original station (left) and Phatiger's Hotel (right) are seen above. One of the stationmaster's duties was to hand-pump water into the water tower. It is believed that the original schoolhouse, moved from Church Street, became the barroom at Phatiger's.

TIMETABLE IN EFFECT DECEMBER 28, 1914.

Buffalo and Southwestern Division of the Erie Railroad

WESTWARD TO JAMESTOWN — EASTWARD TO BUFFALO

*519	‡517	*515	*11	*513	Miles	Station	‡514	*516	*10	*518	*520
P M	P M	P M	P M	A M			A M	A M	A M	P M	P M
8 30	6 00	5 00	12 55	7 50	0	Buffalo	8 05	9 55	10 55	6 05	8 45
8 50	6 20	5 18		8 11	7	Blasdell	7 43	9 35			8 20
9 03	6 32	5 32	1 27	8 24	14	Hamburg	7 32	9 22	10 21	5 32	8 10
	6 39	5 40		8 30	17	Eden Valley	7 23	9 13			8 01
9 15	**6 45**	**5 46**	**1 37**	**8 36**	19	**EDEN** (CENTER)	**7 16**	**9 08**	**10 11**	**5 21**	**7 56**
9 23	6 53	5 55	1 45	8 44	23	NORTH COLLINS	7 08	9 00	10 04	5 14	7 48
9 35	7 01	6 03		8 52	27	Lawtons	6 59	8 50			7 37
9 43	7 08	6 10	1 56	8 59	30	Collins	6 53	8 44	9 52	5 01	7 23
9 53	7 15	6 19	2 05	9 08	34	Gowanda	6 45	8 35	9 45	4 53	7 15
g	g	6 44	g	9 30	38	Dayton	g	8 22	g	g	7 00
		6 48		9 36	40	Markhams		8 08			6 40
10 18		6 55	2 33	9 42	43	South Dayton		8 00			6 30
10 29		7 07	2 43	9 52	48	Cherry Creek		7 50			6 21
10 40		7 18	2 52	10 02	53	Conewango		7 39			6 10
10 58		7 33	3 03	10 17	61	Kennedy		7 16			5 57
11 15	8 15	7 50	3 19	10 35	70	Jamestown	5 45	6 55	8 45	3 55	5 40

* Daily ‡ Except Sunday g Stops at D. M. Tower, Dayton f On signal

D. A. PALMERTON, Real Estate & Mortgage Loans, Eden, N. Y.

D.A. Palmerton sponsored this pocket-sized timetable from late 1914 that informed riders of the number of daily trains running through Eden. Written communications of the day chronicle how friends from as close as Hamburg would write to say, "I am coming out on the train on Sunday. Will you pick me up at the station?" Commuter trains, carrying workers into Buffalo and locations in between, were very popular.

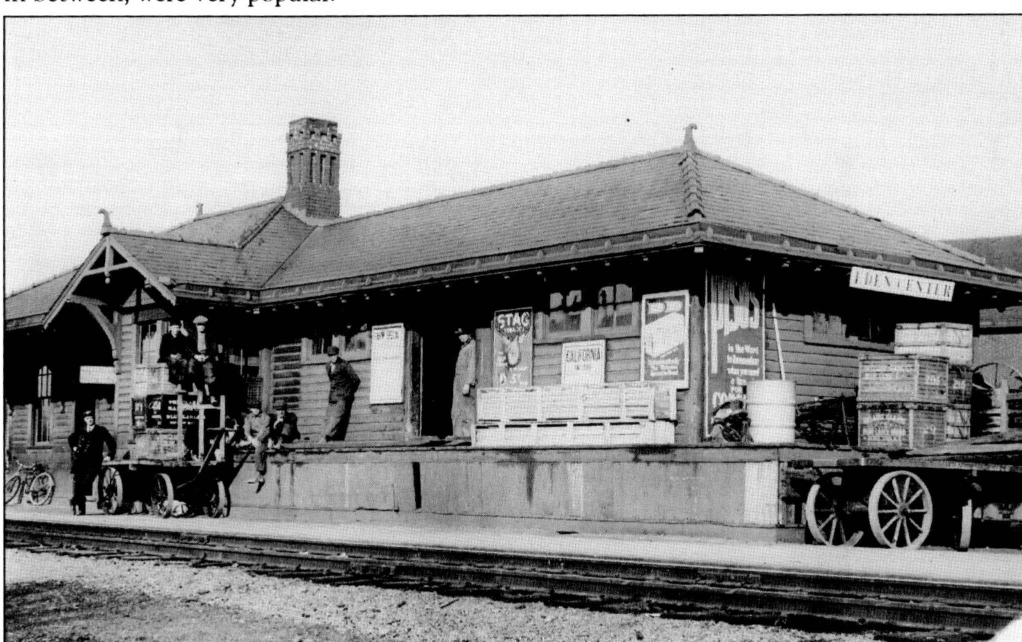

Trains helped businesses prosper and allowed leisure travelers to broaden their horizons. Excursions to Chautauqua Lake and Niagara Falls were very popular. During one week in 1889, over 200 Eden residents rode the train to Jamestown and then boarded the steamships that ferried travelers up the lake to the Chautauqua Institution. After the original one burned in 1897, this attractive new station was erected. Today it is a doctor's office.

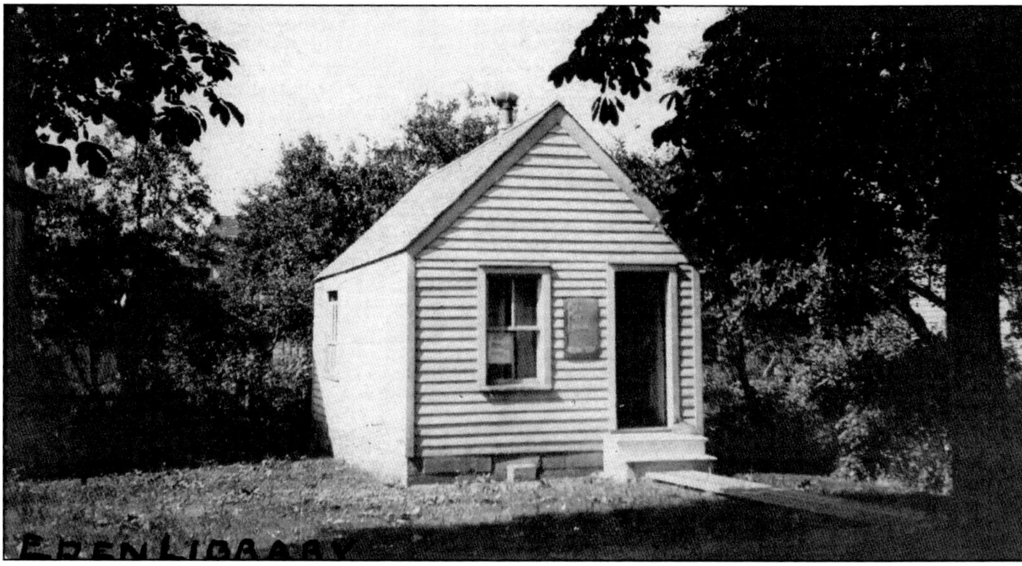

Thanks to a group of farsighted and dedicated ladies, Eden opened its first library in 1911 in a frame building (above) located on East Church Street. A newly formed library association, headed by Martha Hubbell, held a series of dinners and teas to raise funds for the project. Their efforts, combined with many gifts of money, furniture, and books, enabled the group to realize their dream. With 726 donated books on the shelf, the library was formally opened on November 18, 1911. Volunteers loaned out 328 books during the month of December. Those same volunteers had to have believed in their mission, because during that first winter, the building had no heat except for a heated soapstone at their feet! The books must have felt like blocks of ice. The Eden Free Library, whose interior is seen below, occupied the building from 1911 to 1923.

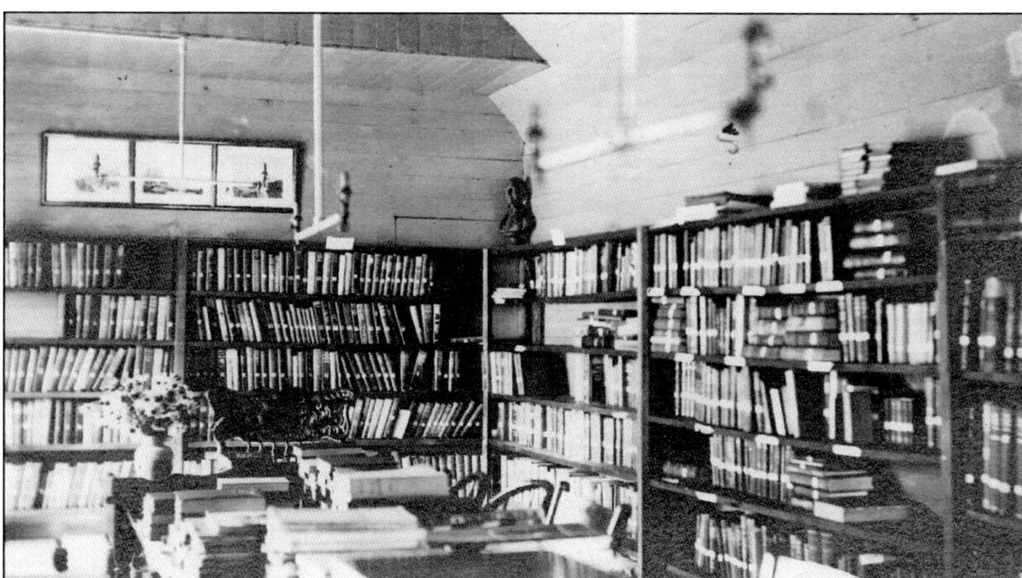

In 1922, the library pooled $3,000 of its funds with the town's to build a town hall. The town government offices were located on the second floor, and the library shared the ground floor space with the newly organized volunteer fire company. The town moved out in 1940, and the library relocated in 1955. The building was torn down and replaced by the current fire hall in 1973.

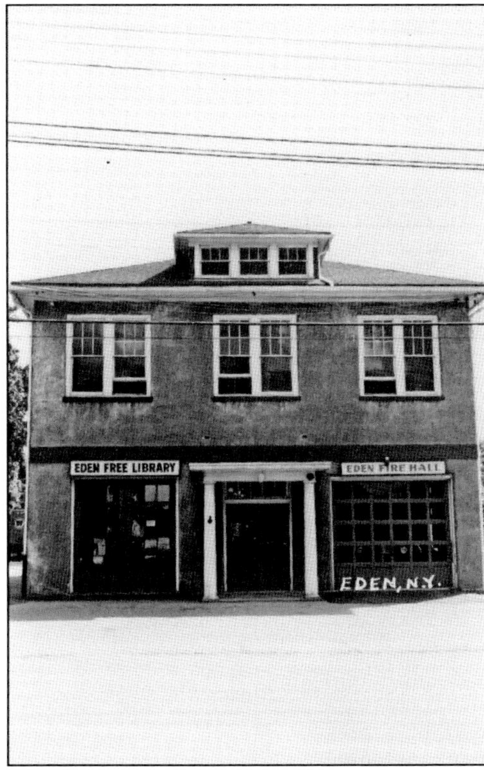

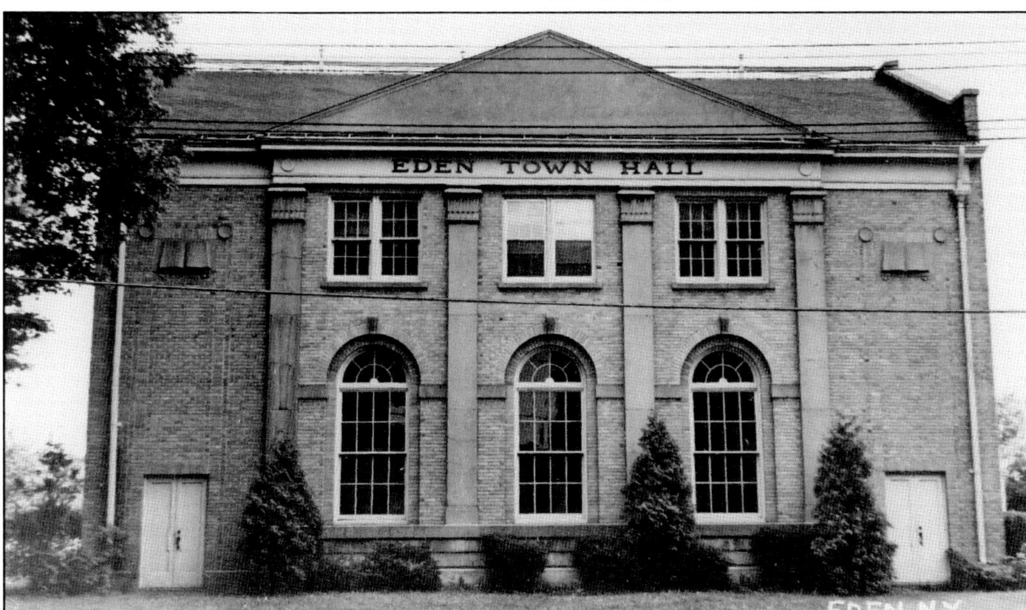

Following the centralization of Eden' schools in 1939 and the opening of the new school in 1940, the town moved its headquarters into the former high school building on East Church Street. Since that time, there have been interior renovations and additions to the building. In 1955, a one-story wing was built on the east side to make room for a new library. Today that space is the Eden Police Department.

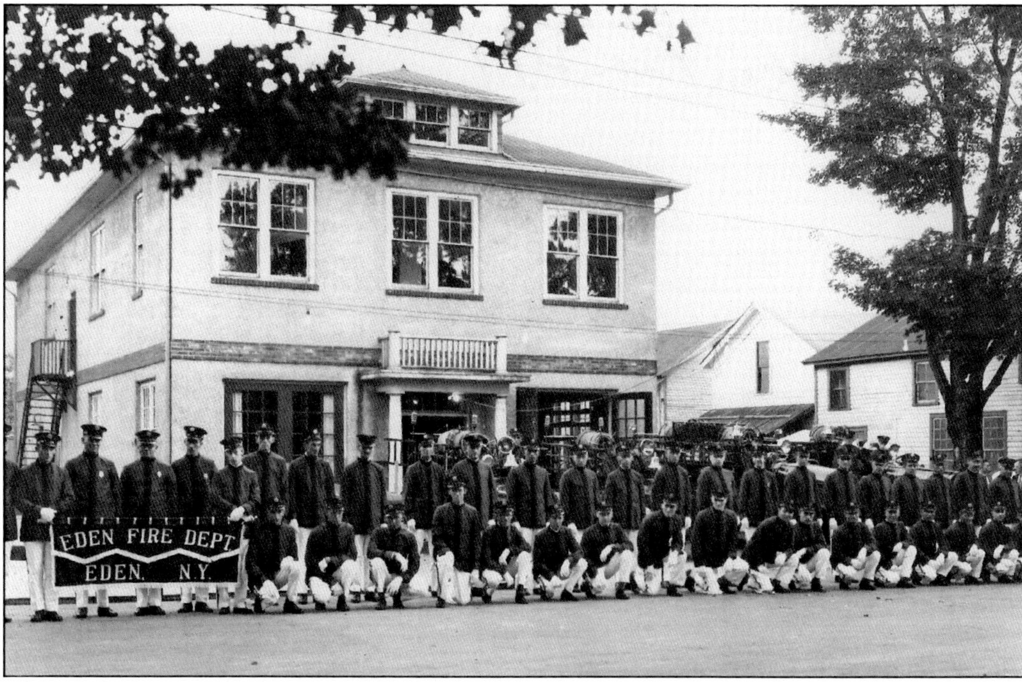

The newly organized Eden Volunteer Fire Company, Department One, is shown above in 1923 in front of the first fire hall on East Church Street. Eden's first fire truck was the Ford Model T shown below. Until public water was installed in 1936, all water for firefighting had to be pumped from farm ponds and wells. Before a siren was installed in the 1950s, a bell located at Roeller's Hotel called the men to fires. That system was backed up by a phone tree dispatch for those not hearing the bell. In the 1960s, a radio dispatch system was inaugurated. The dedication of the fire companies has been evident in their efforts to be professional and in the pride they take in maintaining their equipment. The longest-serving active volunteer is Bill Rice, who joined the company in 1950. Four members, Ron Salzman, Bob Stickney, Harold Greeley, and Clyde Colvin, have been active for 45-plus years.

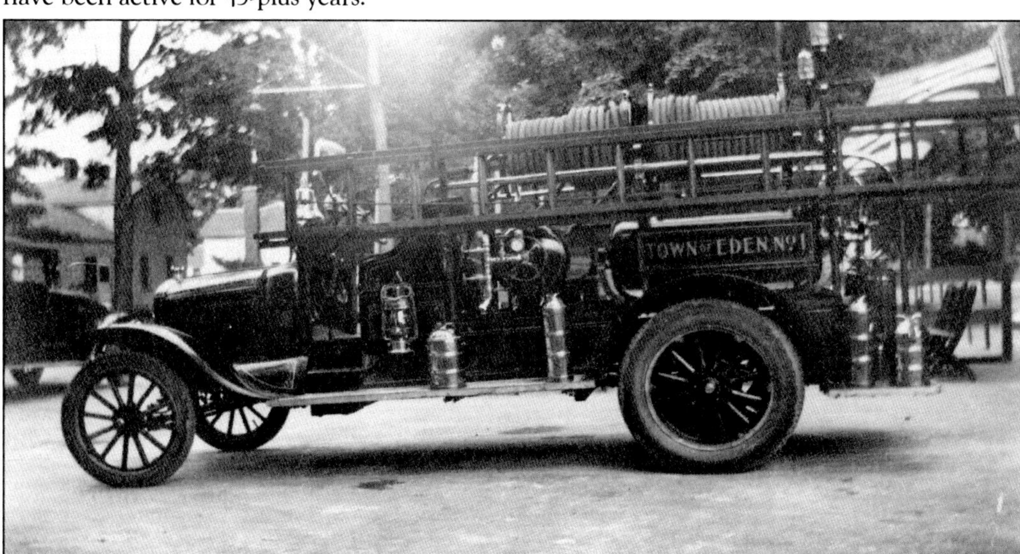

In 1950, the Laing brothers, David, Richard, and Paul, began the first ambulance service in town. A 1938 Buick was converted to meet the needs of the service. This vehicle was used until 1953, when a new Ford station wagon was purchased and outfitted for medical needs. The ambulance service was discontinued in 1968. A volunteer group, the Eden Emergency Squad, was formed the same year. (Courtesy of William Laing.)

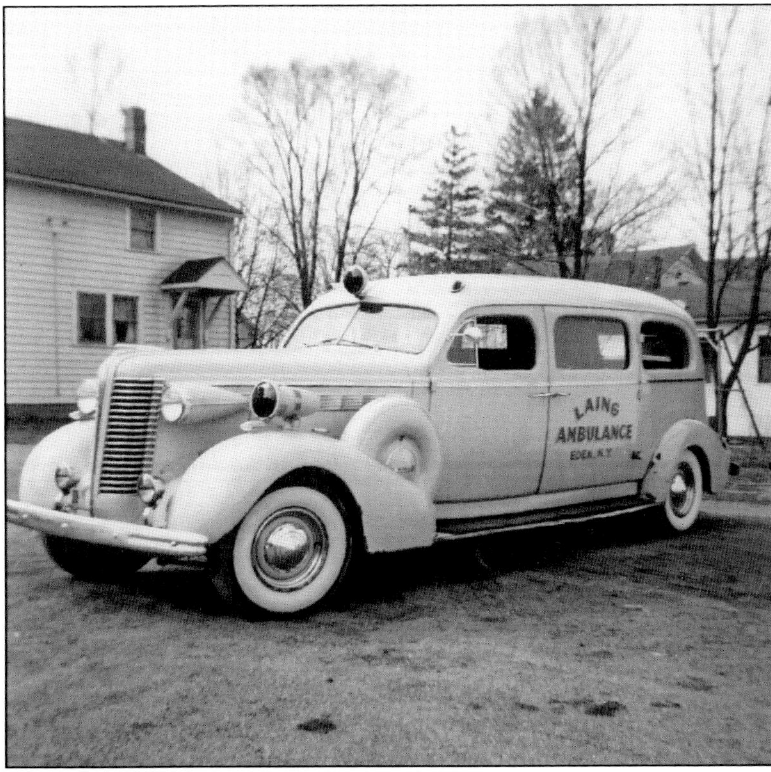

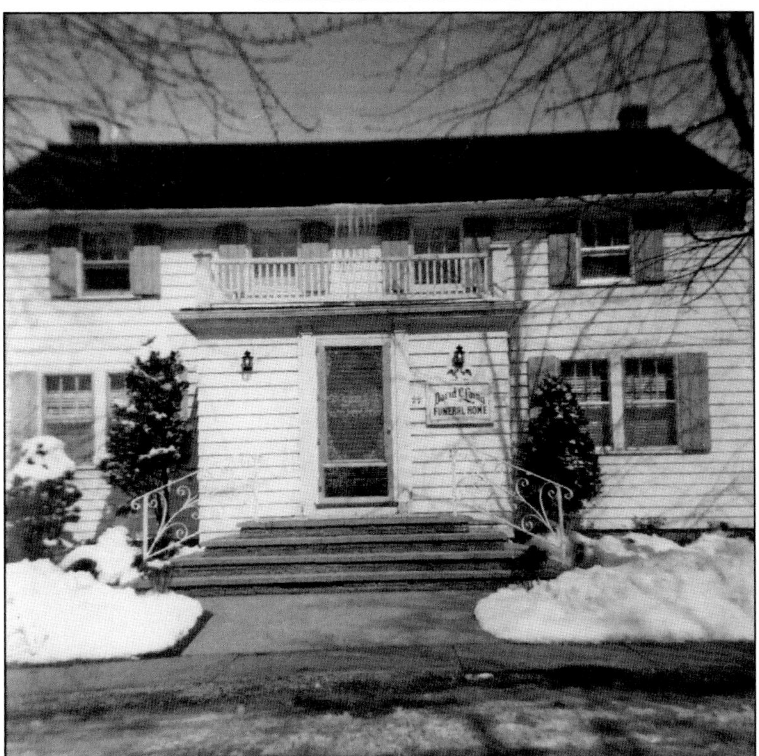

Following in his great-grandfather's footsteps, David Laing opened this funeral home in 1950 in a house at 2724 West Church Street. Part of the house was built from the Lakeley barn, which had formerly occupied the site. Eight years later, Laing added funeral rooms on the front and living quarters at the rear. This photograph shows how the business looked in 1958 and for many years later until a large front porch was added. David Laing's son, William, still operates the business. (Courtesy of William Laing.)

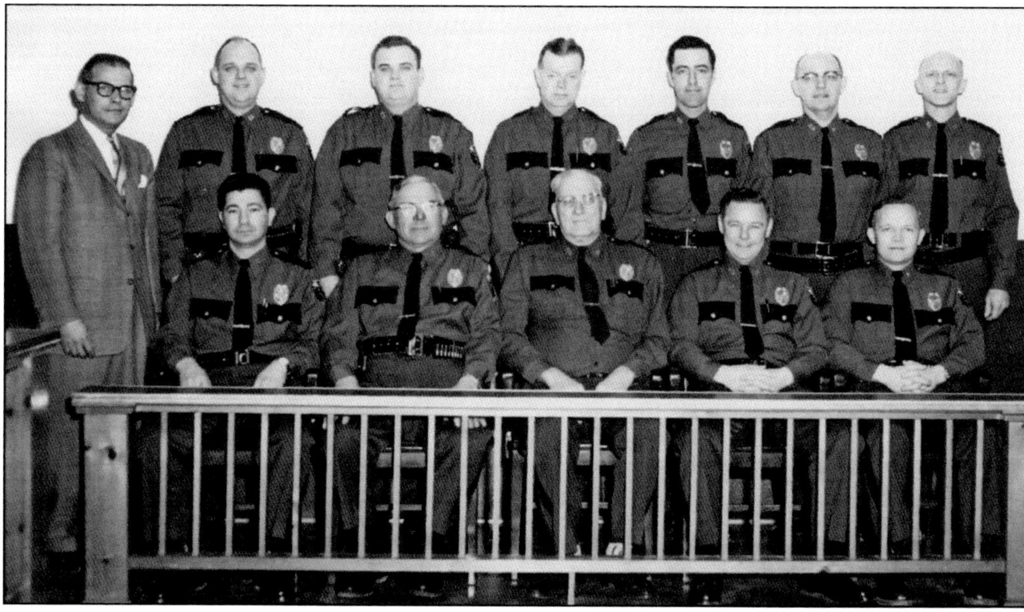

Before 1935, when Floyd Waite was appointed Eden's first police chief, constables had been elected. The police department was a one-man operation for many years. In 1955, to accommodate Eden's growing population, the town board approved the formation of a 12-man volunteer constabulary. Police chief Cleveland Shook was the head of the unit. The photograph above shows Eden town supervisor George Guenther with the newly formed unit. Members include, from left to right, (first row) Michael Eppolito, August Eichler, Chief Shook, Michael Miller, and Donald Wightman; (second row) Supervisor Guenther, David Laing, Paul Laing, Charles Moulthrop, Wilbur Smutz, Franklin Meyer, and Claf Chittenden. Accidents always seem to draw a crowd, as illustrated below in a picture from 1957, which shows Chief Shook responding to a fender bender at Main and West Church Streets.

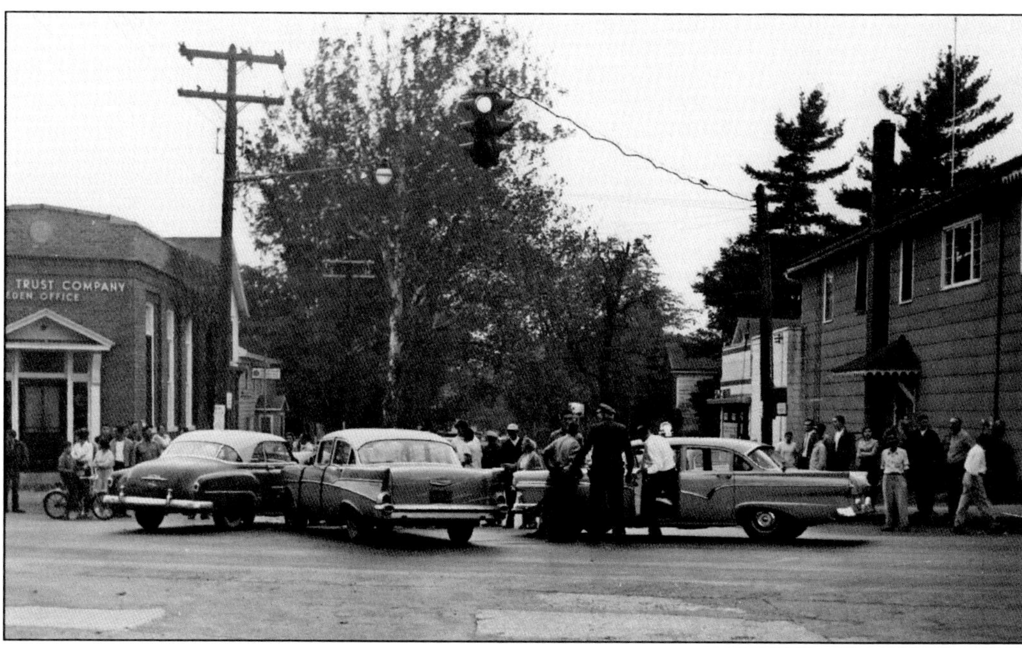

Eight

Early Folk and Other Notables

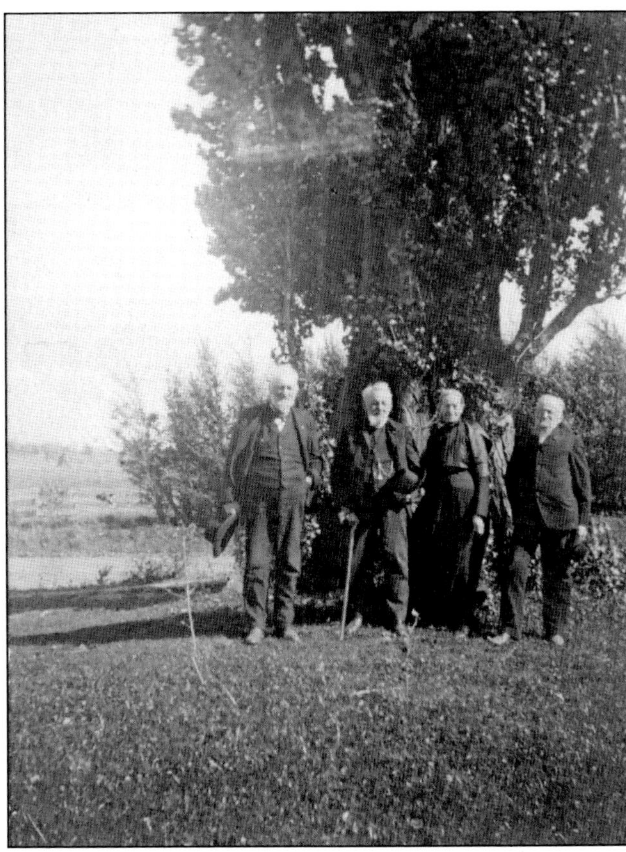

The tree in this photograph is the source of legend. Original settler John Morgan Welch purchased several large tracts of land in the north end of town. According to tradition, he used a poplar stick when he walked from Eden (then Willink) to Batavia, New York, to register his property deed with the Holland Land Company. Upon his return, he stuck the stick into the ground, and it grew into a tree. Shown in 1901 are Welch's sons, Clinton (left), Colonel ?, and Ezra (right), and Welch's niece Marcia Hill.

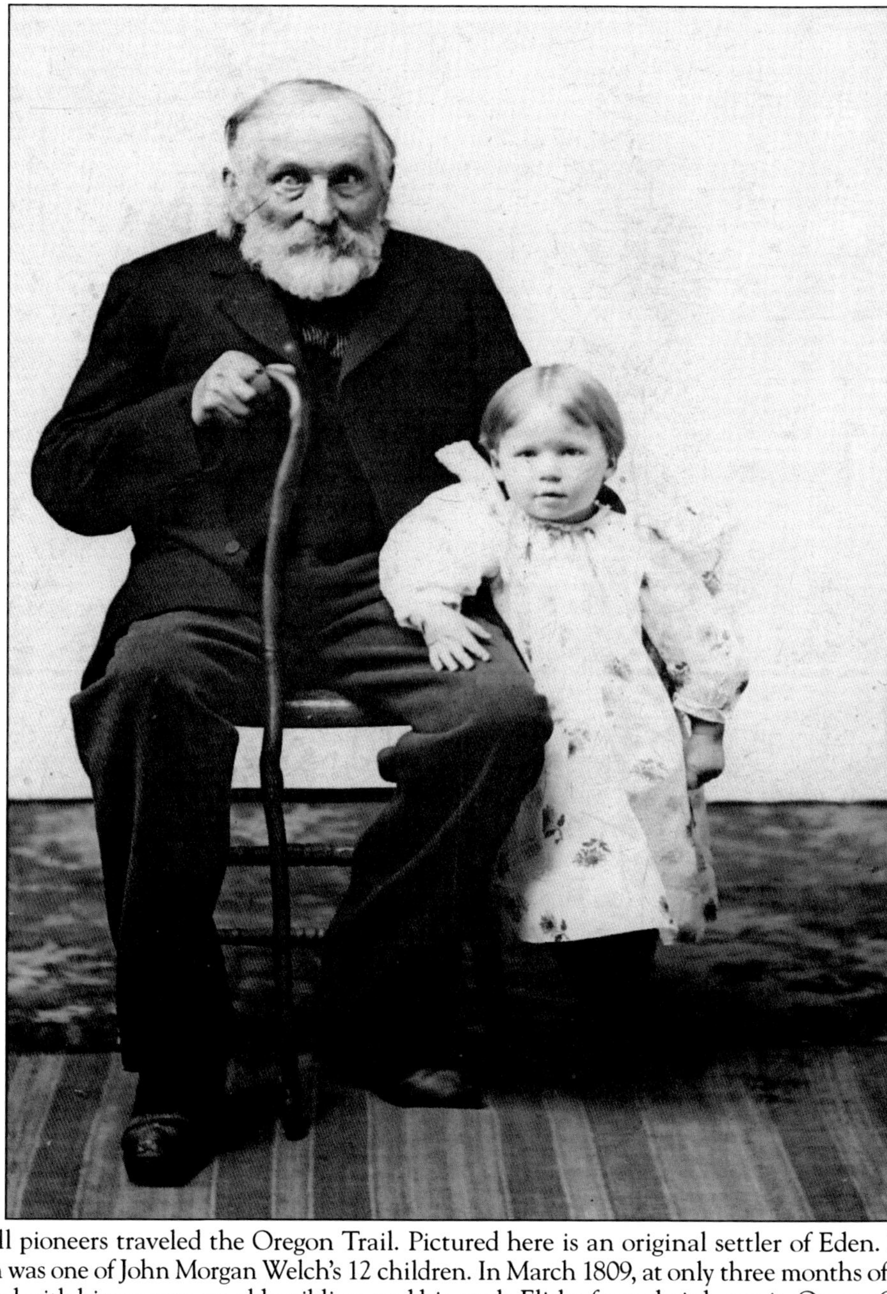

Not all pioneers traveled the Oregon Trail. Pictured here is an original settler of Eden. Nelson Welch was one of John Morgan Welch's 12 children. In March 1809, at only three months of age, he traveled with his parents, an older sibling, and his uncle Elisha from their home in Otsego County, New York, into the wilderness that would become Eden. Carting all their earthly belongings in a wagon pulled by a team of oxen, it took the group two weeks to reach their destination. John and Elisha traveled at the behest of their brother James, who had settled in Eden the previous year with their uncle Deacon Samuel Tubbs. Nelson Welch was a well-respected man. Between 1850 and 1872, he served 11 terms as town supervisor. In 1853, he was elected to the state assembly, one of five men from Eden to eventually hold such an office. His grandson, Nelson Welch Cheney, was among the others. Welch is shown with his granddaughter, Hazel Webster, on his 90th birthday in 1898.

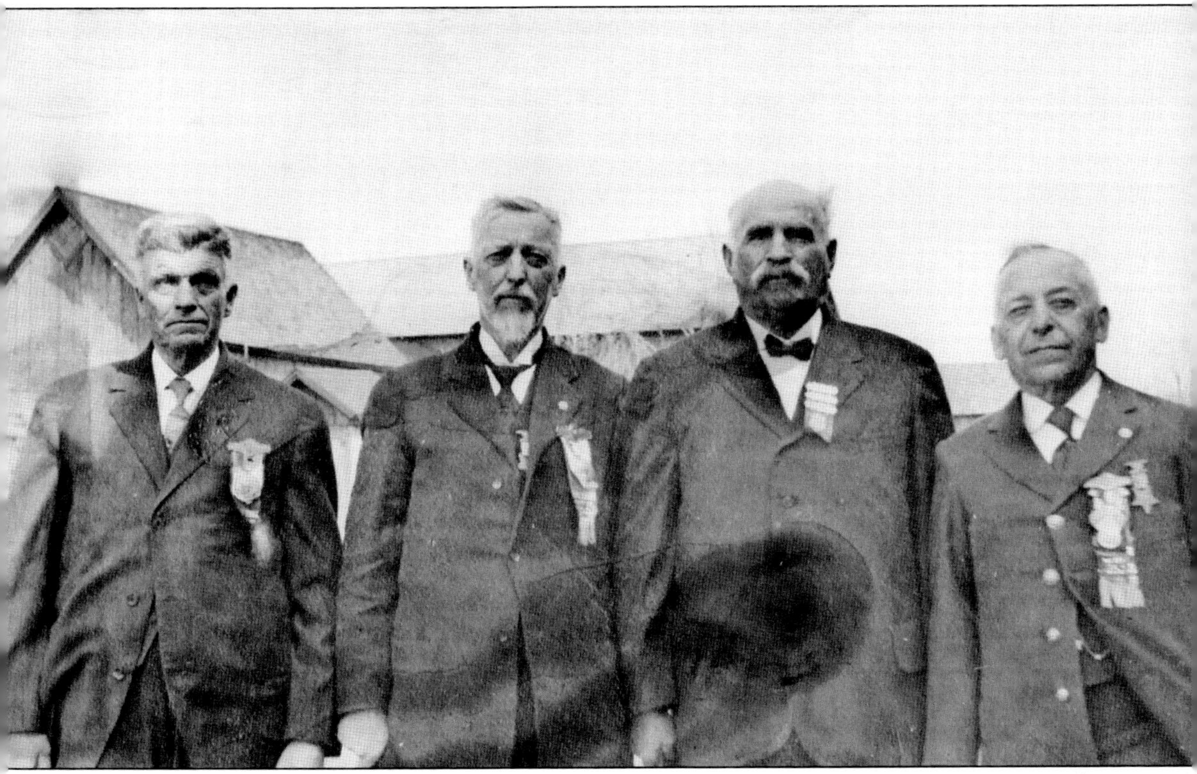

During the Civil War, 50 or more men from Eden joined the ranks of the Union army. Fortunately, most of the men returned. Letters from the field reflect the concern soldiers had about staying healthy. Fever, measles, and small pox were mentioned in a letter from Norman Bartoo. He observed that the army was a "hard place to be sick," and that "the number killed in battle is only a part of whom die." Eden's last remaining Civil War veterans, (from left to right) William L. Laing, James Read, Fred Philippi, and Edward Bauman, were photographed on Memorial Day, May 30, 1917. Laing, a cabinet and coffin maker, served with Gen. William Tecumseh Sherman during the infamous "march to the sea." Laing died the month after this picture was taken. James Read built the first post office and served as Eden's postmaster from 1904 to 1914. He passed away in 1920. Fred Philippi died in 1922 at the age of 78. Edward Bauman's daughter helped form the O.G. Brindley Circle of the Grand Army of the Republic, an organization honoring Civil War veterans.

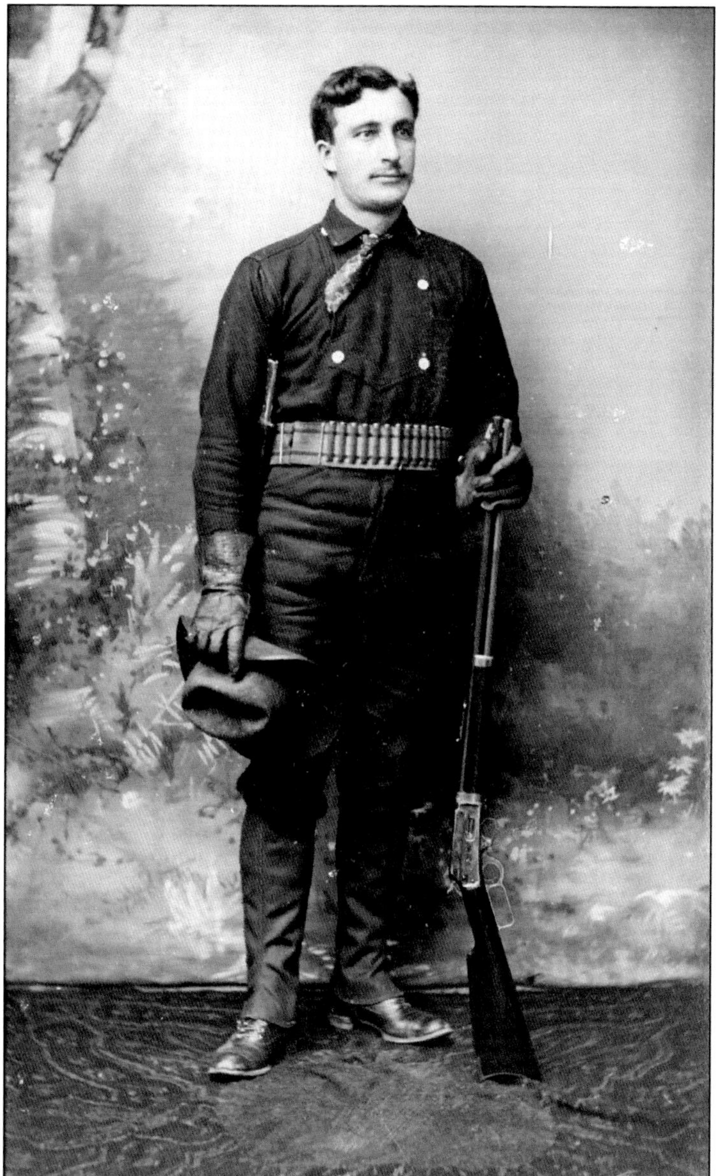

Sharpshooter William Lakely (1874–1936) was perhaps one of Eden's more colorful characters in the early 20th century. During the 1910 Pan American Exposition in Buffalo, Lakely performed as one of the principal shooters in Buffalo Bill's Wild West Show. After the exposition, he traveled for a year with "Wild Bill" Cody. To the delight of his sons and other boys in town, Lakely often amused and awed them by shooting holes through coins and ashes from cigarettes as people walked down the street. He could also light matches using a bullet. Mothers must have been horrified! As a young man, Lakely had traveled to the Pacific Northwest and Alaska. The tales of his harrowing adventures on that journey entertained many in town for years. He worked at the canning factory and owned a bicycle shop. With two others, he owned a secondhand Stanley Steamer, the first car in town. He played on the town baseball team, was a member of the Eden Cornet Band and the Eden Conservation Society, and was a charter member of the Eden Volunteer Fire Company.

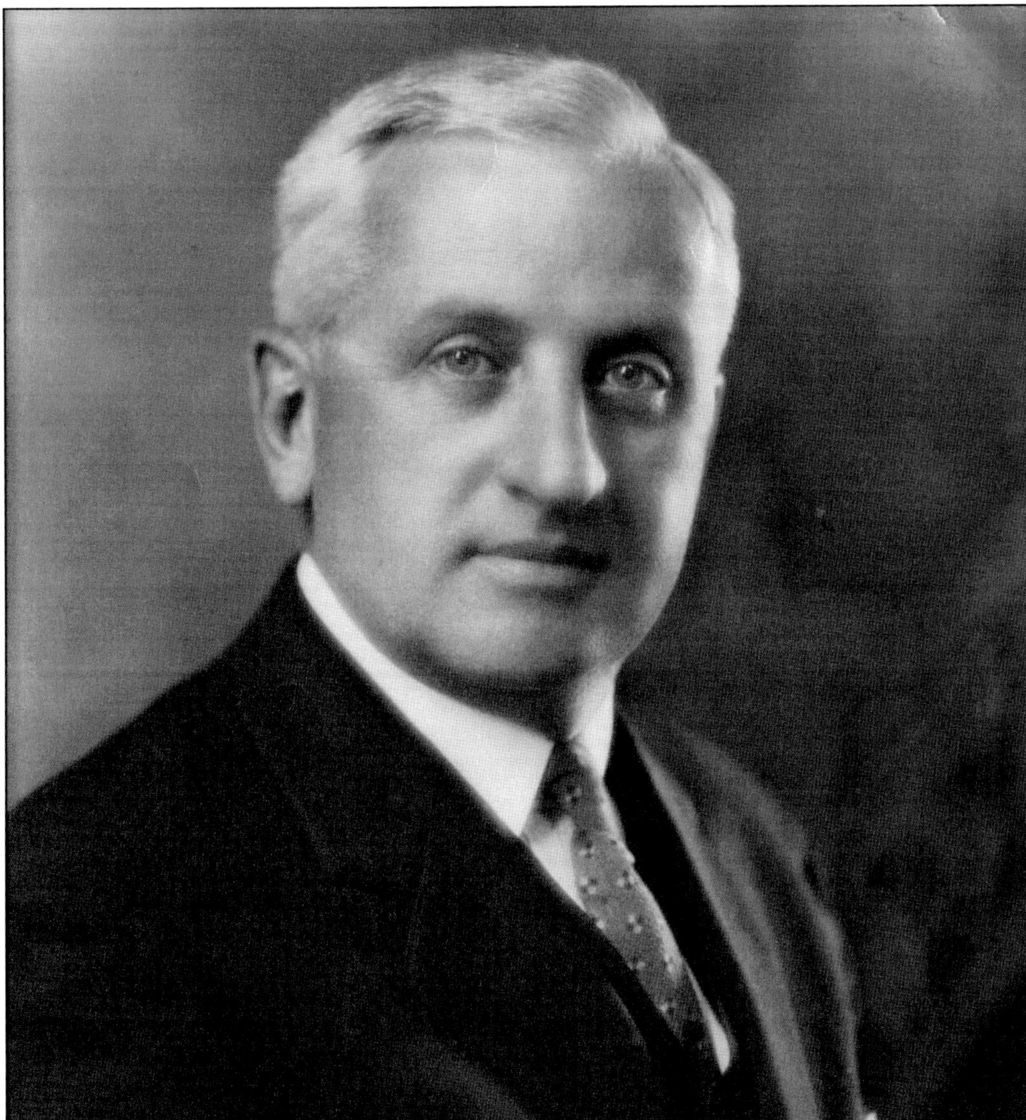

One of Eden's most distinguished citizens, Sen. Nelson Welch Cheney (1875–1944), was the great-grandson of John Morgan Welch, one of the town's first settlers. Cheney's mother was the former Philena Welch. His father, Edgar O. Cheney, was the treasurer of the Susquehanna Railroad. Senator Cheney was born in Buffalo and graduated from Central High School of Buffalo in 1895 and Cornell University in 1899. In 1903, he and his wife, the former Edith Ingram, moved to Eden. Two years later, they built an impressive home at 8362 North Main Street. Cheney was interested in agriculture and reforestation, and eventually, he planted thousands of trees on properties around town. A prominent public servant, Cheney is best remembered for his service in government. For six years, he was the town supervisor. In 1915, he began 23 years of service in the New York State Legislature, first as an assemblyman and then as a senator. He served as president of the Bank of Eden and as director of several other banks in the Western New York area. A member of several fraternal organizations, Cheney was also a director and president of the Erie County Agricultural Society. At the time of his death in 1944, Cheney was serving as the commissioner of jurors of Erie County.

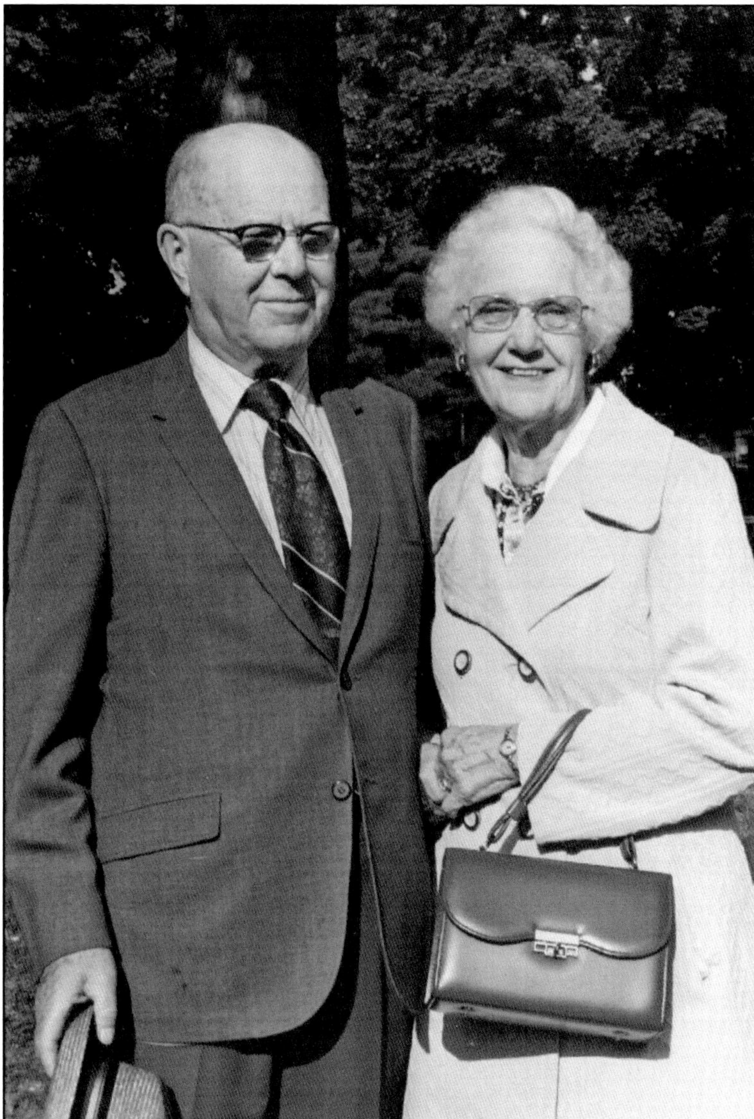

At the young age of 11, Albert Hickman (1893–9185) fashioned a tiny electric motor from dry cells, a handmade magnet, and a knitting needle. A natural and prolific inventor, he never finished high school and was a vegetable farmer. A very uncomfortable, bumpy ride in 1925 to deliver cabbage to Bradford, Pennsylvania, is credited for his initial invention of suspension truck seats. While continuing to farm, he devoted more and more time to his ideas and inventions. Within a few years, he had developed three types of suspension truck seats and had organized Hickman Pneumatic Seat Company. When he died in 1985 at age 92, Hickman held more than 230 US and foreign patents for vehicle suspension systems for a variety of transportation modes. His original pneumatic farm tractor seat is on display at the Smithsonian Institution in Washington, DC. A well-known and highly respected citizen of Eden, Hickman was a faithful member of the Eden United Methodist Church and the Eden–North Collins Rotary Club. This picture shows Albert and Lucille Hickman at Chautauqua Institution, where they spent 55 summers with their family. Hickman helped plan the transportation system around the institution grounds. (Courtesy of Warren Hickman.)

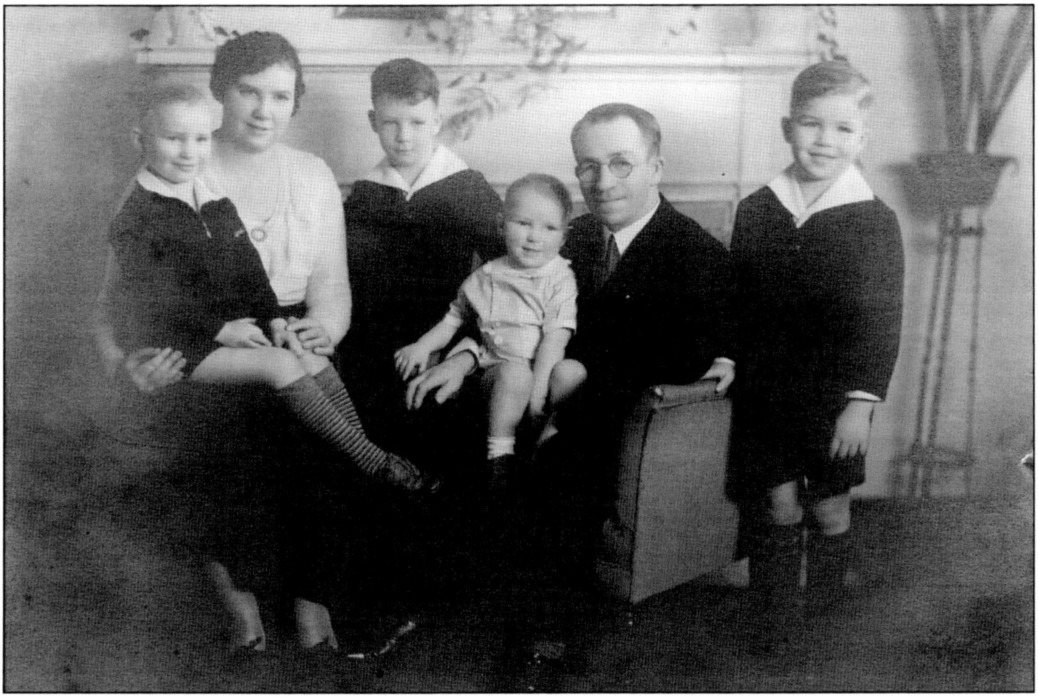

Luther and Ida Cooke Landon both served as supervisors of Eden. Luther Landon served from 1928 until his death in 1937, at which time Ida Landon was appointed to fulfill his unexpired term. She was subsequently elected in her own right and held office until December 1947. One her proudest moments as supervisor occurred in October 1947, when she presided over the opening (below) of the first high-level bridge over Eden Valley. In addition to town government, the Landons were active in a variety of community activities. She started the first Girl Scout troop in Eden and helped organize other activities for the town's youth. He was one of the organizers of the Bank of Eden and also a charter member of the Eden Volunteer Fire Company. The above photograph from 1935 shows the Landons with their four sons, (from left to right) James, Horace, George, and Gordon. (Above, courtesy of James Landon; below, courtesy of George Zittel.)

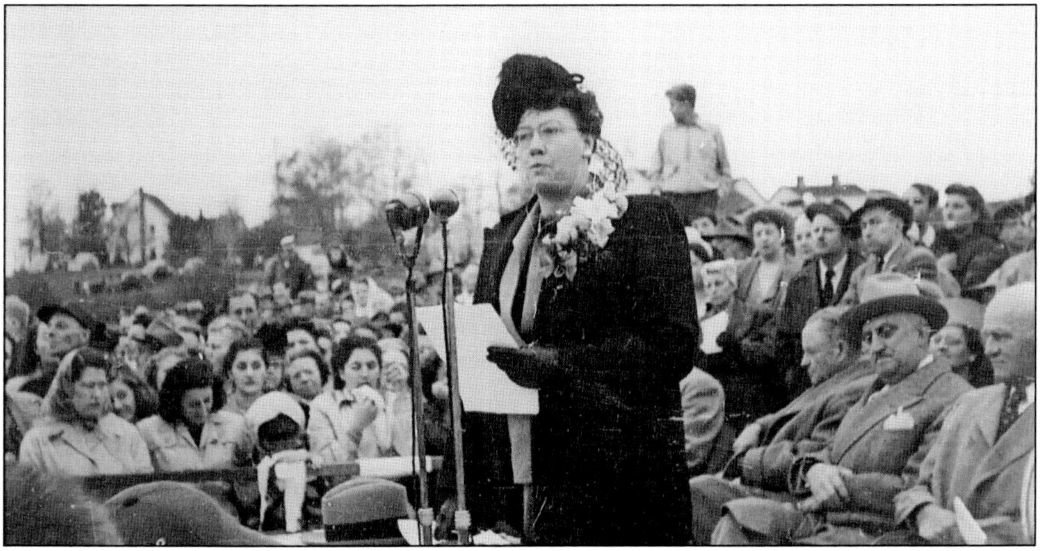

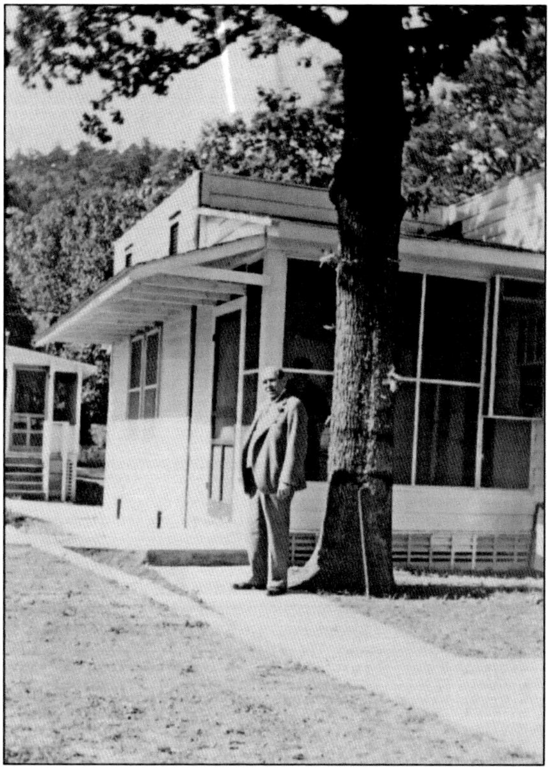

Swiss-born Paul J. Simmen (1872–1941) made his home in Eden for many years. He invented several signal systems for railroads and was the founder and president of the Simmen Automatic Switch and Signal Company. He held 105 patents for devices that greatly improved the safety of train travel in this country. Simmen and his wife lived at 2736 West Church Street from 1921 until his death. He was an avid gardener, and he located his office in a small building among his flowers and plants.

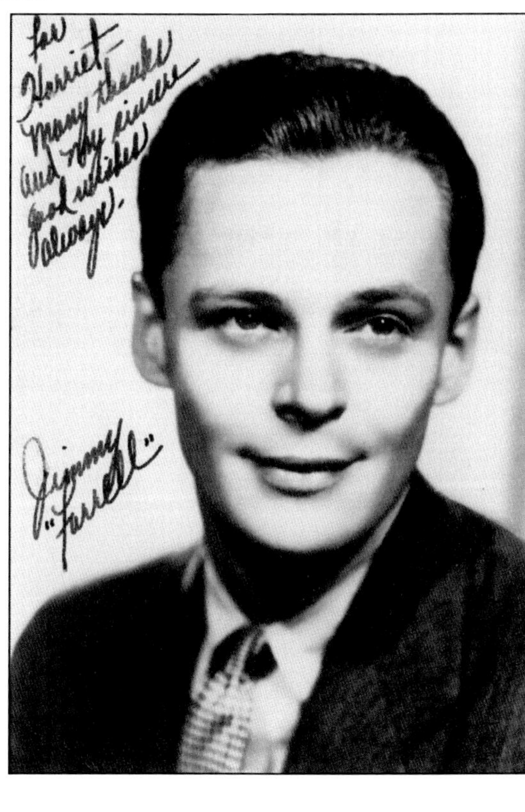

To his friends in Eden, Jimmy Farrell was Jimmy Phatiger. Singing for fun during high school and college led him to enter a talent contest sponsored by radio star Kate Smith in the early 1930s. Winning gave him a start on the radio, where he sang with the Johnny Green Orchestra. He appeared in the 1936 Ziegfeld Follies and other Broadway productions. In 1943, while serving in the Army, Farrell was one of the service men selected to appear in Irving Berlin's movie *This is the Army*.

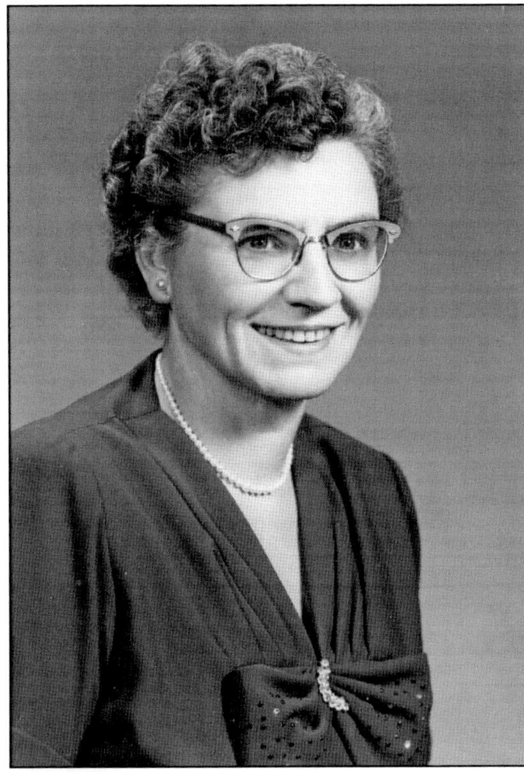

Evelyn Tooley Hunt (1905–1997) was born and raised in Eden. After graduation from William-Smith College in 1926, she went on to become a well-known author and poet. Her works were published in over 40 anthologies and high school textbooks, and she was recognized as the originator of American haiku. In 1962, she was the recipient of the Sidney Lanier Memorial Award in American poetry. Her poem "Taught Me Purple" inspired Alice Walker to write the novel *The Color Purple*. (Courtesy of Donald Hunt.)

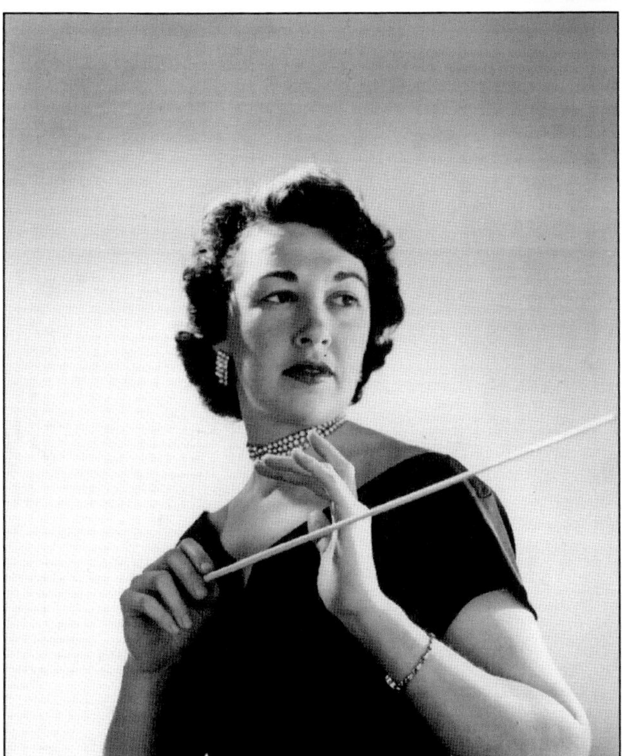

Each year, a music student from Eden Central School is awarded a scholarship in memory of Lucille Burnham Miller. Following graduation from Eden High School in 1938, Miller went on to earn bachelor's and master's degrees from the Cincinnati Conservatory of Music. During her successful career as a pianist and conductor, she made her home in New York City. Her career was cut short by her death in 1970 at age 47.

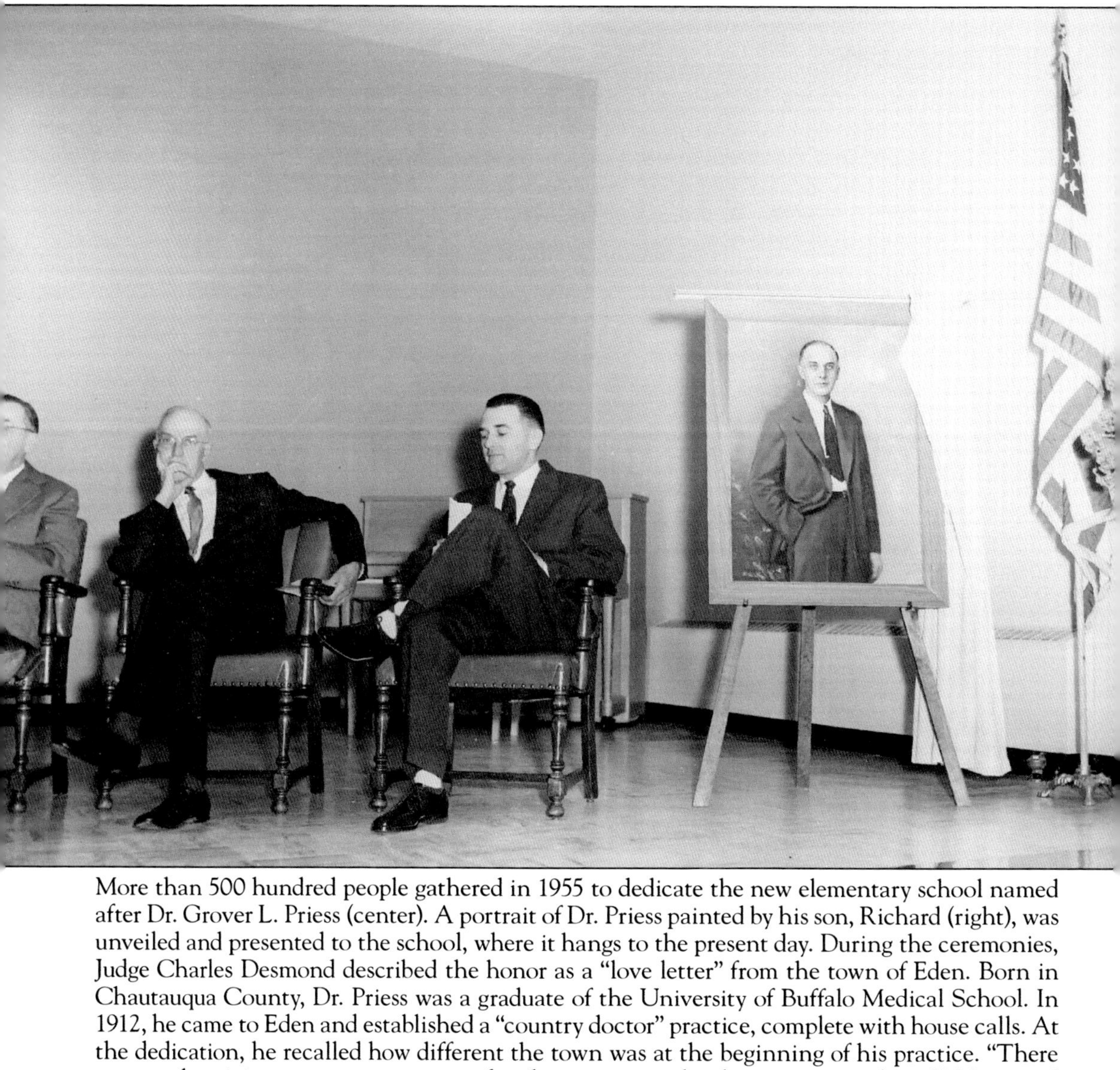

More than 500 hundred people gathered in 1955 to dedicate the new elementary school named after Dr. Grover L. Priess (center). A portrait of Dr. Priess painted by his son, Richard (right), was unveiled and presented to the school, where it hangs to the present day. During the ceremonies, Judge Charles Desmond described the honor as a "love letter" from the town of Eden. Born in Chautauqua County, Dr. Priess was a graduate of the University of Buffalo Medical School. In 1912, he came to Eden and established a "country doctor" practice, complete with house calls. At the dedication, he recalled how different the town was at the beginning of his practice. "There was no electricity, no water system, no fire department and only one improved road." He served as the Town of Eden health officer, was the school district's physician until 1950, and was on the staff of Bertrand Chaffee Hospital in Springville. During his long career, he is reported to have delivered from 4,000 to 5,000 babies, many of whom still remember him with esteem and affection. He retired in 1965 and died at age 78 in 1966.

Bertha Schenkel Johnson (who died in 1960) truly reflected her unofficial title as "Eden's Little Flower Lady." From the 1920s to the 1940s, she made daily trips on the train to Buffalo to sell flowers that grew on her small farm at Route 62 and Sandrock Road. As she stood only 4 feet, 10 inches tall, her bundles of blooms surely overwhelmed her slight stature as she loaded them onto the train. In 1972, four acres of her property were donated to the town and dedicated to her as Little Flower Lady Park.

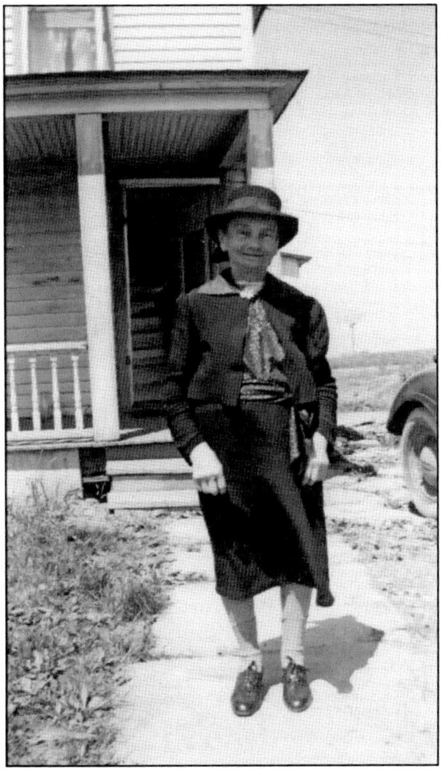

A lady from a more recent generation did her part to preserve local history through her paintings. Thelma Winter (1931–2009) began her painting career later in life after raising four children and teaching music for almost 30 years. Her popular paintings and prints captured images of numerous historical places and structures in Eden, Western New York, and beyond. She was a familiar exhibitor at art shows, where she happily chatted with customers as she worked on her latest picture. (Courtesy of Kate Riedel.)

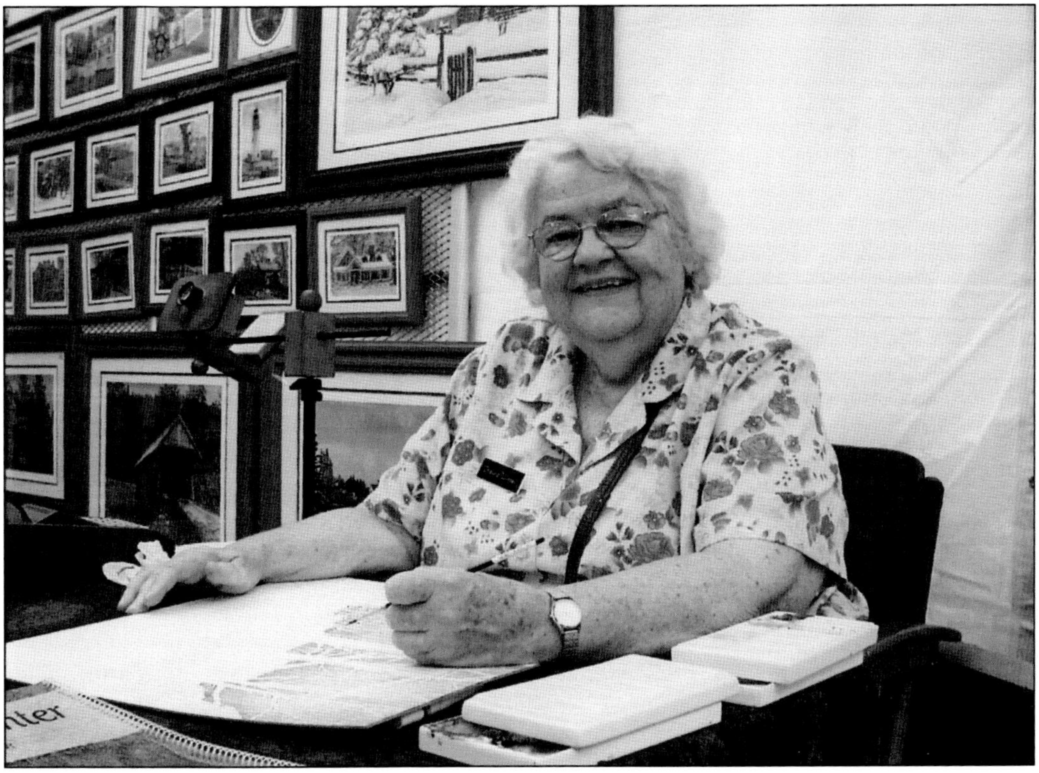

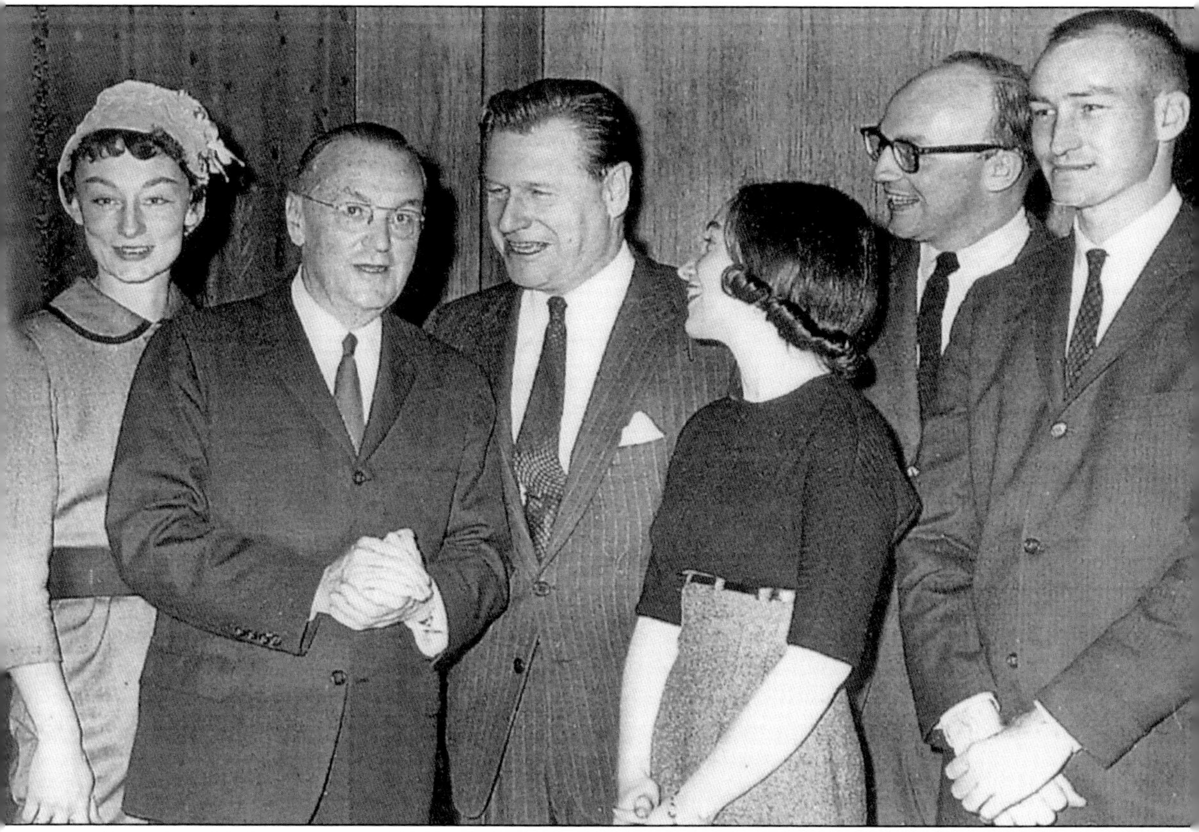

From humble beginnings, Charles S. Desmond rose to become the highest-ranking judge in New York State. Born in 1896 in a room above his father's saloon near Buffalo's Lake Erie docks, he went on to earn a bachelor's and master's degree from Canisius College. After being awarded a law degree from the University of Buffalo in 1920, Desmond established a law practice in the city of Buffalo. In 1946, he and his wife moved their young family to Eden. Judge Desmond had served on the New York State Court of Appeals since 1940, and in 1960, Gov. Nelson Rockefeller swore him in as the Chief Judge of the Court. Following the ceremony, Judge Desmond (second from left) poses with, from left to right, his daughter Sheila Landon, Gov. Rockefeller, daughter Patricia Williams, son Charles Ryan Desmond, and son-in-law James Landon. During his 25 years as a judge, he spent all but one on the Court of Appeals. Following his mandatory retirement from the bench at age 70, the judge returned to private practice and taught courses at the University of Buffalo Law School and Cornell University. Prior to his death in 1987 at age 90, Judge Desmond generously donated a portion of his property to the Eden Library for a new building. (Courtesy of Sheila Desmond Landon.)

Nine

Recreation and Celebrations

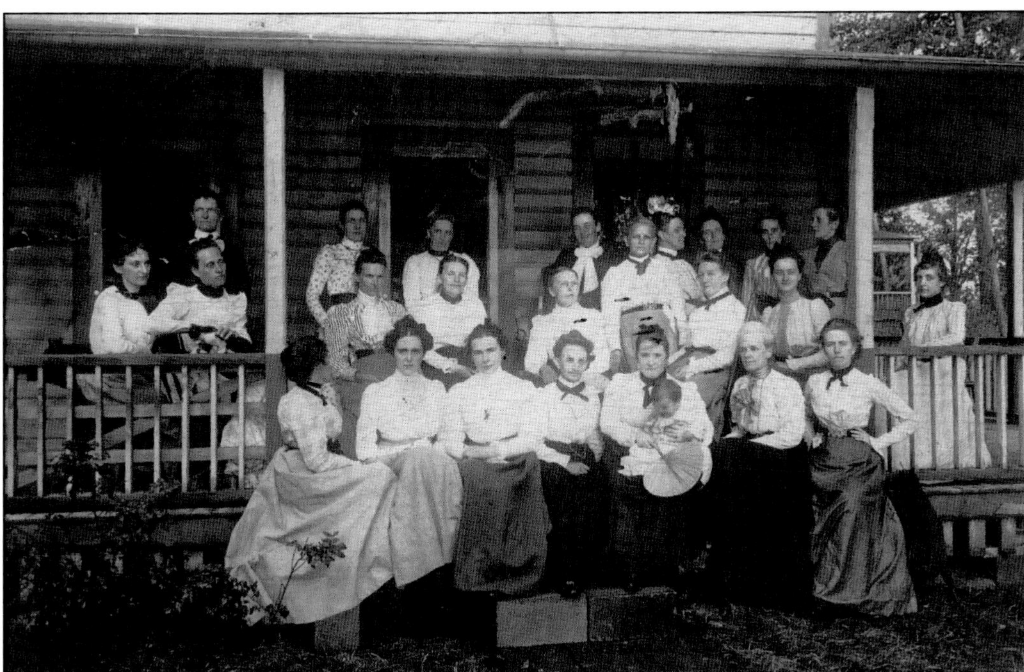

The oldest active organization in Eden is the Up-To-Date Club. It was founded in 1894 and is still going strong. The study club was begun by a small group of chore-weary women from Eden Valley who felt closed off from the world and wanted to broaden their horizons. They researched and wrote educational papers dealing with literature, music, and topics of national importance and interest. Bimonthly meetings, accompanied by elaborate meals, were held in members' freshly and thoroughly cleaned homes.

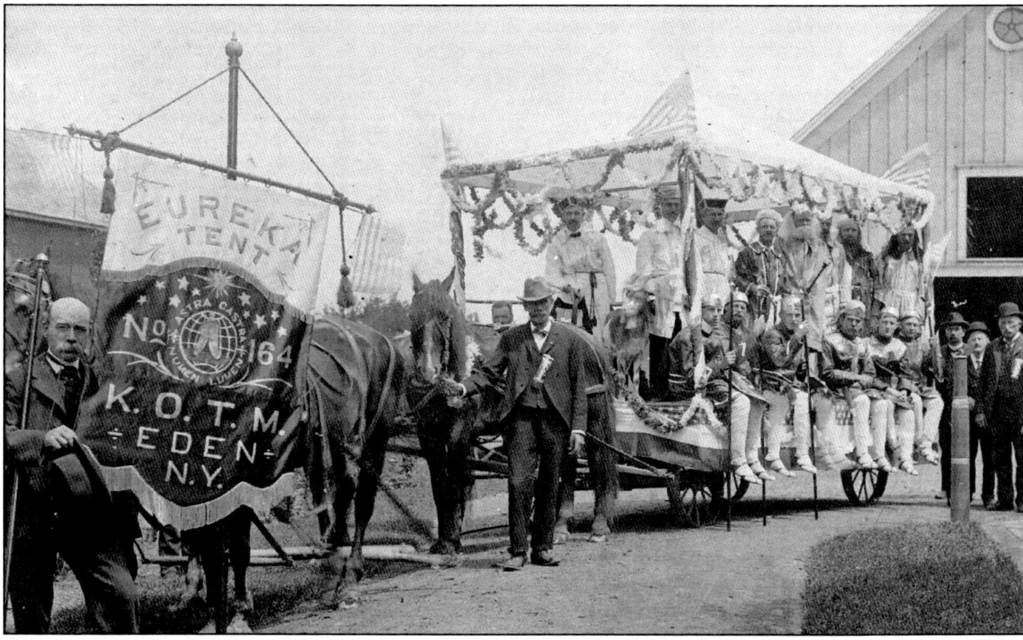

Little is known about the Knights of the Maccabees, one of several fraternal groups that had a presence in Eden during the 1880s or 1890s. It appears that the Eden "tent" or chapter was related in some way to the Royal Templars of Temperance, a society espousing total abstinence from alcohol. Membership in the Maccabees provided the benefit of life insurance.

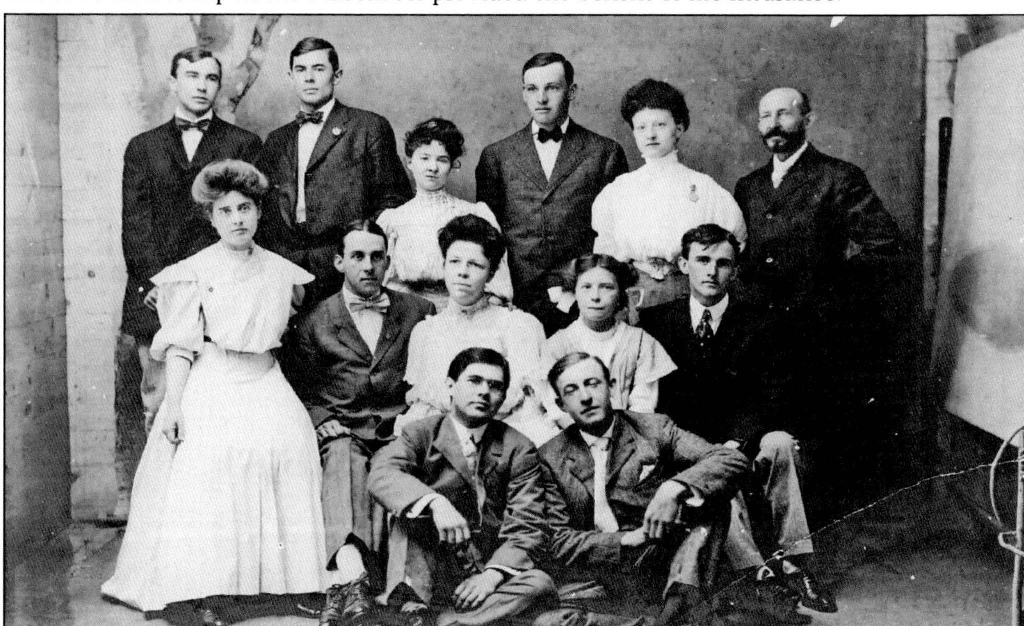

The members of the Eden Dramatic Club pose for their group picture in 1907. One of their plays that year was entitled *Tony the Convict*. The group, organized in the 1890s, held its productions in Hutchinson Hall on West Church Street. The hall, which was built as a Congregational church in 1828, was purchased by John Hutchinson in 1890. He created an entertainment venue that was used until 1922. The fire hall now stands on the site.

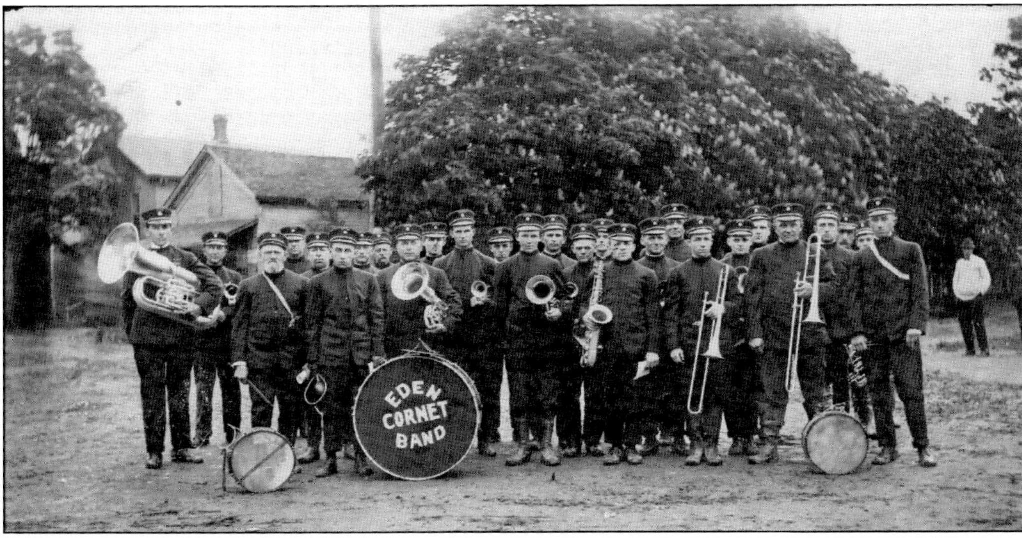

This picture from 1909 shows the Eden Cornet Band assembled at the intersection of Main and Church Streets. The horse chestnut tree in the background stood where the Four Corners Café is today. Earlier photographs indicate that the band was formed as early as 1880. Music and drama groups were popular recreation in the earlier days. Home talent dramas were often presented, and at one time, there was a "singing school" in town.

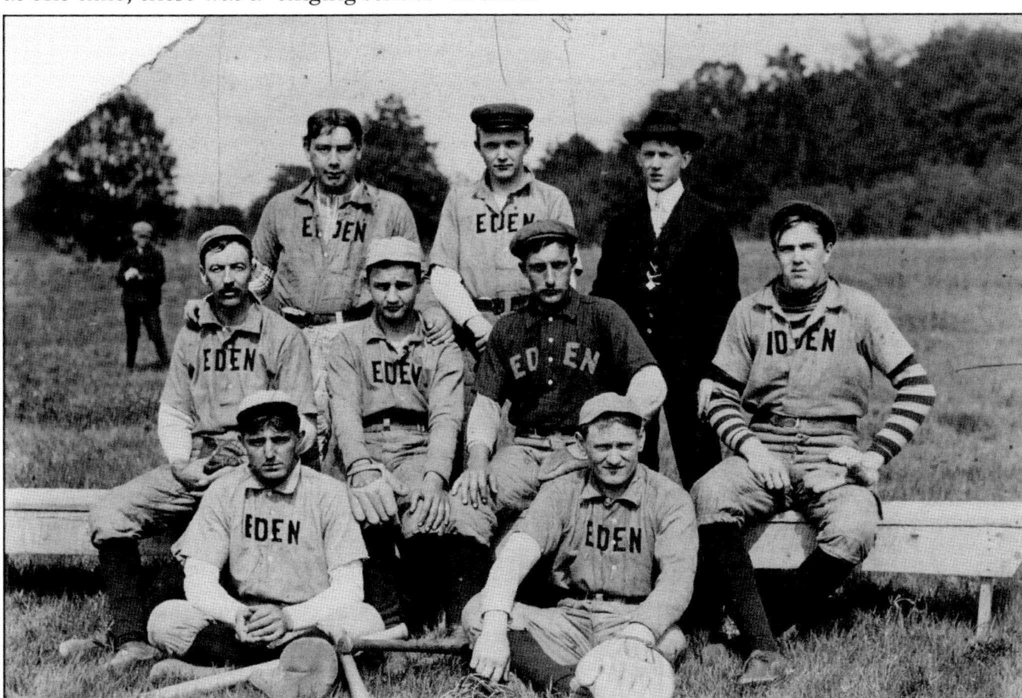

Sports, especially baseball, have a long history in Eden. The Eden baseball team was small, but they look like they took the game seriously. The men who posed in 1902 for their team photograph are, from left to right, (first row) Arthur Ernst and Andy Wiggins; (second row) F. Kaufman, Herbert Webb, William Lakely, and Horace Cassell; (third row) ? Trevallee, William Phatiger, and ? Roeller.

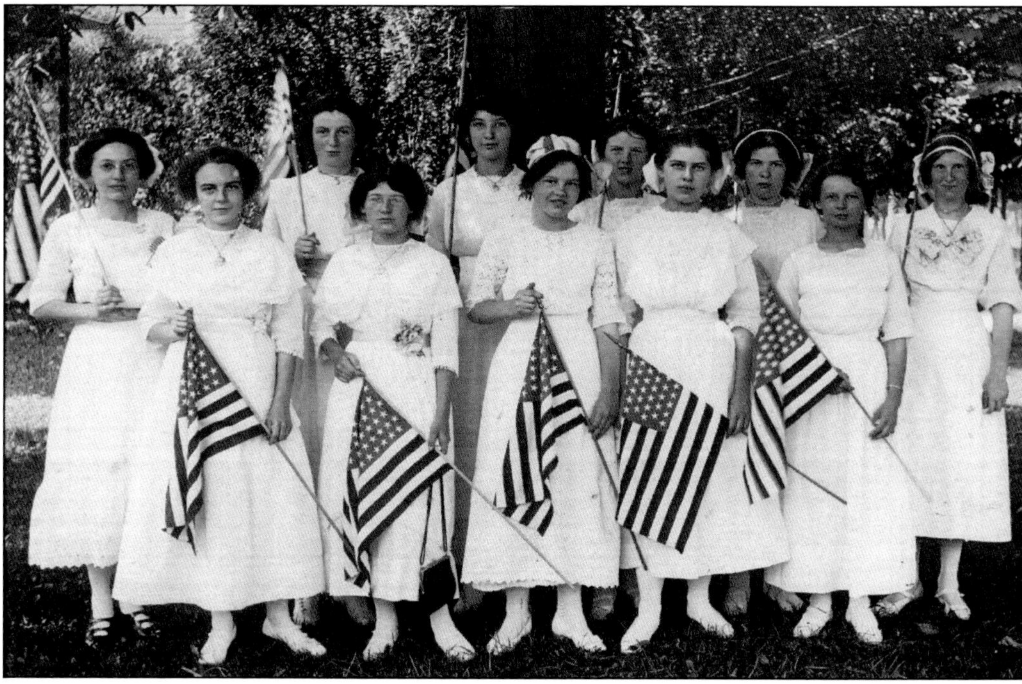

Patriotic celebrations were commonplace in the early 20th century. Fourth of July was probably the town's biggest public celebration of the year. Buildings were adorned in red, white, and blue bunting, and flags flew everywhere. The town's people turned out in their best attire to watch or participate in parades, picnics, and other festivities. The upper photograph shows the young women of the flag drill team posing in beautiful white dresses before ceremonies in 1911 or 1912. The gaily decorated truck in the lower picture is seen turning the corner from Main Street onto West Church Street during a Fourth of July parade in 1917, the year the United States entered World War I. Chances are that patriotic fervor was running higher than usual that year.

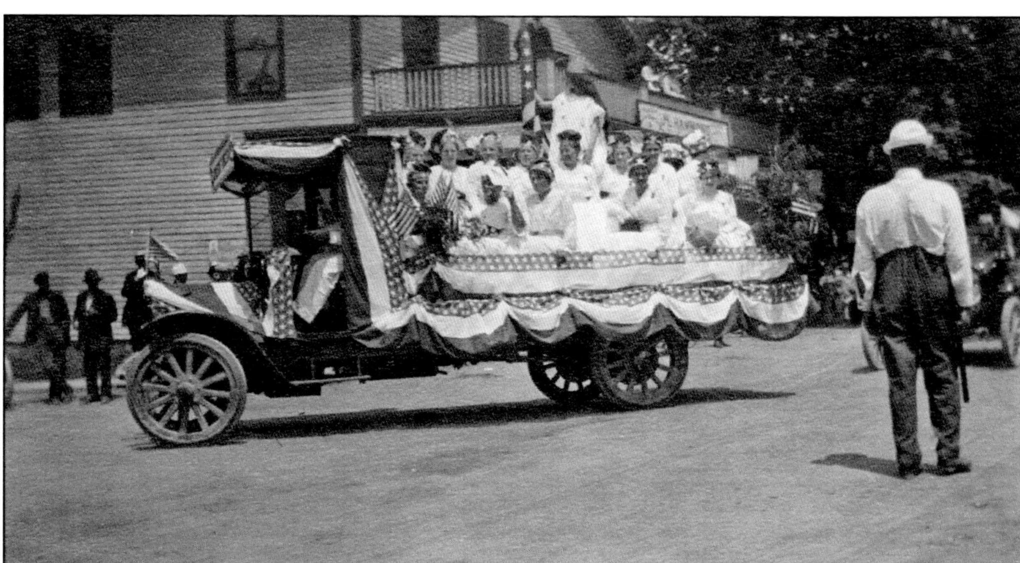

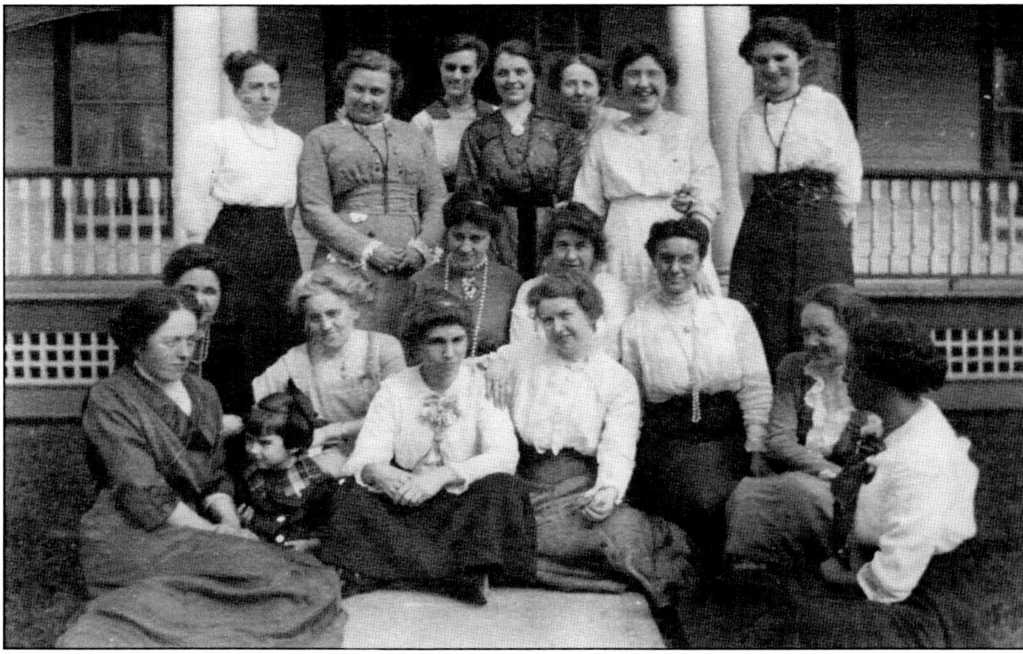

In this 1914 photograph, Lorene Landon's home (known now as the Asa Warren House) was the meeting place for the Stitcheri Club. The previous year, the women had organized the group as a social center "where old friends meet and new comers are welcome." Over their 70-year history, they contributed to a number of charitable causes, sewing for soldiers and the needy and delivering Christmas baskets.

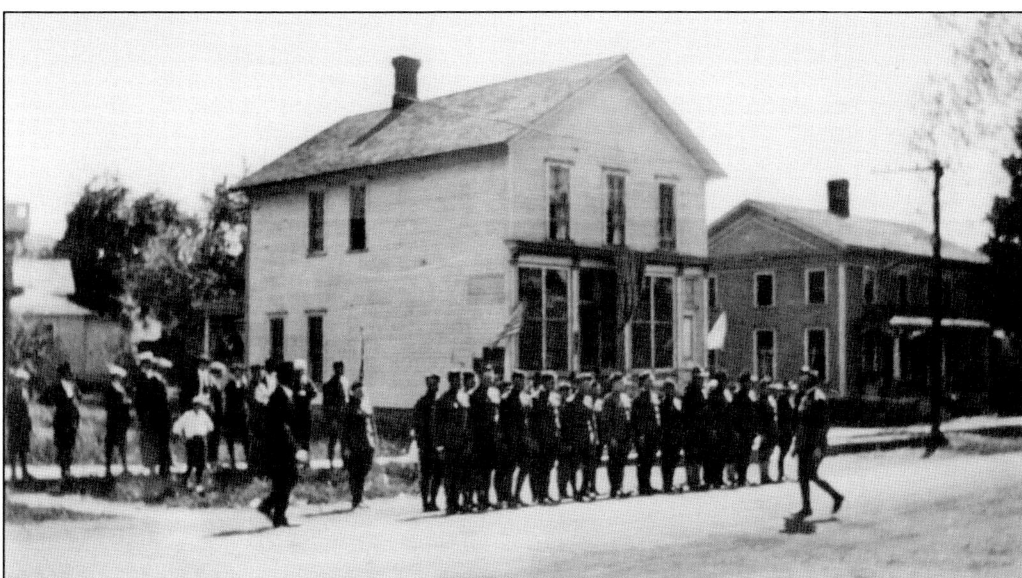

World War I veterans who shared common experiences, problems, and goals formed the American Legion in the United States. Eden's newly organized Newell-Faulkner Post No. 880 musters for a parade in 1920. It remains an active and important organization. From 1930 on, the Legion has sponsored a patriotically themed essay contest. Winners are recognized at their annual Memorial Day services, a duty assumed from the O.G. Brindley Circle in the 1930s.

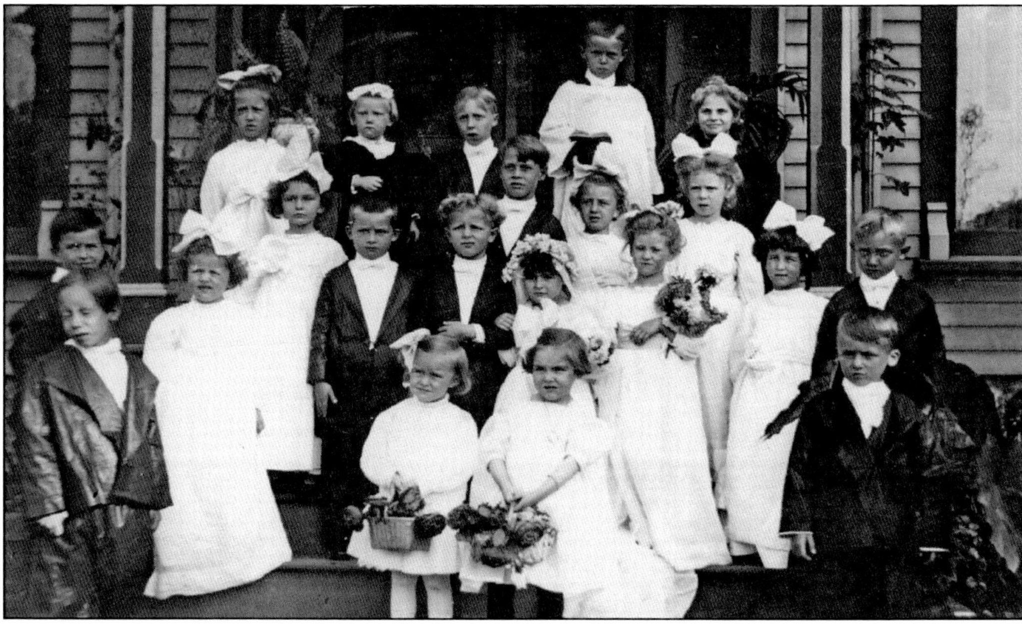

Pastimes for children were quite different in the early 1900s. From the expressions on their faces, it is hard to guess if this event was recreation for these children or their parents. A "Tom Thumb Wedding" was presented around 1909 in the town hall, which was then located in the Redfield Building. After the performance, the actors pose in front of Dr. Shaw's across Main Street.

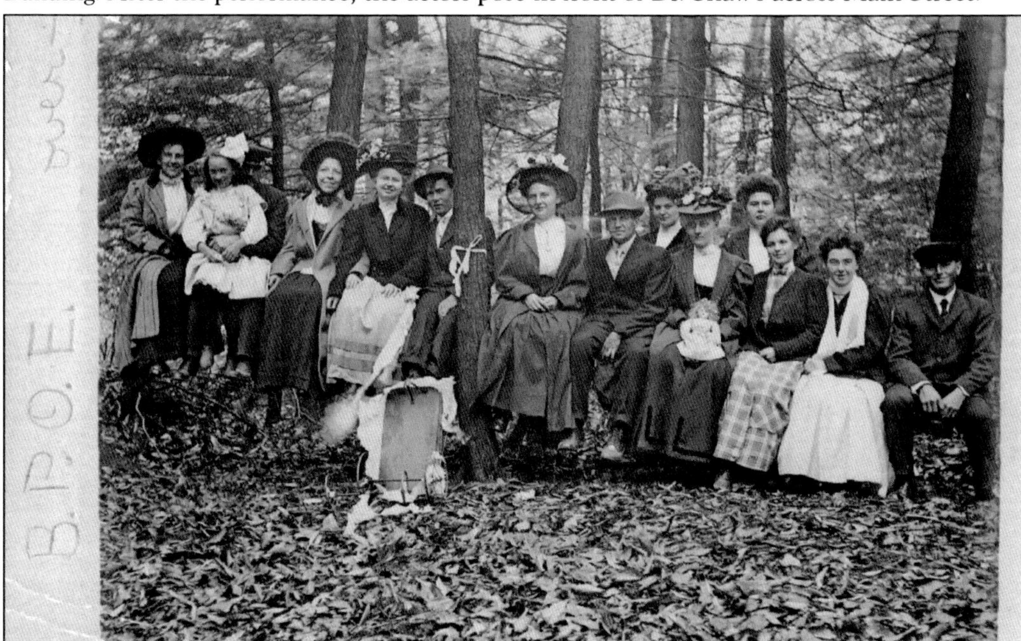

Several images in Eden's historical files show this group on various outings. This postcard has B.P.O.E. written in the margin, and no, this is not a group from the Elks Club (Benevolent and Protective Order of Elks). This c. 1900 photograph simply captures a group of good friends (Best People of Eden) as they enjoyed time together. Unlike many pictures of the day, these people are smiling!

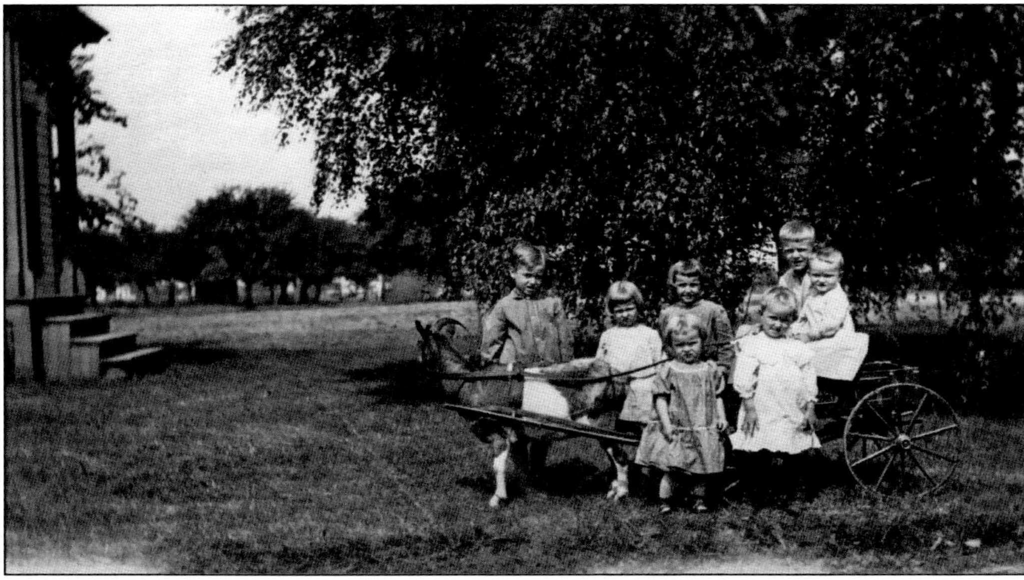

The youngest family members found entertaining uses for their four-legged farm friends. This photograph from 1910 shows a group of Agle cousins dressed in their Sunday best and enjoying a ride in the goat cart. Pictured from left to right are (first row) Loretta Agle Zittel and Martha Agle Fisher; (second row) Herman Agle, Evelyn Agle Saar, Adeline Agle Feasley, Elmer Agle, and unidentified.

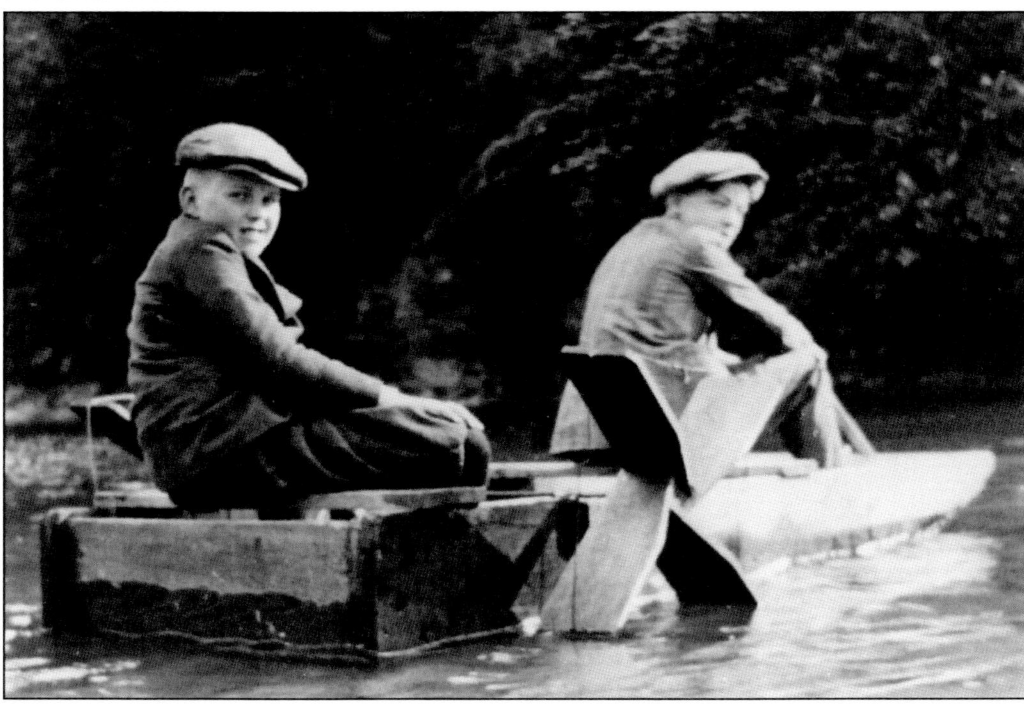

Recreation for children in the 1920s was more about physical activity and being outdoors than it is today. Children were more apt to create their own entertainment, as is shown by these boys in their homemade paddleboat. Around 1925, Edwin Kromer (left) and an unidentified friend take to the waters above the falls and dam at Kromer's Mill. (Courtesy of Marvin Cohoon.)

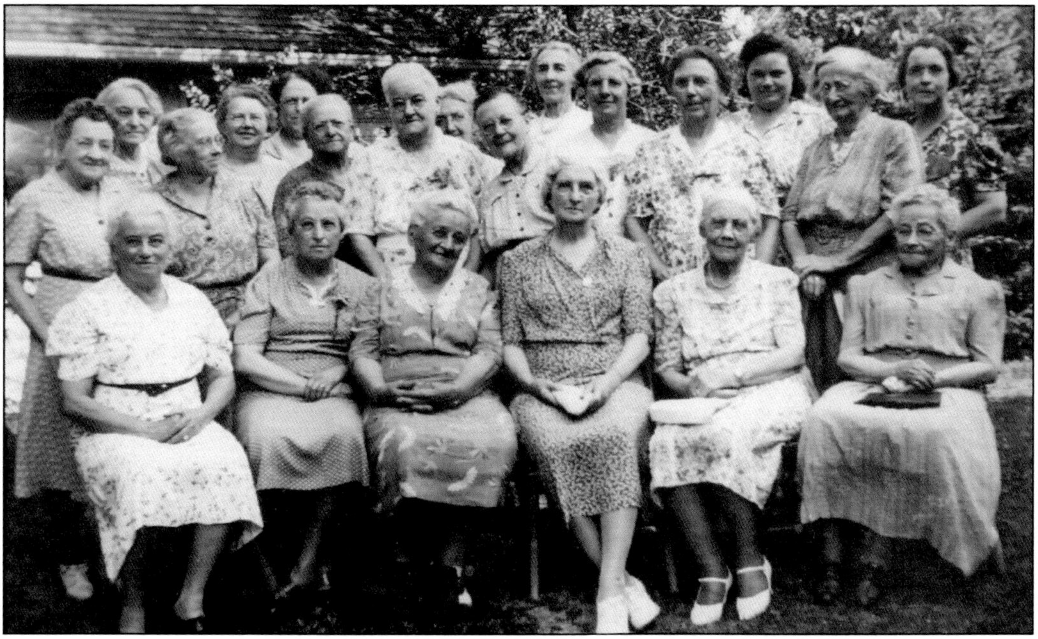

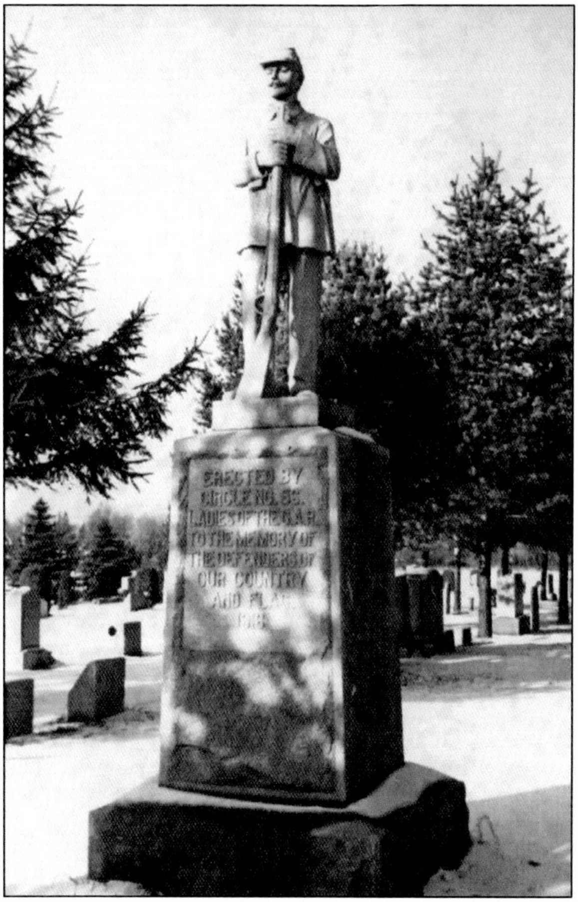

The GAR or the Grand Army of the Republic was a fraternal organization composed of Civil War veterans from the Union army. Wives, mothers, and other relatives of veterans often started auxiliary organizations called circles. In 1909, the O.G. Brindley Circle No. 56 of the GAR was formed. Pictured in 1941, the group sought to foster patriotism among young people. A primary duty of the circle was to conduct an annual memorial service for deceased veterans. One of their first projects was to erect a monument honoring and commemorating the devotion that Civil War veterans had for their country. After raising the necessary funds, the soldiers' monument was dedicated in the Evergreen Cemetery at the 1916 Memorial Day observances. The once-vibrant circle waned as members aged and passed away. It disbanded in the 1940s. The GAR formally dissolved in 1956 after the death of Albert Woolson, the last Civil War veteran.

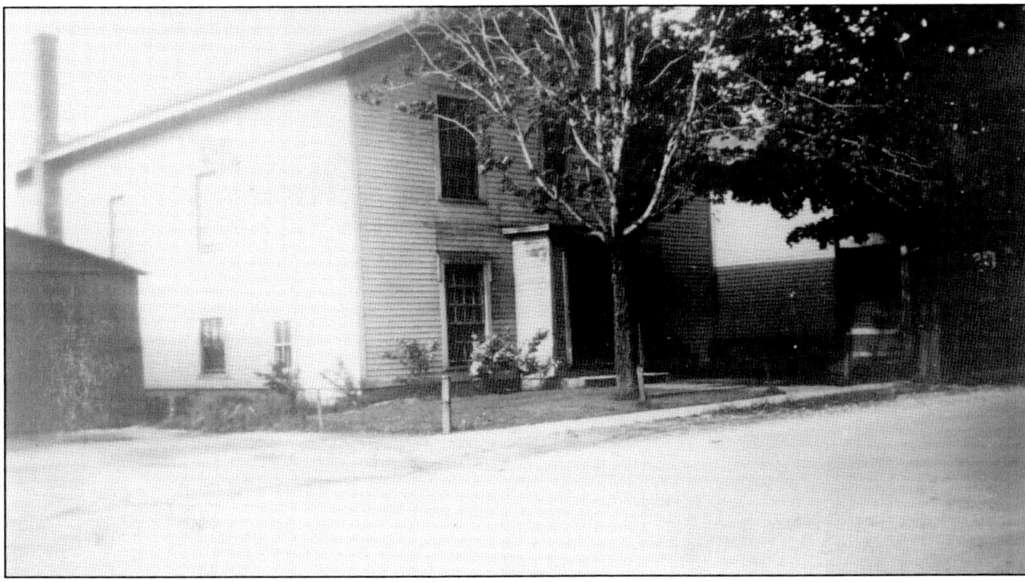

The building seen above had several uses over its lifetime. It was home to the German Evangelical Church, the Odd Fellows, and the American Legion. It is best remembered as the Grange Hall. The National Grange was founded in 1867 on the premise that farmers should work together for their mutual economic and political well-being. In later years, non-farmers joined for social and educational benefits. Records show that the Eden chapter, organized in 1910, numbered most of the people in town as members at one time or another. Membership in the 1950s, when community service was a component of the Grange's program, was strong. Dinners, card parties, and dances were among the many activities held for fundraising and fellowship. If the c. 1945 photograph below is any indication, theatrical productions must have been on the program as well. Grange activities ceased in the late 1970s. The building, located on West Church Street, was demolished in 1989.

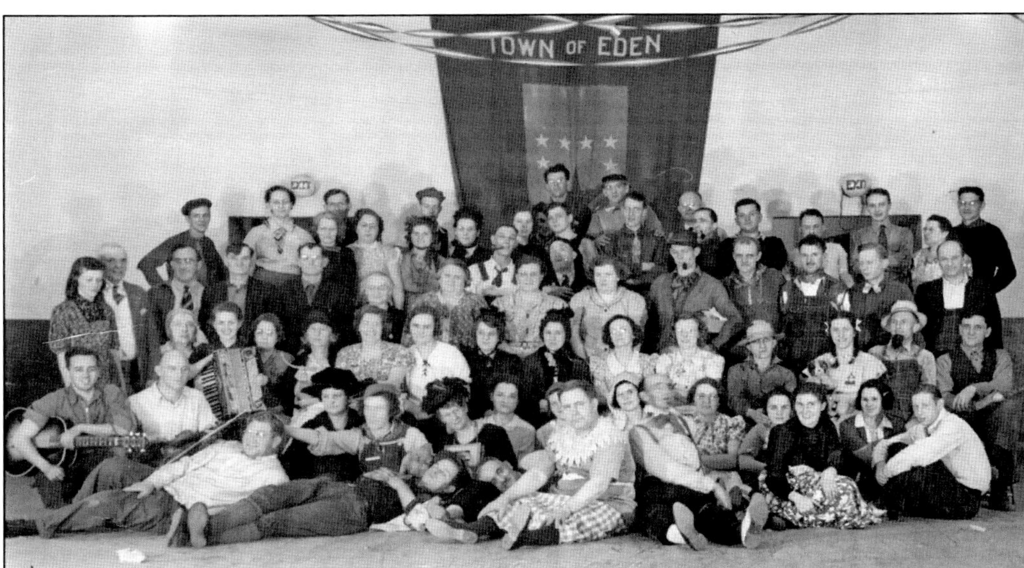

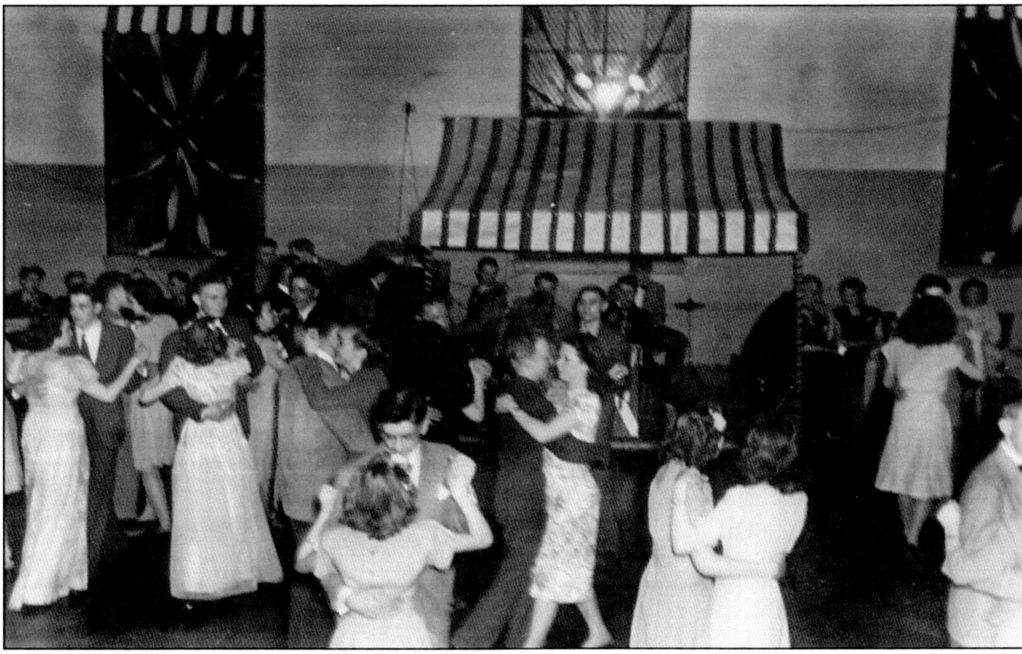

In 1944, junior and senior high school students worked with interested adults to organize Teen Town. With minimal guidance from adults, the teenagers took all responsibility for the program and its activities. It was active for 10 successful years, after which the school student council assumed the duty of event planning. In 1953, a gala ninth anniversary party was held with a live band providing the dance music.

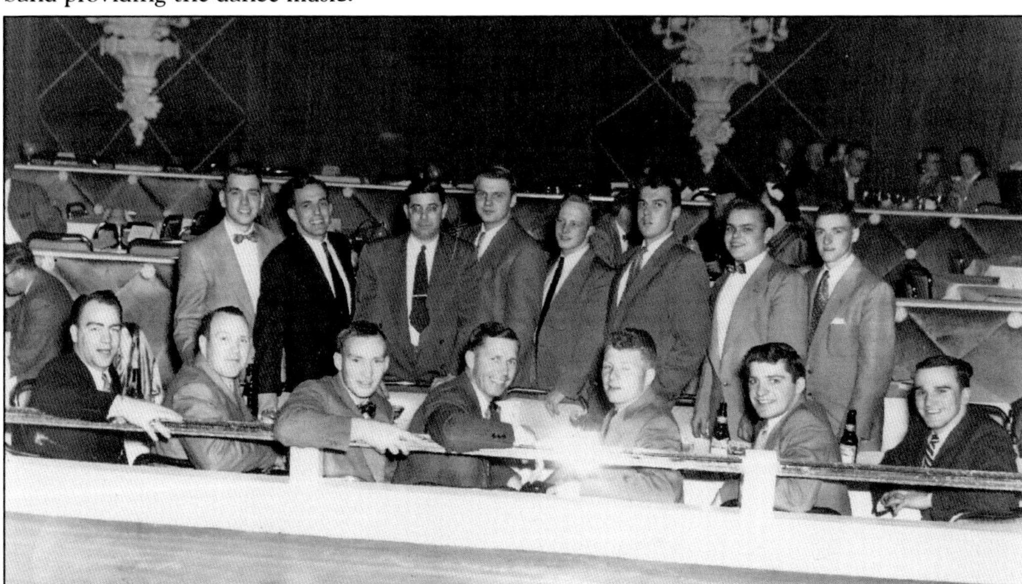

The Town of Eden basketball team celebrates at the Town Casino in Buffalo in 1953. Frank Meyers, an appliance dealer, sponsored the team. A few of these gentlemen still live in Eden. Shown are, from left to right, (first row) Gordon Landon, coach Tom Connors, Jim Landon, Jerry Nelson, Joe Reagan, Ed Walker, and Bill Argenteri; (second row) Jack Smith, Robert Crowe, Burt Ball, Jim Walker, Jim Kennedy, Harry Bearsch, Larry Szal, and Ray Klein.

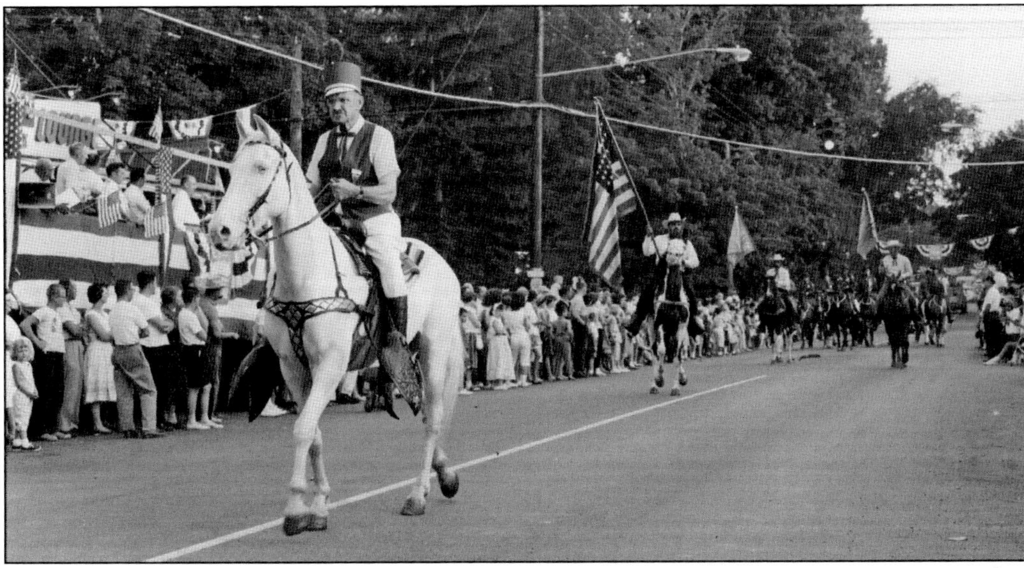

The Town of Eden celebrated its 150th anniversary in 1962. Howard Hill had the honor of acting as the grand marshal of the Sesquicentennial Parade. Hill was the great-great-grandson of John and Jemima Hill, who were the first to settle in what was initially known as Hill's Corners and then as Eden Center. As he sat astride his white horse, Howard Hill was within feet of his ancestral homestead. (Courtesy of Julia Hill Laing-Meyers.)

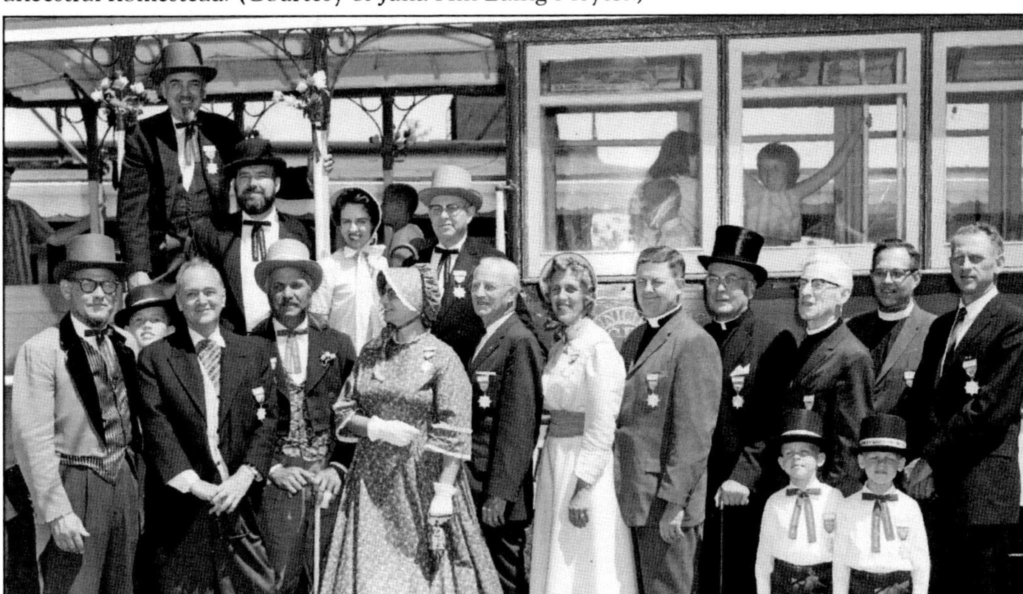

Members of Eden's Sesquicentennial Steering Committee and other dignitaries posed in period costume during the festivities. From left to right are (first row) Town Supervisor and Committee Chairman George Guenther, unidentified, Judge Charles Desmond, Clayton Wittmeyer, Evelyn Tooley Hunt, Rev. Walter Meisenheimer, Audrey Segebarth, Reverend Schauer, Father Norman George, Rev. Earl Woodell, Rev. Arlan Brandt, and Rev. Wayne Baldwin; (second row) Kenneth Savage, Ferris Randall, Julia Hill Laing, and Albert Hickman. Twins William and Harry Laing are seen at the lower right.

Consistent with our mission to preserve history on a local level, this book was printed in South Carolina on American-made paper and manufactured entirely in the United States. Products carrying the accredited Forest Stewardship Council (FSC) label are printed on 100 percent FSC-certified paper.

MADE IN THE USA